Another Fine Dress

Role-Play in the Films of Laurel and Hardy

Jonathan Sanders

CASSELL

Cassell
Wellington House
125 Strand
WC2R 0BB

215 Park Avenue South
New York
NY 10003

First published 1995

British Library Cataloguing-in-Publication Data
A catalogue record for this book is available from the British Library.

ISBN 0–304–33196–1 (hardback)
    0–304–33206–2 (paperback)

Typeset by York House Typographic

Printed and bound in Great Britain by Biddles Ltd,
Guildford and King's Lynn

Contents

To Paul

Chapter one

Ringing the Changes

I LIKE to think that Howard Hawks's 1952 comedy *Monkey Business* was intended as a tribute to Laurel and Hardy. Marilyn Monroe, a 'dumb blonde' secretary, is named Miss Laurel, and Cary Grant plays a professor whose absent-mindedness is conveyed in the opening scene partly through his Stan Laurel-like inability to position himself on the correct side of the door he is closing. But these are incidentals. The film concerns a rejuvenation drug which, when taken by the stuffy professor and his wife, induces a behavioural regression first to that of teenagers and then to infancy. It's in the second of these roles that the scene most obviously inspired by Stan and Ollie occurs: a tit-for-tat confrontation where the adult spouses slosh paint over each other. However, the debt to Laurel and Hardy's films is much broader. The professor notes that the drug induces a 'complete reversal of the normal behaviour pattern'. As Robin Wood comments in his perceptive analysis of Hawks's movie, the characters do not become the youths that they were; rather, the drug 'releases all the things they *weren't*' (Wood, 1968, p. 80) but that, at least as adults, they wish to be. The drug is merely an agent which removes restraints, enabling the characters to try out new roles and vent their normally suppressed desires.

Stan and Ollie also have a great capacity for changing and varying roles. Charles Barr has written that they 'preserve the fluidity, the "overlapping" quality, the moment-to-moment inconsistencies of childhood' (Barr, 1967, p. 6). This mutability reflects the period in which Laurel and Hardy formed their cinematic personas – the 1920s, America's 'Jazz Age', described by

2: *Another Fine Dress*

Joan Mellen as 'in general a decade of experimentation in lifestyles, [when] films echoed the public's thirst for liberation from repressive sexual norms' (Mellen, 1977, p. 27). Stan and Ollie's regression to a childlike state is only the first stage of a fluidity which often embraces those around them. In their world, women and men, even humans and animals, are interchangeable; anything seems possible.

Sometimes, the metamorphosis is effected by a drug comparable to that in *Monkey Business*. Indeed, it's a rejuvenation formula which causes Ollie's regression to an ape at the end of *Dirty Work* (a moment echoed in the title and action of Hawks's movie). In *Leave 'Em Laughing* an overdose of laughing gas frees Stan and Ollie from all sense of responsibility, transforming them into anarchic infants whose playful aggression disrupts the order of traffic and the authority of a policeman. Alcohol produces similarly subversive behaviour in several of their films, possibly in reaction to the 1920 Prohibition law which was still in force when most of them were made.

But in general Stan and Ollie have no need of such external influences; it's in their nature to change, sometimes in their attempts to integrate into society, sometimes in their rebellion against it when their best efforts fail. The films present a series of experiments with different identities and roles, which are assumed by putting on and taking off the dress appropriate for each masquerade. Although Stan and Ollie are most familiar to us in their ill-fitting suits and derby (bowler) hats, they frequently dress up for part or all of a film, donning the costumes of children, women, animals and, less obviously, of men. The uniforms worn in the many films where they join a military or other male organization are as much dresses as the drag used in their female impersonations.

In their 1927 prison comedy *The Second Hundred Years* – a prototype film in several ways – Stan and Ollie wear convict uniforms which, together with the jail's rituals, stifle their individuality. They break out by masquerading initially as painters then as French police chiefs; liberation from the prison of conformity is achieved through role-play. In order to be painters, they simply turn their uniforms inside out, symbolizing the chameleonic reversibility of their personas and an inversion of the jail's values. Their appropriation of the visiting VIPs' formal clothes and taxi elevates their social status in a particularly marked way: they become 'guests of honour' at a dinner party hosted by the governor of the very institution where they had previously been dishonoured guests. Like poor Cinderella, transformed by costume and conveyance into a lady, they are admitted to life's ball. But their masquerade is also circumscribed by time and space: when the equivalent of midnight arrives, they must leave the 'ballroom' and return to their cells. They will be rescued from their daily drudgery not by a prince but by the next masquerade . . .

Often, the new guise is effected not through a costume change but is merely implied by more subtle means such as gesture, speech and visual metaphor, or by means of a parallel or role reversal with another character. Two or more identities may be displayed by the same person simultaneously. Whether these are in mutual contradiction or harmonious coexistence, the effect is to blur the boundaries of each identity. Laughter comes with our recognition that society's carefully labelled stereotypes are being inverted, undermined and subjected to fluctuation. Childhood and adulthood, masculinity and femininity, heterosexuality and homosexuality: polarities such as these are synthesized into comic ambiguities, which in turn are combined with each other to create a world in perpetual flux. During the half-century since Laurel and Hardy's final Hollywood film was released in May 1945, the role-play with which we conform to or challenge society has become much more complex and sophisticated. The team's anticipation of this, through their ironic representation of social and sexual roles *as* roles, makes their films even more relevant today than when they were made.

Career outline

Before I begin my analysis of Laurel and Hardy's 106 films – thematically in this introductory chapter (which will also consider how their cinematic personas were shaped in films prior to their teaming), then chronologically in the main body of the book – it may be useful to outline their careers. Since this volume is concerned exclusively with their work, I will not include details of their private lives; for this type of biographical information, readers are referred to the books of John McCabe and Randy Skretvedt listed in the bibliography.

Stan Laurel was born Arthur Stanley Jefferson in Ulverston, Lancashire, England, on 16 June 1890. A showman's son, he grew up against a music-hall background and decided to become a comedian at the age of fifteen. He eventually joined one of Fred Karno's pantomime troupes, which also included Charlie Chaplin. In 1910 he sailed with Karno to the United States where he settled several years later, touring the vaudeville circuits under the new surname 'Laurel' with a variety of acts and partners. By 1917 he was making short films while continuing his theatrical career.

Oliver Hardy was born Norvell Hardy in Harlem, Georgia, USA, on 18 January 1892. He adopted the name Oliver in honour of his father who died in the year of his birth. Hardy's early career was primarily as a singer in vaudeville, but by 1914 he was working as a comic actor for the Lubin Film Company. By 1917 he had appeared in over 100 one-reel films. In most of those he made for the Vim Comedy Company he co-starred with Billy Ruge in a series called 'Plump and Runt', where the physical disparity between the two comedians is seen as a precursor of Laurel and Hardy. In another series, made in 1917 and 1918 for King Bee, he partnered the Charlie Chaplin impersonator Billy West.

Around this time Laurel and Hardy's paths in comedy films crossed briefly when they both appeared, by chance, in *The Lucky Dog*, a two-reeler made for G. M. Anderson. However, they went their separate ways, Hardy into films, where he played the villain for comics such as Jimmy Aubrey and Larry Semon, Laurel back to vaudeville, interspersed with bursts of cinematic activity. He too supported Semon, who regarded him as a scene-stealer, but not in the same films as Hardy. However, Laurel more often appeared as a leading comedian. He starred in a 1922 series of two-reelers (some of which were spoofs of serious movies) for Anderson, a 1924–25 set of twelve for Joe Rock and, between these, a series of one- and two-reelers for Hal Roach, the comedy producer under whom he was reunited with Hardy in 1925.

5: *Ringing the Changes*

By this date, however, Laurel saw himself not as an actor but a writer and director. It was only by accident that he returned to acting in 1926 and that, consequently and coincidentally, he began to appear in Roach's All Star series of films with Oliver Hardy among the other players. The official Laurel and Hardy series did not commence until *Should Married Men Go Home?* in 1928, though by then the two comics had been teamed deliberately many times before. Throughout the period with Roach, Laurel wrote the scripts for their films with a team of writers and gag men. He was also heavily involved with direction and editing, guiding the men who nominally performed these functions. The opening titles of the films did not usually credit Laurel for any additional work, though it was reflected in his salary. This was considerably higher than that received by Hardy, who mainly confined himself to acting. This book is not especially concerned with the question of authorship, but my assumption is that the Roach films were collaborations, with Laurel more or less at the creative helm. The credited directors are not mentioned, since unity of style – so unobtrusively apt for the material – throughout the Roach period is much more marked than the distinguishing characteristics of any particular film or group of films by one 'director'.

All the silent films Laurel and Hardy made together were two-reelers of about twenty minutes' duration. This length was retained, with an occasional extension to three (and on one occasion four) reels, for the forty Roach sound shorts in which they starred between 1929 and 1935. They also appeared in a smaller number of feature films, mainly from the same studio, but in 1939 the team left Roach – who had increasingly compromised Laurel's creative control – in the hope of gaining complete independence. The decision proved to be disastrous: the films made in the 1940s for 20th Century Fox and MGM were written and directed by people who neither understood Laurel and Hardy's comedy nor granted them the freedom to make their own creative contributions. After an ill-fated attempt in 1950 at making a film away from Hollywood, the team finished their careers, as they had begun them, with successful theatrical tours. Oliver Hardy died on 7 August 1957. Stan Laurel was awarded an honorary Oscar in 1961. He died on 23 February 1965.

Boys will be boys

Fans of Laurel and Hardy, following the example of some of their screen wives, usually refer to them as 'the boys'. The epithet is an affectionate one which crystallizes the ambiguities of age in the duo's personas: 'boy' can mean a child, a youth, or a man who lacks maturity and experience. The three ages of infant, teenager and adult which Cary Grant lives separately in *Monkey Business* are present in Stan and Ollie simultaneously. Pluralized, 'the boys' brings a suggestion of brotherhood, either biological or in the sense of friendship between adult men. Yet in the latter definition 'the boys' usually refers to a group larger than two (as in 'a night out with the boys'), so this meaning does not eclipse but fuses with the earlier alternatives.

It's significant that when either Stan or Ollie is being censured for childlike behaviour, the reprover resorts to specificity: in *Come Clean* Mrs Hardy contemptuously tells her husband that he has 'the mind of a four-year-old child'; in *The Live Ghost* Ollie himself criticizes Stan for acting 'like a three-year-old child'. These moments are both awkward, for they explicitly tell us something which we already know and which Stan and Ollie's behaviour usually only implies – together with a range of other identities. Moreover, while it's true that Stan has a mental age even younger than Ollie's, three and four are both exaggerations of the degrees of infancy which they typically display. Five and ten respectively would be my rough assessment of their *average* psychic ages, but both can behave as if they are much younger or much older. The instability – the tension between infancy, adolescence and their physical maturity – is the crucial factor.

In this respect particularly, both Laurel and Hardy (but especially Laurel) owed a debt to Harry Langdon – a much greater one, in my estimation, than is acknowledged by most commentators. Langdon was the baby-faced comedian, contracted by the slapstick comedy producer Mack Sennett in 1923, whose humour was largely based on an infant-like innocence and bewilderment in the sophisticated atmosphere of 1920s America. He was at the height of his success – both critical and commercial – in the team's formative years of 1926 and 1927. At this time

Langdon, as Walter Kerr puts it, 'was simply in the comic air' (Kerr, 1975, p. 265), his many mannerisms being absorbed, perhaps unconsciously, even by well-established comedians like Buster Keaton. Ultimately, Langdon's influence on the team was much broader and deeper, consisting of more than merely external traits. The ambiguity of his comic persona – the all-important face has been described as 'a strange mixture of discordant opposites' (Mast, 1979, p. 166) – provided Laurel and Hardy with a model of instant and infinite variability in terms of gender, sexuality and, especially, age. James Agee's famous description of Langdon as 'an elderly baby' (Agee, 1949, p. 8) – the ex-vaudevillian was aged forty when he came to films – is an oversimplification. Walter Kerr comes nearer to his fascinatingly complex image when he refers to 'the three ages of Harry' (Kerr, 1975, p. 272) – baby, pubescent teenager and fully grown (often married) man: all of which he was, and was not, simultaneously. As I have already suggested, Laurel and Hardy's films – at least those made from late 1927 (ironically, the exact moment when Langdon's career went into sudden decline) – exhibit very similar contradictions of age. For example, in *Their Purple Moment*, made in February 1928 and the first co-starring film in which both are married, they also pick up girls with a coyness that suggests a first-ever date with the opposite sex, and by the end of the movie they are hurling food like naughty infants.

There is evidence that Stan Laurel was modelling his persona on Langdon's at least twelve months before his gradual teaming with Oliver Hardy got under way at the studios of Hal Roach (Sennett's chief rival) around September 1926. By this date, Laurel had been a screen comic for ten years. Most of his pre-1925 films present a brash, go-getting (if sometimes stupid) character modelled on those of Charlie Chaplin and Harold Lloyd. In the one-reel chase comedy *White Wings*, made for Roach in 1923 before his permanent association with the producer began, Stan somehow balances a liberally wrapped baby on his shoulders, so that the infant's head seems to replace his own. As he runs from a cop, he projects an extraordinary adult-baby image, but it remains just a one-off sight gag, a disguise that has nothing to do with Stan's character. However, two years later in the tellingly titled *Half a Man*, one of his Joe Rock two-reelers, Laurel has transformed his earlier persona into 'a simple child of nature'. His performance, exaggerating some of Langdon's characteristics, has little subtlety; he skips along a beach and, bidding farewell to his parents, he alternates between sobbing in his mother's lap and equally earnest lollipop-licking. Soon, Stan finds himself on board a boat with a predominantly female crew of whom – in the Langdon manner – he is terrified. One of the women calls him 'baby', attaches a bib-like napkin to his collar and fork-feeds him.

However, by the time of *On the Front Page*, made at the Roach studio in 1926, Laurel has discovered less obvious ways of conveying infantile qualities, no doubt encouraged by the more sophisticated style being cultivated in the All Star series. He plays an English butler, introduced as he lies asleep in bed, his exhalations blowing back the peak of the nightcap that hangs over his face. A stone, thrown through the bedroom window, lands in his mouth, and he swallows it. Betraying a childlike anxiety, close to tears, he tries to cough it up, first grasping at his throat, then his stomach (a gag re-worked with an apple in Laurel and Hardy's 1929 short *The Hoose-gow*). Stan's master is a gutter-press editor whose reporter son is told to rake muck on a racy countess. To furnish the newspaper with a suitable scandal, the reporter draws Stan into a plot to seduce her. The butler refuses, protesting, 'Women scare me, sir,' but the reporter repeatedly coshes him on the head, rendering him into the dopily submissive state of an infant. At several points, as the plan is put into effect, Stan is so gripped by fear that he cries, contorting his face in a manner that would later become a trademark expression indicative of his immaturity. Instructed by the reporter, who is preparing to photograph the action on a balcony outside a window, Stan puts his arms round the Countess's waist but, once his hands are in position, he doesn't know how to proceed. Clinging to her, he's like a virginal boy with a mature woman, his bouts of terror alternating with overzealous lunges into the mysterious world of sex. And the reporter-photographer's presence reminds us that it's all play-acting, performed under duress, so distancing Stan further from genuine sexual desire.

Meanwhile, Hardy's wide range of previous film roles had included at least one that exploited his naturally boyish appearance, which in real life earned him the nickname 'Babe'. In the King Bee two-reeler *Playmates* (1918), he and Billy West play children on an oversize set – an idea used briefly by Harry Langdon in the 1920s and more extensively by Laurel and Hardy in *Brats* (1930). However, the remainder of *Playmates* finds Hardy in the heavy make-up (bushy black eyebrows and moustache) which was necessary to transform his naturally cherubic features into the older and villainous ones that, according to cinematic convention, complemented his bulky physique. In most of his early films, both comic and serious, he was typecast as the heavy. By 1925, when he made *Stick Around* (a two-reeler modelled on Chaplin's 1915 *Work*) with the diminutive Bobby Ray, the comic hero and heavy have entered a very marked power relationship. Hardy is the lazy boss in a two-man paperhanging outfit; he makes his assistant Ray into a beast of burden who must pull the cart bearing their materials through the streets. Even when they arrive at their place of work for the day, Ray is loaded with all the equipment and forced to do all the work while Hardy rests. Of course, the lackey proves to be an anarchic child who accidentally subverts the discipline of the boss/father-figure. Through the characters of Ray and Hardy, *Stick Around* provides an outline of the later Laurel and Hardy relationship, but mainly in the context of very crude slapstick.

Hardy's screen image was gradually softened when he went to work for Roach. Yet he remained a dominant personality, so when he was accidentally co-starred with Laurel in *Duck Soup*, their relationship is largely characterized (as in *Stick Around*) by the big man's power over the smaller one. This, more than Laurel's childlike moments in the film, suggests a dimension of the relationship to come. In their next few films together, made in late 1926 and early 1927, Stan develops the infantile manner he displayed in *On the Front Page*, especially in relation to women. The personality is still largely based on Langdon's. When, in *Slipping Wives*, Stan is cradled in the arms of the woman he is supposed to be seducing, the image echoes similar sequences in Langdon's films, such as the final shot of *Saturday Afternoon* (1926) when Harry, in the front passenger seat of a car, receives a maternal cuddle from his wife as she drives. But on the whole, Laurel at this point lacks the subtlety and unhurried tempo which Langdon had by now brought to his films. The frantic lollipop-licking in Laurel's solo film *Half a Man* is still present two years later in *Why Girls Love Sailors*. The dice game of *Sailors Beware!*, shot about April 1927, suggests he has at least learned to slow down, though the eye-blinks here are more rapid than Langdon's – or indeed Laurel's of later years, when the ocular suggestion of childlike fatigue would be integral to his mature persona.

In early 1927 Laurel's infantilism usually exists independently of Hardy. When the latter is given a substantial role in the same film, he's usually an adult authority figure, but not necessarily in relation to Stan. After *Duck Soup* their scenes together were infrequent until they made *Do Detectives Think?* around May 1927. Here, Stan sees Ollie as a paternal protector, rushing to him for safety when frightened. Ollie pompously pretends to be in command, delegating the most dangerous work to Stan, but his behaviour betrays a childlike terror at least as great as Stan's. Already, Ollie has been established as, according to Charles Barr, 'a childish father-figure' (Barr, 1967, p. 67). However, a strong child–parent relationship does not emerge until later in the same year with *Putting Pants on Philip*, in which Hardy is actually cast as Laurel's uncle. Two films further on, in *Leave 'Em Laughing*, they have managed to absorb the essentials as bed-sharing friends in a boarding-house, Ollie implicitly playing the long-suffering parent to Stan's child with a toothache.

This inter-generational dimension of their screen relationship is present at some point in most of their mature films. It's important to note that Stan's passivity and helplessness is at least partly a result of Ollie's way of treating (sometimes punishing) him like a child. In *The Live Ghost* he refuses to let Stan have responsibility for his own money ('You can't spend it unless I'm with you'), so he should not be surprised to find that his repressed friend is, as he remarks later in the film, 'getting to be absolutely childish'. In *Come Clean* Stan's insistent craving for ice-cream may be childlike, but Ollie is equally determined to play the father-figure, accompanying him to the shop, relaying the assistant's question about the desired flavour and paying for the purchase. It's no wonder, then, that Stan upsets a container of straws, fulfilling to perfection the infantile status which Ollie has designated for him. Like an over-protective parent, Ollie prevents Stan from learning: in the 1933 film *Twice Two*, Stan attempts to buy ice-cream on his own, but he is unable to accomplish the task.

Their roles are unmistakable in this scene from *Come Clean*, yet they are not subjected to emphasis – Stan does not, for instance, cry on hearing that his favourite flavour is sold out – and within a few minutes the duo revert to the married men they were at the start of the film. The ease with which they were able to slip in and out of the child–parent relationship (and, incidentally, of their movie personas) is illustrated by an impromptu gag they perform within the documentary footage of their 1932 British tour. During a civic reception at Tynemouth, Hardy presents toys to a stream of children as part of a charity programme. Laurel joins the queue, his hands held out, and is automatically given a toy by Hardy, who, suddenly noticing who the recipient is, withdraws it in mock anger. By 1932 the team's fans would have recognized this role-playing as a natural extension of their screen relationship.

But even in the mature films Stan did not need Ollie to convey his childlike qualities. One of the most prominent of these was his identification with animals. Stan's relationships with the eponymous dog in *Laughing Gravy* and Ethel in *The Chimp* often seem closer than that between him and Ollie. He treats animals as his equals, addressing them as if they were able to comprehend English: in *Way Out West* he politely asks the mule to wait, a request repeated to the dog he befriends in *Air Raid Wardens*. A little later in that film he seems to imitate, albeit unconsciously, the mutt's movements as he pursues it on his hands and knees. When Ollie impersonates an animal, it's always for a specific purpose. On his suggestion, both yowl like cats in *Night Owls* to allay the fears of the people inside the house they are noisily attempting to burgle. But later Stan repeatedly lapses into the feline masquerade simply because he identifies with the animal kingdom. In *Be Big* Ollie compares Stan to a sphinx, an inscrutable combination of felinity and humanity, and in the freaky final scenes of *Dirty Work* and *The Flying Deuces* Ollie physically metamorphoses into a talking chimp and horse respectively, thus embodying the synthesis of human and animal which seems to be Stan's ideal object of affection.

12: *Another Fine Dress*

Another reliable guide to Stan's infancy is drink. His compulsive sucking of milk from the baby's feeding bottle in *Their First Mistake* seems entirely apt. When he enters the adult world of alcohol, he is unable to cope: in *The Devil's Brother* and *The Bohemian Girl* his carefree imbibing of wine suggests a youngster who knows he likes the taste without realizing its effects. The same is true, though, of Ollie: in *Them Thar Hills* both believe they are drinking mountain water, when in fact the well from which it's drawn is polluted with whisky. Conversely, in *Blotto* they manage to lose their sobriety on 'liquor' that turns out to be cold tea. Either way, the effect of drinking is to push the boys towards the extremes of emotion they often display (itself another index of their immaturity). In Stan's case, this may be weeping or, after his excessive intake of wine, a drowsiness that extends his inherently dopey demeanour. (Stan's tendency to lose consciousness is another inheritance from Harry Langdon whose films, Joyce Rheuban notes, frequently present him 'drunk, dazed, drugged, falling asleep, or waking up' (Rheuban, 1983, p. 69).) However, when the boys are together, alcohol – real or apparent – tends to facilitate a hysterical laughing jag in which they feed off each other's mirth. Both regress to infancy, no longer constrained by adult propriety.

Ollie's father-figure is not, therefore, any more constant than Stan's child-figure. In some films, Stan brings about an equalization of their psychic ages, releasing Ollie from the responsibilities and inhibitions of his nominal adulthood by involving him in childlike play. In others, Ollie does not need any assistance to regress to an age even younger than that we associate with Stan. At the climax of *Sons of the Desert* his loss for words in the face of his irate wife's impending assault is represented by a babyish sound effected by his blowing into a glass. After he falls into a cake during the magic act in *The Hollywood Revue of 1929*, he addresses the camera in the monosyllabic words of a toddler – though Stan still seems to be his junior here for *he* is unable to speak at all.

Despite the inter-generational aspect of Stan and Ollie's relationship, the sense that they are *also* both infants is simultaneously conveyed. *Brats* dramatizes this paradox by casting them as both the fathers and their children. This (except for their cameo appearance in Our Gang's *Wild Poses*) was the only occasion when Laurel and Hardy played actual children. The gimmick succeeds because the relatively mature aspects of their personas are also represented through their roles as parents; equilibrium is preserved despite the overtly childish behaviour of their younger selves. However, the dangers of pushing Stan and Ollie too far into an infantile world are illustrated by the over-explicit 'schoolroom' sequence in their first feature *Pardon Us*.

An even riskier undertaking was the introduction of real children in their films. Even if the youngster didn't steal the show, there was a danger that the physical maturity of Stan and Ollie would be highlighted by the direct comparison. (This had not been a problem for Chaplin in *The Kid* (1921), in which he reared a boy, since Charlie, though an unlikely parent, was not a particularly childlike persona.) Yet the team flouted the old theatrical adage, 'Never act with children or animals' on both counts – and these gambles, like that of *Brats*, paid off due to careful preparation. In some ways, the child-adoption films are merely an extension of those in which the boys live with an animal – in *Angora Love*, for instance, they even refer to their goat as a 'kid'. Each sub-genre features the trio as a kind of family unit in which Stan constantly interchanges with the infant or pet. The team chose to appear with girls rather than boys in *Pack Up Your Troubles* and *The Bohemian Girl*, presumably because the gender difference helped to deflect attention from the similarities of psychic age. In both films the girl is merely adopted – they describe themselves as her 'uncles' – though in *The Bohemian Girl* Ollie's wife initially leads him to believe that he is the father. Even though they are married in many films, Stan and Ollie (except in the ironic *Brats*) never have children of their own. Naturally, parallels between each girl and Stan are developed, but the fact that this involves not only regression but also his feminization (another advantage of casting a girl) adds to the richness of the humour.

In *Pack Up Your Troubles* the child's father, soon to be killed in action, tells Stan and Ollie that his absent daughter would 'go crazy about you two', thereby blessing their later role as her surrogate parents. But the statement also functions, I think, as a reference beyond this film to Laurel and Hardy's popularity among children. This does not mean that their work was specially designed to appeal to them, as Laurel confirmed in an interview with John McCabe: 'We made our pictures principally for adults, of course, but they were always loved by kids, too. I hadn't realised how much kids watched us and loved us until the television reruns started.' (McCabe, 1975, p. 149.) Indeed, in Britain at least, the films have usually been broadcast within children's TV. Although there are certainly aspects of Laurel and Hardy to which children can relate, the programming policy is regrettable, for it trivializes the movies, encouraging viewers to 'grow out' of them. My own experience, in contrast, has been to grow into these often complex works, and to discover their true depths.

Masculine women and feminine men

If Stan Laurel took a long time to discover the child within his persona, he seems to have been quicker to explore its femininity. In his vaudeville days he wrote a sketch which required him to adopt 'an old biddy guise' (McCabe, 1975, p. 24). Indeed, drag – both male-to-female and female-to-male – was a mainstay of the British music-hall tradition in which Laurel had learned his craft. His boyhood hero Dan Leno, a comedian to whom he bore a striking physical resemblance, was a famous pantomime dame. Most of the silent cinema's male clowns impersonated women at some point, even Chaplin in *A Woman* (1915), but Laurel – perhaps encouraged by the soft facial features that enabled him to be unusually convincing in feminine guise – seems to have made a speciality of drag.

In *The Sleuth*, a 1925 two-reeler for Joe Rock, he offers two quite different female impersonations. The plot makes little sense – a deficiency found in other Laurel films – though here it functions as part of the parody of incomprehensible detective mysteries. Private eye Stan is hired by a woman to spy on her husband for unspecified reasons. He arrives at the couple's home in the guise of 'the new maid' (a precursor of his several maid masquerades with Hardy), all coy smiles and giggles when greeted by the lecherous husband. The feminine daintiness of Stan's hand-on-hip walk is soon punctured by a pratfall, but despite this he remains successful in his efforts to attract the husband when the two take tea together on a sofa. The detective's motive for his elaborate ruse is not explained, but he clearly does not welcome the husband's attentions: he breaks crockery on the flirt's head and fends off a wandering hand by scalding it with tea. Although he soon abandons the maid's costume, appearing in most of the film as a man, Stan dons drag again for the final scene. Now he is being chased by the husband and three henchmen who, on removing a screen, find a vamp reclining on a couch. The villains are deceived: when the vamp tosses a rose in their direction, they fight over the prize, pummelling each other unconscious as Stan, fanning himself, looks on with a bored yawn. Thus, he defeats them by pandering to their masculine desires and competitiveness, while he adopts the role of feminine passivity. Indeed, it's striking that this and the earlier sofa scene are almost the only occasions in the film that Stan is able to keep reasonably still; when he tries to be an active male, he literally runs around in circles, to no great comedic effect.

Laurel's solo appearances in Roach's All Star series rely even more heavily on drag. *Eve's Love Letters*, released in May 1927 (after the first fruits of the accidental pairing with Hardy), casts him as a butler who helps his married mistress to recover the incriminating missives of the title. However, most of the two-reeler is occupied by Stan's impersonation of a flapper who flirts with his/her master. By acting as an *agent provocateur*, Stan enables the errant Eve to expose the double standards of her jealous husband Adam, in a bedroom farce so typical of Roach at this time. The implicit comparison with biblical archetypes highlights its comment on the sex war, which was a topical subject in the 1920s, the decade in which many women began to gain independence and power.

The butler obviously relishes the joke played on his master, but he concentrates on concealing his masculinity rather than projecting femininity. His costume comprises simply a hat (obscuring his eyes and hair) and a long cape, both of which he is able to don or remove instantly. Indeed, he spends much of the film frantically alternating, out of his master's sight, between his butler and flapper roles, a procedure which succeeds in confusing Adam, especially since Eve is also constantly oscillating between her normal appearance and that of an identically dressed flapper. The masquerade climaxes with the butler pretending to beat the 'flapper'

– now just a dummy – into submission behind a sofa. Much of this scene is shot from the husband's viewpoint, the amazing spectacle he witnesses framed by parted curtains. The suggestion of a stage highlights, for us, the artificiality of Stan's performance, including his manhandling of the 'flapper'. Stan's tough masculinity is as much a pretence as his femininity. His lightning ability to shift gender, and his sharing of the flapper role with Eve, are the significant factors in this film. A man, it seems to say, can play a female role just as effectively as a woman. Yet Stan makes it clear that he was only putting on an act; he denies his femininity. When Adam tries to prove his innocence before his wife by asking the supposedly loyal butler if there has been a woman in the house, Stan replies with ironic truthfulness, 'Nothing like a woman, sir.'

But Laurel didn't have to resort to drag to lose his masculinity. *Half a Man*, which I have already examined for evidence of his burgeoning infantilism, is also a film about gender reversal. The Captain of the boat Stan boards tells him to 'be a man' – an imperative that, like the film's title, alludes both to our hero's lack of maturity and his lack of masculinity. But it's difficult to be a man, at least in the traditional sense, in a world where women appear to have usurped their role. The contemporary popular song 'Masculine Women And Feminine Men' summarized the topsy-turvy gender relations experienced during the 1920s, and this phenomenon is also reflected in the film. Stan finds the female members of the boat's crew intimidating enough at sea when they playfully chase him round the vessel. But after it sinks, and they repair to a desert island, they turn into a savage pack of man-hungry predators whose libido has apparently increased tenfold. Stan is the only man on the island, a situation which exaggerates the surplus of women after the decimation of the male population in World War I.

'There are only two times when women need men – day and night,' proclaims one of the film's titles, reflecting male fear that women were now assuming the active role in sexual relations. To the sex-starved females on the island, even half a man is better than none. They hunt and catch Stan, though when they divest him of his pants they seem shocked by their action and avert their gaze – perhaps a hopeful suggestion by the male film-makers that the new woman did not have the courage of her convictions. Nevertheless, Stan is forced momentarily into the role of the self-sacrificing heroine; like the virgin pursued by a rapist in D. W. Griffith's *The Birth of a Nation* (1915), he threatens to jump off a cliff if the aggressors come nearer. The gender reversal is made even clearer in a later scene, described as 'Beauty and the Beast' by a Griffith-like title, in which the tribe's butch matriarch stalks the cowering Stan. After a discreet cutaway to the other women, who shield their eyes in horror, Stan emerges with a shredded shirt and the Beast in hot pursuit. But Beauty is saved by the arrival of competition – the male crew members of the sunken boat.

This comic inversion of the traditional power relationship between man and woman would appear to be another instance of Laurel emulating Harry Langdon. *The Chaser*, a 1928 Langdon feature, is explicitly a film about gender reversal: Harry is forced to exchange roles and clothes with his wife, who brings her female friends home to observe his humiliation. But even in Langdon's earlier shorts of 1924–26 women were insidiously dominant. On one level, this was another aspect of the child in Harry – his wives were more like mothers – but his over-powdered face and pencilled eyebrows accentuated the effeminacy inherent in his face. 'The least virile and most sexless of all the comedians' (Mast, 1979, p. 166), Langdon disliked being an object of erotic desire – for anyone. In *The Chaser* he attempts suicide after a salesman and an iceman make passes at him – though eventually he submits to his role to the extent of proffering his cheek to the milkman, who duly delivers a kiss! Women's desire for him, however, was usually only in his imagination, as in the bedroom scene of the 1926 feature *The Strong Man* (which evidently inspired a similar scene between Stan and Lola in Laurel and Hardy's feature *Way Out West*). Here, the deceitful Lily chases and wrestles with Harry, who mistakenly believes she is out to seduce him, but Lily is interested in the money inside his clothes, not the body they cover.

Similarly, in Roach's *On the Front Page*, released two months after *The Strong Man*, Stan's enforced seduction of the sophisticated Countess in her boudoir proceeds only because she, tired of intrusive reporters, has decided to teach one of them a lesson. She assumes the role of a vamp whose active sexuality intensifies Stan's inherent fear of women. The reluctant seducer becomes the terrified object of seduction, chastely protecting his virtue by folding his jacket over his breast – an effeminate gesture that would recur in the *Way Out West* bedroom scene. In short, the humour derives from Stan's unconvincing masquerade as a man – just as, in other films, it derives from his successful impersonations of women. The process of feminizing Laurel's persona was well under way by the time he met his cinematic soul mate.

Oliver Hardy's ample size limited his potential in drag, though in one of his early comedies with Billy West he appeared, incredibly, as a pigtailed teenage girl, even posing in a swimsuit like a Sennett Bathing Beauty. As already mentioned, Hardy gradually specialized in heavies, and in other embodiments of masculine authority such as policemen. But in the films of the 1920s at least, both villains and comic cops were set up to be defeated, to have their proud masculinity undermined. This process was intensified in Hardy's early Roach films. In *Yes, Yes, Nanette!* (1925) – co-directed by Laurel – he plays a newlywed girl's burly ex-boyfriend who humiliates the timid groom (James Finlayson). But eventually the worm turns and he physically ejects Hardy from the bride's home; Ollie's apparent masculinity is actually as fragile as his maturity. A title sarcastically describing him as a 'refined steam-fitter' points to a genuine contradiction in Hardy's evolving persona.

This strange mixture of gentility and coarseness is also evident in another Roach marital comedy, *Along Came Auntie* (1926). Here, the inconsistency is suggested even by his character's name, Vincent Belcher, and by the fact that although a musician, he is a peculiarly insensitive one. The plot, a prototype for Laurel and Hardy's *That's My Wife*, makes another comment on the period's changing sexual standards. The old morality is represented by a wealthy aunt ('an antique', puns a title) who bitterly opposes divorce. Her niece, who will receive a fortune only if she conceals her second marriage, clearly embodies the new morality, not to mention the easy credit consumerism of the decade – we are told she 'buys things she can't pay for'. Her impecuniosity has led her to take in a boarder who just happens to be the first husband, played by Hardy. As in *Yes, Yes, Nanette!*, he has been supplanted by a weedy rival

(Glenn Tryon). Hardy retains his masculinity, but mainly in contrast with Tryon who, as part of the scheme to deceive the visiting aunt, is forced to drag up as his own wife and share the marital bed with his amused predecessor. Moreover, Hardy's earlier masculine display – a frenetic fight throughout the house with Tryon – is explained to the amazed aunt as 'a boyhood game'. He may be male, but he is isn't really a man.

Along Came Auntie was made for Roach just a few months prior to *Duck Soup*, the film in which Laurel and Hardy made their first co-starring appearance. Here, the gender roles established separately in the 'solo' films of each actor come together. During the masquerade which forms the bulk of the film, Laurel, drawing on his experience in drag, plays the maid. Hardy, whose gentrified tramp character explicates the class paradox implied in his earlier parts, plays the master. Yet the fact that they are explicitly acting out roles reminds us that gender is not fixed but a performance which can be altered. This theme is continued in *Slipping Wives*, their next film, in which a somewhat effeminate Stan is engaged to play the conventionally masculine role of lover to a wife who wants to make her neglectful husband jealous. He is comically unconvincing, but he puts on a bravura demonstration of gender fluidity in his mimed portrayals of Samson and Delilah, delivered within his masquerade as the lover.

Most of the team's early co-appearances go to some lengths to contrast Stan's femininity with Ollie's masculinity. *Why Girls Love Sailors* casts Ollie as a burly Second Mate who flirts with Stan, in drag again. *With Love and Hisses* is an army comedy which, like so many examples of the genre, relies on a crude opposition of 'sissy' and macho stereotypes. The Stone Age setting of *Flying Elephants* enables the distinction to be made even more clearly, though – as in most of these early efforts – it's Stan who, ironically, emerges as the victor in a contest of masculinity.

In other films, Stan was implicitly feminized not through drag or in contrast with Hardy but by the role reversal with women already evident in some of his solo movies. His sexual submission in *Slipping Wives* revives this theme, much more strongly stated in *Love 'Em and Weep*, where all three male characters are threatened or assaulted by a formidable gallery of aggressive women. Stan is subjected to the deepest humiliation, in that he is symbolically 'raped' by one of them. This, and *Their Purple Moment*, in which the boys are faced with money-grubbing wives, weapon-wielding flappers and a hyperactive female gossip, are prototypes for the many films in which Stan and Ollie come into conflict with women.

William K. Everson has written that the team's 'constant vendetta against women', comparable to that of W. C. Fields, 'undoubtedly alienated a large percentage of the female audience'. (Everson, 1978, p. 271f.) The vendetta is reflected not only in the action of the films but in the coldness and aggressiveness of most of their female characters. These include gossips, scheming vamps or, most often, monstrous harridans who threaten men with axes, shotguns or knives and pots and pans (in the world of Laurel and Hardy, as in Hitchcock, the traditionally female domain of the kitchen becomes an arsenal of lethal weaponry). The sympathetic exceptions tend to be very old or very young – females who are unlikely to present a sexual threat to the boys.

The relationship between Laurel and Hardy and women, as characters in and spectators of their films, deserves a book to itself. The subject was aired in a 1988 edition of BBC Radio Four's *Woman's Hour*, in which even some of the team's most prominent male admirers recognized the misogyny in their movies. 'Ladies don't like Laurel and Hardy', admitted Bill Cubin, curator of the Laurel and Hardy Museum in Ulverston. The female interviewees were keen to connect this notion with the portrayal of marriage in the films. Cubin's wife Lucy argued that male viewers identified with Stan and Ollie as 'henpecked husbands', a role which she felt men, despite their complaints, 'quite enjoy ... whereas women don't like the idea of being a nagging wife'. This points to an element of masochism in the pleasure which (heterosexual) men derive from the films.

Movies of the 1920s tapped into the male fears of emasculation that emerged in the wake of growing female independence. This was symbolized above all by the increased mobility of the many women who learned to drive the automobiles that were changing lifestyles all over the United States during the years of economic boom. *Love 'Em and Weep* makes direct references to this phenomenon as part of its feverish anxiety about men 'losing control'. Women were now occupying the driving seat. But when boom turned to bust in the Wall Street crash, the emasculator men feared most was the Great Depression, as unemployment – or the threat of it – weakened male authority and caused much tension between husbands and wives. Many of Laurel and Hardy's films are a masochistic reflection of this, the pain channelled and assuaged through comedy. The 1930 short *Hog Wild* presents Ollie as a harrassed husband whose failure to erect an aerial for Mrs Hardy is an index of his wounded masculinity.

The boys are equally inadequate when, in some of their other 1930s films, they attempt the household duties normally performed by women. This particular role reversal is another reflection of a common situation during the Depression. As Joan Mellen notes, 'Many jobless men had to take over domestic chores and child-rearing; they were early "house-husbands" while their wives, who could get work, became "breadwinners"' (Mellen, 1977, p. 96). She continues, 'No film chronicles this role change', but several of Laurel and Hardy's come close to doing so. Stan and Ollie's efforts to clean, cook, wash, iron and care for children usually occur when women are absent, though not because they are at work. It was in keeping with the films' misogyny that the boys' humiliation should be blamed on female tyranny rather than economic forces and the government's policies. *Live Bait*, an unproduced story outline probably written (by Laurel) in 1932, presents Ollie's wife as 'a domineering clubwoman who is preparing a luncheon for the Political Rights of American Women group. Mr Hardy and his friend are ordered to peel potatoes and onions' (Skretvedt, 1987, p. 249). Perhaps the overt satire of this inversion of traditional roles was, on second thoughts, considered inappropriate. The scene seems to have been reworked within the remoter nineteenth-century gypsy world of *The Bohemian Girl*. Otherwise, the team's final two-reeler *Thicker than Water* comes nearest to it when, at the insistence of Mrs Hardy, the boys wash and dry the dishes – the one kitchen duty which men have often been expected to undertake. Much more startling are the child-rearing films, particularly *Their First Mistake* where Stan and Ollie seem to compete with each other for the vacancy of 'mother'.

This more covert type of feminization gradually replaced (with rare exceptions) Laurel's drag of the earlier films. In *That's My Wife*, a late silent, he is still cross-dressing but the interest resides less in Stan's somewhat reluctant performance as a woman than in the fact he is masquerading as Ollie's spouse – and at Ollie's instigation. *Another Fine Mess*, a sound remake of *Duck Soup*, presents Stan in a double masquerade where he alternates between maid (his only role in the original) and butler. His gender fluidity, similarly displayed in *Eve's Love Letters*, complements the childlike aspect of his persona: Stan resembles an androgynous infant who, unaware of society's need for conformity, does not yet identify as masculine or feminine. *Twice Two* extends the idea of gender duality in a bold experiment: Stan and Ollie simultaneously play themselves and their twin sisters, Ollie's female half called Fanny. (Equally bizarre is a comic strip in the 12 November 1938 issue of the British children's weekly *Film Fun*, which presents the boys as film actors in drag as 'Fussy Fanny' (Ollie) and her mother (Stan), thus feminizing and inverting their usual inter-generational relationship.) Drag is minimized in the climax of *Chickens Come Home* where Ollie (then Stan) becomes the lower half of an artificial creation headed by Mae Busch. Male and female coexist in one 'body', the join simply concealed by the woman's long coat.

But the team were finding even subtler means to convey femininity, often by little more than a line of dialogue such as Ollie's complaint in *Bonnie Scotland* that he must become 'the mother of invention', delivered with a sigh and a camp clasping of his hands beside his head. It's not surprising to discover that the elaborate, over-genteel mannerisms Hardy used frequently in their films were based on women – his mother and an aunt who was 'very much the grand lady' (McCabe, 1989, p. 103). However, it's usually Laurel who parodies popular images of women, as in the bedroom scene of *Way Out West* and his baring of a leg to halt a stagecoach in the same film. This aspect of Stan's persona was exploited in a 1989 Electricity Board magazine advertisement which used a still from *Come Clean* of him taking a bath fully clothed. Via a balloon, Stan avers, 'Total water heating or not – I'm not doing a nude scene.' On one level this visual ventriloquism simply feminizes Stan, because most people still think of 'nude scenes' as a female preserve. But the juxtaposition of the 1931 image with 1989 words implicitly acknowledges the increased cinematic display of male bodies since Laurel and Hardy's heyday in order to poke fun at the idea of Stan as a masculine sex object.

The musical numbers which feature in many of their longer films also contribute to the feminization process. Stan and Ollie's songs and dances allow an extra degree of gender playfulness, the soft-shoe shuffle and the duet in *Way Out West*, for example, both displaying androgynous qualities. In some of the military films the duo's numbers function as part of their transgression of male authority and discipline. Their spontaneous self-expression in these peculiarly graceful musical interludes liberates them from the rigid conformity that other men seek to impose on them. Their dustcart dance in *Bonnie Scotland*, though wordless, is perhaps the clearest example of their subversion of masculine values.

Yet due to their misogyny the boys are constantly embracing male organizations in their efforts to escape from the female domain of the home. This may be the temporary refuge afforded by the masonic type of fraternities to which they belong in several films. But in others they are removed to male communities which seem to offer a more permanent safety zone: the army, the navy, the Foreign Legion and even prison are offered as preferable alternatives to the world of women. University, as portrayed in *A Chump at Oxford*, and the police force, of which they are members in *The Midnight Patrol*, also qualify as exclusively male domains.

Stan and Ollie's discomfort in the uniforms which these institutions require them to wear symbolizes their inability to integrate. In *A Chump at Oxford* they arrive in the wrong one, in other films they wear the right outfits incorrectly or are unable to fit into them. These difficulties draw attention to the uniforms as mere get-ups: masculinity, like femininity in the drag films, is only a costume, a masquerade. But if this is true for Stan and Ollie, it's also true for their peers. Inside these male organizations the boys remain outsiders only because they are less skilful at playing the role of men. In *Be Big* they belong to a fraternity whose uniform is a riding outfit, worn merely as fancy dress at a stag party. Stan and Ollie struggle with their uniform for so long (significantly, their problem is matching themselves to the butch boots) that they have not even left home for the party when their wives return. But their failure lies only in their inability to put on the disguise of masculinity.

Perhaps they don't even want to. Deliberately or otherwise, they break the rules and disrupt order. Stan and Ollie repeatedly undermine conventional masculinity with a highly individual blend of bourgeois and feminine behaviour. This is illustrated by the dug-out scene in *Pack Up Your Troubles* where the boys calmly proceed with their morning toilet despite the massive raid in progress above their heads. Earlier, they have been found cuddled up together in a bunk. Their love for each other, whether sexual or not, is another subversive force in these hierarchical communities, most of which foster division and hatred between men. Transgression of masculine roles also occurs in the boxing match of *Any Old Port* where Stan transforms the tough sport into a dance by hugging rather than hitting his opponent.

Laurel and Hardy's parody of 'male' genre movies is not limited to their overt spoofs of war films, Westerns and prison pictures. The boys' tit-for-tat battles, with each other and with third parties (usually men), are scenes of combat that have been transferred from the rugged, exotic locales of 'male' genres to the mundane urban world of high streets, homes and shops. The ritualistic aspects of combat are, in a fashion, retained but the phallic weaponry of guns is replaced by soft substances, such as mud and many types of food (including eggs, a female product). The favourite targets are clothes, possessions and homes, not human bodies. The comedy of these scenes lies not only in their suggestion of children at play but also in the feminization and embourgeoisement of traditional depictions of male combat.

Mocking eroticism

In Stan Laurel's earliest films his comic persona is clearly that of a determined heterosexual. He might not 'get the girl' as often as, say, Harold Lloyd but there's seldom any doubt that he wants to. However, in the mid-1920s, the ambiguities of age and gender in his revised Harry Langdon-like persona are supplemented by contradictions concerning his sexuality. The desert island comedy *Half a Man* supplies love interest for him, but the role of the heroine, dubbed 'The Girl', is as perfunctory as her anonymity suggests. Although she wears a dark naval uniform to distinguish her from the other female crew members dressed in white, she is still a member of the pack of man-hungry women from whom Stan runs away in terror. To avoid being raped, he flees momentarily to The Girl with cries of 'Save me!', but this hardly prepares us for the film's conclusion where Stan embraces her on a beach. This moment of token heterosexuality seems a self-conscious act designed to parody the romantic happy endings of more serious films. These are parodied in a different way in *The Soilers* (1923), a spoof of the popular Western *The Spoilers*, when Stan becomes the object of homosexual desire from a 'sissy' cowboy (an early example of the feminization of a butch stereotype) who throws him a potted petunia and exclaims, 'My hero!'

Stan himself displays his strongest sexual signals when masquerading as heterosexual *women* in *The Sleuth* and other drag films. His flirtatious behaviour with men in these films might suggest that he has homosexual desires, but the fact he's in a woman's costume reassures us that it's all an act, a mere ruse motivated (though seldom clearly) by the narrative. In *Eve's Love Letters* his female impersonation facilitates the heterosexual reunion of his employers, but his own sexuality remains obscure. Casting him as a butler in this and at least two other solo films of 1926 and 1927 (*Get 'Em Young*, another drag film, and *On the Front Page*) highlights his subservience to the desires of others. As a butler, Stan is the epitome of English impassivity and asexuality, a dummy whom his employers tailor to their needs of the moment when they embroil him in their sophisticated schemes involving sex and/or marriage. When ordered to play the role of the virile heterosexual male who must seduce the Countess in *On the Front Page*, it seems more foreign to his nature than when he is required to impersonate a woman. Nor can he cope with being the object of (apparent) homosexual desire: he is affronted when his master's son uses him to demonstrate how the Countess should be kissed. Physical love of any kind, real or simulated, is anathema to him. But perhaps it was just that he hadn't met the right partner yet.

Oliver Hardy, in his earliest appearances, is remarkably successful for a movie fat boy at 'getting the girl'. In the 1914 Lubin one-reeler *The Servant Girl's Legacy* he wins the heroine's hand by virtue of his constant love, while that of his rivals is financially motivated. A year later, in *Something in Her Eye*, the girl announces that she will marry 'the best fighter' among her various suitors. Hardy, a clean-shaven cherub, is defeated by foul play but she elopes with him anyway. Of course, when he was cast as the moustached villain the tables were turned. In the Larry Semon two-reeler *Kid Speed* (1924) Hardy plays Semon's unscrupulous rival in a car race that, like a jousting tournament, will decide who wins the fair lady they both desire. This time Hardy loses both the contest and the girl.

But in this and other films where he supported Semon, the girl was secondary to the prize of the rival's humiliation in the stunt-studded fights and chases that, even when not as explicitly competitive as the *Kid Speed* race, functioned as contests of masculinity. In *Stick Around*, where Hardy is partnered with Bobby Ray, the focus on the two male protagonists has become sharp enough to produce a scene of ironic homosexuality. When the head decorator and his lackey both drink bootleg liquor, their power bond melts into an affectionate one, sealed when each man kisses the other's cheek. 'I've always loved you, bossy,' declares Bobby and the scene fades with Hardy cradling his diminutive assistant against his chest. In its depiction of a male relationship where love and conflict alternate – perhaps even coexist if Ray has 'always loved' his boss – this film anticipates the mature Laurel and Hardy. However, Stan and Ollie's mutual affection, like their occupation of master and servant roles, would almost always be conveyed more subtly and ambiguously than Bobby and Ollie's.

The overt homosexual (rather than merely effeminate) images in *The Soilers* and *Stick Around* reflect the increasing sexual frankness of 1920s cinema. This is even more evident in many of the films produced by Roach from around 1925. The themes of sexual and marital relations dominated the All Star series in which Hardy eventually met Laurel. The scene in *Along Came Auntie* where ex-husband Hardy shares a bed with his replacement imitates a similar one in *Should Sailors Marry?* In this slightly earlier (1925) comedy of remarriage, Hardy has a minor role as a dignified doctor while the villainous part of a wrestler in which he would once have been typecast goes to Noah Young. The latter is so desperate to receive alimony from his ex-wife – a typical comment on the role reversal of the period – that he takes *her* place on her second wedding night in order to prevent the escape of the groom (Clyde Cook) from whose savings both hope to benefit. The new husband, a weedy sailor called Cyril, contrasts strongly with his butch predecessor, so that the long scene in which the two men share a bed represents an alternative marriage of masculine and feminine, while the wife common to both is displaced to another room.

As we have seen, many of Stan and Ollie's early co-appearances are also marked by gender difference, indicating that their screen relationship initially imitated the heterosexual one of wife and husband. This is made more explicit in films such as *Sugar Daddies*, where Stan masquerades as Ollie's 'little wife', and *Why Girls Love Sailors*, in which Ollie responds in kind to Stan's slap and tickle. Stan's drag inhibits homosexual interpretations of such scenes but when, flirting with a sheriff in *Duck Soup*, he loses the protective mask of his female attire – yet retains the complementary gestures – his appearance becomes that of an effeminate gay man. He conveys this impression, this time without the excuse of any female impersonation, in his characterization of Cuthbert the 'sissy' private in *With Love and Hisses*. Confirmation of Cuthbert's supposed sexuality is provided by Ollie's homophobic stare at the private's hand resting on his shoulder.

Ollie, at this stage, is often portrayed as a womanizer. Stan cannot even *pretend* to be one in *Slipping Wives*, though the wife he is supposed to seduce does not enhance his intended image as heterosexual lover by introducing him as the author of 'fairy stories'. In *Putting Pants on Philip* he is, for once, a real woman-chaser. Yet even here Stan is feminized and/or homosexualized in the scene, parodying cinematic representations of rape, where Ollie takes his inside leg measurement by force. As Joyce Rheuban has noted, this is a close reworking of a gag situation 'laden with innuendo about transvestism, homosexuality, rape, and loss of virginity' in *The Sea Squawk*, a 1925 two-reeler in which Harry Langdon appeared as a kilted Scotsman two years before Laurel (Rheuban, 1983, p. 215). *Putting Pants* shows a rare degree of sophistication, however, in its insistence that Stan is not homosexual – quite the reverse – despite his deflowered maiden act. The 'feminine men' of the 1920s were not all gay.

It's not until *Should Married Men Go Home?*, which happens to be the first of the official 'Laurel and Hardy Series', that we see a prototype for what I will term the 'bachelor intruder' films – those in which Stan competes with Mrs Hardy for Ollie. *Married Men* takes some trouble to establish Ollie's devotion to his wife and the difficulty of the choice he faces. Moreover, the boys' heterosexuality is affirmed when they pair off with girls at the golf club. But by the time of *That's My Wife*, Stan is actually living with the Hardys in a tense *ménage à trois*, and he not only precipitates the wife's immediate departure from the narrative but literally replaces her in an extended female impersonation. The team were sufficiently confident with the 'bachelor intruder' theme to use it for their first talkie, *Unaccustomed As We Are*. *Blotto*, the only movie in which Stan but not Ollie is married, reverses the basic set-up. *Our Wife*, however, returns to the original pattern with a vengeance; here, Ollie ends up legally wedded to Stan, who no longer needs drag to assume the role of his spouse. The cross-eyed judge who marries the two men, instead of Ollie and his bride, cannot see 'straight' in either sense. *Their First Mistake* takes the situation to its furthest extreme: Stan and Ollie conceive the idea of a baby to divert Mrs Hardy's attention from their friendship. It was not, however, the last of these films. As late as 1938, in *Block-Heads*, Ollie's wife was telling Stan, 'Not content with wrecking my home, you want to take my husband away from me.' Stan's home-wrecking is not confined to the destruction of property.

1938 also saw *The Wedding Party*, a pilot script, written by Laurel, for a projected Laurel and Hardy radio series that never materialized. The sketch, recorded before a live audience, has been preserved in sound and published in John McCabe's book *The Comedy World of Stan Laurel*. Its interest lies partly in its reversal of the 'bachelor intruder' theme. Here, as Stan is about to be married, Ollie tells his pal's bride (Patsy Moran), 'You took poor little Stanley away from me. You broke up *my* home.' (His emphasis.) By now, Stan and Ollie were so firmly established as a couple that the unmarried woman could become the intruder in *their* domestic bliss. The theme's weirdest variant is suggested in *The Fighting*

Kentuckian (1949), one of three sound feature films which Hardy made without Laurel. Here, 'Ollie' – or rather his revised character Willie Payne – almost becomes the bachelor intruder in the marriage of John Wayne and Vera Ralston. As Duke drives off with his bride at the end of the film, he remarks regretfully, 'We can't take him with us on our honeymoon, can we?' In lieu, he takes Willie's hat.

Stan and Ollie's image as a domesticated couple had been established in a number of movies which open with the boys living together on their own. *Leave 'Em Laughing* presents them as lodgers whose bed-sharing (repeated in many later films) was perhaps inspired by that of the first and second husbands in earlier Roach comedies. The presence of an animal in several of the team's boarding-house films reinforces their status as a couple, bonded by a pet rather than a child. *Early to Bed* (set in 'Hardy Manor') eliminates all other characters, except a dog, in order to focus on the Stan–Ollie relationship. It contains a scene, comparable to the 'rape' in *Putting Pants on Philip*, which illustrates a recurrent motif in the Laurel and Hardy oeuvre that I will call the 'mock-erotic': a non-sexual act presented in a sexually suggestive manner, sometimes satirizing conventional cinematic imagery. The bedroom scene of *Way Out West* is a heterosexual specimen, but the mock-erotic moments are often gay. The sequence in *Liberty* where passers-by mistake the boys' furtive efforts to exchange pants for a homosexual assignation is one of the longest and clearest examples. The reworking of this gag in the drag comedy *That's My Wife* adds an extra layer of deception; here, their vigorous efforts to find a necklace that has got lost in Stan's dress are misinterpreted as not only sexual but heterosexual.

More subtle mock-eroticism occurs in the boot-removal scenes of *Be Big*, a film whose most overt parallel with sexual activity never made it to the screen. The original scripts of this and other Laurel and Hardy vehicles outline gags that were apparently never shot, or at least removed from the final cuts. The film-makers clearly exercised self-censorship in their mock-eroticism. They knew exactly what they could and could not do with the Stan and Ollie personas. It was not only a question of yielding to prevailing standards of taste and decency. The period of Hollywood cinema in which Laurel and Hardy made most of their films was not as 'innocent' as many commentators have claimed. Before 1934, when the Hays Production Code became much stricter, a great amount and variety of sexual innuendo managed to pass through the censors, as these and many other 'pre-Code' films testify. But more explicit sexuality, even if allowable, would have been inappropriate; Stan and Ollie are not gay, any more – or any less – than they are heterosexuals, women or children.

However, to deny that homosexual humour is present in many of their films is, I think, to diminish their stature and richness. Yet many writers have attempted to do so. Even Charles Barr, in his otherwise admirable and considered study of the team's work, finds 'something rather absurd about discussing this seriously at all'. Invoking a 1960s brand of psychoanalytic prejudice, he tries to dismiss the gayness as merely another component of Stan and Ollie's childlike behaviour with the suggestion that 'homosexuality itself consists of a fixation at a certain level of immaturity' (Barr, 1967, pp. 57–58). This absurd generalization perhaps has some validity in relation to the boys, especially Stan: his psychic age is reflected in a failure to see any reason to stabilize his own gender, and in the similarity of his behaviour to both women and men. Both are illustrated in *The Wedding Party* radio sketch, where he appropriates the bridal veil, answers to the 'sweetheart' epithet Ollie intends for Patsy, and responds to Ollie's request to 'kiss and make up' by depositing a smacker on him instead of the bride. When Stan does behave like a heterosexual male, it seems that he is yielding to society's pressures, not to his own desires. In another radio sketch, with Lucille Ball, he declares that though he has chased girls he 'never knew why'.

Mentally a little older, Ollie feels greater pressure to play a heterosexual role, which is why he, more often than Stan, is trapped in a loveless marriage. In *Their First Mistake*, asked to clarify whom he prefers, his wife or Stan, he replies, 'We won't go into that,' but emotionally the films are always weighted in favour of the relationship between the two men. Their love does not need to speak its name, but in *Our Relations* Stan and Ollie, both married, perform a little ritual after every occasion when they happen to speak in unison. This celebration of their togetherness also emphasizes the exclusion zone around them which their wives are forbidden to enter. When, in two of the 'bachelor intruder' movies, *Blotto* and *Their First Mistake*, the wife's physical proximity forces the husband to feign a verbal denial of the friend who is telephoning, the narrative focuses on reuniting the two men. It is they, not the estranged spouses, who have to 'kiss and make up' – metaphorically, at least.

The female characters' negative qualities make Stan and Ollie appear all the more vulnerable and sympathetic. The warm intimacy of their bond, sometimes extended to incorporate other men, is emphasized by contrast with the miserable marital relationships. However, in the talkies especially, women are displaced from narratives that, logically, demand their presence. In *Beau Hunks* the vamp who drives her men to the Foreign Legion is reduced to a photograph that is promptly torn to pieces. The eponymous Ethel in *The Chimp* behaves alternately like the wives and girlfriends of earlier movies then, later in the film, she supplants her human namesake, whose role is little more than a photograph. However, the most radical usurpation of the woman's role occurs in the movies where either Stan or Ollie somehow 'becomes' the other's wife. In the double-identity film *Twice Two* it works both ways: they are married to each other's twin sister. But it is in *Their First Mistake* that the apotheosis of this and other themes in Laurel and Hardy's work is reached . A fascinating masterpiece, it shows how Stan alone is able to contain the multiple identities of child, wife and the friend who may – or may not – be Ollie's lover. Here, the ambiguities of age, gender and sexuality are fully synthesized.

These three ambiguities, representing the human (and occasionally animal) aspects of Stan and Ollie, are central to my analyses of the films. However, I will be discussing, in less detail, the following issues which also involve opposing forces.

Class conflict and masquerade

I have already touched on the issue of class in relation to gender. Stan and Ollie's bourgeois values are often allied to the femininity with which they disrupt masculine authority in the military films. The combination is not, however, confined to that sub-genre. When Stan dons drag, the performance is usually linked to upward mobility. In the Fox feature *Jitterbugs* he elevates his social status when he masquerades as a Boston lady whose image of wealth is designed to attract money from others. Similarly, Stan's performance as Ollie's spouse in a swanky nightclub in *That's My Wife* is motivated by his pal's desire to secure the 'fine new home' promised by a rich uncle: femininity is thus employed to squeeze cash from patriarchy. But, as that example demonstrates, Ollie has the greater class pretensions. In *Duck Soup* and *Another Fine Mess* Stan's maid masquerades merely bolster Ollie's assumption of the master's role.

Ollie's bourgeois pomposity dominates the early silent *Putting Pants on Philip*, where his role as Piedmont Mumblethunder establishes, albeit in extreme form, the condescension he would show towards Stan throughout their movies. When Ollie really does inherit a fortune in *Early to Bed*, his inherent snobbery leads him to employ his friend as the butler of 'Hardy Manor'. This is one of several films in which wealth, or the expectation of it, momentarily severs the boys' friendship. Huge sums need not be involved: in *Brats* even the prize of a nickel for the first one in bed produces violent conflict. When Stan's (presumed) inheritance is at stake in *The Laurel-Hardy Murder Case*, Ollie insists on receiving half of it. The situation is reversed in *Oliver the Eighth*, though earlier in this film Ollie has explained to Stan that his new 'social position won't permit' their association to continue.

But on the whole, the boys share the same class. This changes from film to film and is usually defined by work and home, or the lack of them. They may be unemployed or tycoons, tramps or householders. The variability of their social, economic and marital statuses only serves to focus attention on what is constant about their personas and their interrelationship. This is a further illustration of the fluidity of which the duo are capable while remaining essentially the same Stan and Ollie.

Conformity and rebellion

Charles Barr has written that Stan and Ollie 'are supreme liberators from bourgeois inhibition, yet essentially they are, or aspire to be, respectable bourgeois citizens' (Barr, 1967, p. 6). This tension between conformity and rebellion is, on one level, another aspect of their class fluidity. The duo may oscillate between both poles of behaviour within one film. In *Perfect Day* they appear to represent the epitome of bourgeois conformity: both married, they intend to go on a Sunday picnic with their wives, but their respect for 'the day of peace' is overridden by the destructive violence in which they become embroiled with their neighbours. Ultimately, they erode the social standards and responsibilities which their homes and marriages initially seem to celebrate.

Rebellion in Laurel and Hardy films typically takes the form of reciprocal destruction, in which the violence intended for people is usually redirected on their property. Clothes, possessions, merchandise, cars and even homes all become fair game. Some of these are fashioned into weapons, which are then used to assault other property or the human body. This is, of course, a feature of their childlike behaviour, but it also represents a much more extreme regression to primeval instincts, and a rebellion against the consumerism of twentieth-century civilization. Yet the exhilaration of the conflict is often followed by a poignant sense of loss – possibly of material possessions but, more importantly, of humanity – because it occurs in the context of their aspirations to integrate with society.

Moreover, the savagery is so intense in some of the films that violent moments have been cut in reissue and/or TV prints: the key scene in *Our Relations* where the boys insert and crush a light bulb in James Finlayson's mouth, and their use of kettles to scald their enemies with boiling water in *Pack Up Your Troubles* have both been excised, presumably for fear of imitation by children. A comic hanging sequence in *The Devil's Brother* and the Bogeyman scenes in *Babes in Toyland* – a film Charles Barr considered 'not altogether suitable for children' (Barr, 1967, p. 90) – were also subjected to censorship long after these movies were first released. The rebellious humour of the 1930s was made to conform to modern tastes.

Narrative and spectacle

The scenes of reciprocal destruction in Laurel and Hardy films are displays of spectacle which momentarily halt the narratives. Tit-for-tat not only parodies the combat rituals in 'male' genre movies, as I have already suggested, but it also offers similar pleasures to, say, the Western shoot-out in which the combatants and their actions are spectacularized. The difference is that Stan and Ollie's violence, besides being comic, rarely resolves the narrative but rather transforms it into a perpetual cycle of futile actions. Moreover, the deliberate pace with which tit-for-tat is usually conducted emphasizes the element of spectacle.

'They're so *slow*' is, in my experience, the most commonly voiced criticism of Laurel and Hardy's films. Many of them do not provide such basic narrative pleasures as surprise (the action is more likely to be deliberately predictable), the building of climaxes or variations of pace and location. Maybe this was the fault – if it be one – of Stan Laurel, who 'in story construction was just impossible' (Hal Roach, quoted in Skretvedt, 1987, p. 292). The objection that the films are slow is incontestable. *Perfect Day* devotes all of its twenty minutes to the impediments which delay the departure of the would-be picnickers; it's a film about progress defeated by repetition. Even the much-loved three-reeler *The Music Box* seems determined to challenge the viewer's patience with its cyclical action. After Stan and Ollie have finally installed the player-piano they have spent the entire film delivering, the narrative still does not progress; instead, they pause to celebrate their achievement with a dance. Musical numbers like this (mainly in the longer films) retard narrative development even further. But, of course, the point is that the musical and comic spectacle often incorporates and transforms the narrative. Sometimes this occurs in an explicit way: in *The Devil's Brother* earlier events are recalled during the boys' laughing jag, and near the end of *Way Out West* Stan (aping Harry Langdon in *The Strong Man*) recapitulates his adventures in mime.

Way Out West is atypical among Laurel and Hardy films in that the narrative moves to a conventionally happy resolution. Stan and Ollie finally recover the misappropriated deed and rescue the heroine from her wicked guardians. But more frequently the traditional success story pattern in 'male' genres is subjected to comic inversion: the boys usually fail – miserably and spectacularly – to accomplish their set objective. This formal 'failure' to provide conventional narrative pleasures is an appropriate echo of the failure of masculine endeavour which the narratives represent.

Despite the unusual degree of creative autonomy which Laurel and Hardy enjoyed during most of their years with Roach, their films were not made in a cultural vacuum. Since many of them have attained an international 'classic' status, there is a tendency to think of them as timeless and universal, but they were of course products of their own time and place. Therefore, where it seems particularly relevant and interesting, the following analyses suggest ways in which, perhaps unconsciously, they reflect the broad developments in the social and economic history of the United States during the three decades which they span. I also attempt, in some cases, to relate them to other films, not only comedies but the serious movies which Laurel and Hardy's parody or allude to. Another influence, on Laurel at least, was the British music-hall in which he grew up. He maintained his link with it in later life by collecting books on the subject and gramophone records by its stars. In a few instances, I suggest how specific music-hall songs may have inspired situations and characterizations in Laurel and Hardy films.

Throughout the book I refer to 'Stan' and 'Ollie' even when their characters are officially given different names. As I explain, this applies mainly to the early films. To preserve the chronology of the team's creative development, I discuss the films in their order of production, rather than their release for exhibition. The few exceptions are clearly stated in the text. On the whole, I do not discuss the foreign-language versions of certain early talkies, in which Laurel and Hardy speak their lines phonetically in French, Spanish and so forth. Judging from the examples I have seen or read about, these films – though fascinating – usually follow the English prototypes closely as far as Stan and Ollie are concerned.

This book is not intended as a definitive or exhaustive account of Laurel and Hardy's work. It offers a series of personal readings, developed over repeated viewings, which emphasize the aspects that have given me the greatest pleasure and interest, especially in my adult life. Since most of these aspects have received only superficial, if any, discussion in earlier books, I hope to shed new light on well-known films and to promote further study of certain neglected or undervalued ones. Although my approach is not primarily evaluative, I do not attempt to disguise my enthusiasms or antipathies.

Of course, my interpretations – though always closely based on the details of each film – may not always be in accord with the film-makers' intentions. Since Laurel and Hardy's films were more collaborative than most made in Hollywood, there was probably a wide range of intentions, most of them unknowable today. However, in some instances I advance reasons which, in addition to the evidence from within a given film, lead me to believe that a certain line of comic thought was deliberately pursued. The intelligent reader will not, however, make the mistake, so frequently committed in tabloid 'newspapers' and popular biographies, of assuming that a creative artist's interest in particular themes, usually sexual, necessarily correlates with his or her private life.

It's surely one test of a film's (or any artwork's) value that it should be capable of producing different meanings in different contexts. If Laurel and Hardy's more conservative fans (and critics) are determined to adhere to the orthodox view that their films are little more than simple-minded slapstick interspersed with catch-phrases, then neither this book nor any other will alter their rigidity. But the rest of us, like Stan and Ollie themselves, do not need to conform.

Chapter two

All Stars into Co-stars: The Early Silents (1926–27)

THE LUCKY DOG is a rather crude and frantic two-reeler, typical of its time, which has been estimated at various dates between 1917 and (more probably) 1920. But it is known that the film was not released in its extant form until 1922 when it appeared in Metro's Sun-Lite Comedy Series. Usually noted only for the first, accidental co-appearance of Laurel and Hardy, it is basically Laurel's show, while Hardy has a relatively minor role as a tough robber. In both their main scenes together, he threatens Stan with a gun, albeit ineffectually: like most of Ollie's attempts to harm Stan in their later work, his threats backfire, almost literally so here. In the film's second half Ollie's masquerade as a top-hatted Swiss count also anticipates the class pretensions that would become central to his persona. However, *The Lucky Dog* is most interesting for its revelation of several traits which would become regular features of Stan's persona, particularly his association with animals, which recurred in many Laurel and Hardy movies including the last one, *Atoll K*, made over three decades later.

In *The Lucky Dog* Stan plays a brash wise guy who at the start of the film is being violently ejected by his landlady for non-payment of rent. At one point in this scene he briefly makes the open-armed gesture of incomprehension that, magnified and slowed down, would become a Laurel trademark. Lying in the road and suffering from concussion after his unceremonious ejection, he imagines – and director Jess Robbins visualizes for us – a group of (female) fairies dancing round his head: a hint of the fey, otherworldly tendency in Stan's later character. One of the fairies begins to kiss him, but the vision fades and he finds that in reality a stray dog is licking his face. Although Stan does not want the mutt – he even tries to dump it in a dustbin – it follows him.

Chaplin's contemporaneous *A Dog's Life* (1918) equates its tramp hero with a 'thoroughbred mongrel': both sleep rough, scavenge for food, etc. *The Lucky Dog* does this less explicitly (or sentimentally), and there's no sense that Stan himself identifies with the animal, but the film compares his pursuit of a young lady (Florence Gillet) with the dog's interest in her poodle, which she's entering in a show. A top-hatted gent accompanies her, but neither Stan nor his mutt are classy enough to gain access to the dog show – 'thoroughbreds only' are allowed. The canine comparison is extended when, to further his romance, and avoid the doorman, he tries to gain entrance on all fours, but his anarchic presence disrupts the orderly show.

Finding himself outside again, he gives his mutt to the lady, apparently as a replacement for the poodle she seems to have lost in the fracas. Stan's romantic interests are conveyed via the dog, which he kisses as he hands it to her, just as it 'kissed' him earlier in the film. In one respect, he does 'get the girl' (Stan, like his mutt, goes home with her), and is therefore a 'lucky dog'. However, the physical intimacy with the animal – not matched by any with the girl (at least in the slightly ragged print currently available) – suggests a childlike bond stronger than the adult heterosexual one he apparently desires. That remains as illusory as the fairy's kiss – the dog is reality. It is also sexless according to Stan, who does not know 'whether to call it Henry or Henrietta', prefiguring the gender ambiguity of Laurel's later screen persona, who does identify with his pets. It's also worth noting that in *The Lucky Dog* Stan's pursuit of the mutt to a street corner, where robber Ollie lurks, serves to introduce Laurel to Hardy. Lucky indeed!

It may even have been lucky that for the next seven years or so the two comedians went their separate ways. If *The Lucky Dog*

to-do husband and wife come to rent the house, Ollie decides that he will impersonate the Colonel and that Stan must masquerade as the maid. They go into the maid's bedroom, where Stan changes into her uniform. Thus, the power element in the   screen Laurel–Hardy relationship is established, with Ollie donning the clothes of the master and Stan adopting a role as his servant. Moreover, the relationship is reinforced by traditional gender stereotyping: Ollie, whose thickly stubbled chin confirms his masculinity as much as his poverty, must adopt the male role to be dominant; Stan must be feminized to be submissive. (In the remake Stan has to be both maid *and* butler, showing how complex their gender and power relations had become by 1930.) The gender roles are further emphasized when Ollie pairs off with the husband – in a fruitless search for a billiard room – and Stan remains on the sofa with the wife.

Although the sofa scene is much shorter than that in the sound remake, even here the extent and detail of Stan's female impersonation is remarkable. Questioned closely by the prospective mistress of the house, he giggles, swishes his hand, bashfully looks away from her and covers his eyes. Reminiscent of his similar laughter in the park-bench scene with Ollie, Stan again occupies the left of the two-shot, the repetition suggesting that his femininity is a component of his everyday behaviour. One does not sense (in the sofa scene at least) a desire on Stan's part to relinquish his role, to declare he's really a man – the source of humour in most cinematic female impersonations. His masquerade exceeds the requirements necessary to convince the lady, so that the scene, unburdened by narrative purpose, becomes a spectacle that's an enjoyable end in itself, both for the viewer and for the impersonator.

However, in a later scene, when the lady instructs him to prepare a bath, Stan – terrified of seeing her naked – becomes like a frightened child or animal (the two images often reinforce each other in Stan's persona). To avert his gaze, he dunks his head, ostrich-like, in the bath-water. When she pulls him out, he makes an open-armed gesture of resignation, then turns to find her still clothed. His relief is expressed through laughter and a Harry Langdon-like hand-on-mouth pose which confirms his immaturity. We are reminded that he's really a man (who shouldn't be in a lady's bathroom) but not 'a real man' (who would be sexually excited by the prospect of seeing a naked young woman). Stan's childlike nature is also conveyed by glimpses of his 'cry' at several moments in the film, notably when the lady announces that she wants to keep the maid on when they rent the house. In another scene Stan is momentarily cradled in Ollie's arms, an image – suggesting the latter's authority over Stan is paternal – that would recur in several of their movies.

Towards the end of the film, Stan has to confirm his femininity twice by using appropriate gestures for the benefit of a new spectator. The first instance involves the real Colonel, who has returned for his bow and arrow. When the unidentified visitor insists on entering, Stan uses a hand-on-hip gesture to convey his maid(en)ish outrage at the intrusion. On the second occasion, Stan encounters the sheriff, and coyly tries to seduce him with a simpering smile and a playful pat on the cheek. Retreating to the house for safety, he turns back to reinforce his image – as in the sofa scene, this exceeds necessity – by striking a feminine hand-on-ear pose; however, the fact he has lost his dress (torn away by a nail) severely undermines the illusion and, incidentally, gives his seductive posture an effeminately homosexual appearance. In the final sequence, the duo are marched off to fight fires, their shared reluctance to embrace this macho occupation suggesting that Ollie's masculinity was more of a pose than Stan's femininity. Their unsuitability for the job is evinced by the final shots of their hose spinning crazily out of control, the force of the water whisking the boys into the air. It would be several films later before they returned to earth as the 'Stan' and 'Ollie' who are embryonically apparent in *Duck Soup*.

Nevertheless, their next joint effort, **Slipping Wives**, made for the All Star series around October 1926, is a more interesting film than commentators have suggested. It's basically a reworking of Jacques Deval's farce, *Her Cardboard Lover*, of which there were several Hollywood versions including MGM's 1932 adaptation for Buster Keaton, *The Passionate Plumber*. Laurel, like Keaton, is the dumb, sexless would-be gigolo unsuitably chosen by a bored wife (Priscilla Dean) to make her neglectful husband (Herbert Rawlinson) jealous. A clean-shaven Hardy is cast as Jarvis the butler, but his role is by no means small and, moreover, it allows him to pair off with Stan in several scenes. In the first of these Stan, playing a beret-wearing paint delivery man called Ferdinand Flamingo (compare his ostrich-like behaviour in *Duck Soup*), rings the doorbell and is told by a haughty Hardy to use the servants' entrance. Although Ollie is supposed to be the servant in this film, he affects the same air of superiority as his gentrified tramp displayed in *Duck Soup*, and once again tries to subjugate Stan. But Stan insists on using the main entrance and a fight ensues, ending with Ollie falling into the paint. For the first time in a 'Laurel and Hardy' picture, Stan causes Ollie's (literal) downfall, but the latter manages to preserve a vestige of dignity by meticulously wiping paint first from his eyes, then his fingers – a series of gestures, accompanied by a camera-look, that would be repeated in later films whenever Ollie was covered in mess.

Stan's comic unsuitability for playing the wife's 'lover', even for appearance, is conveyed through his childlike and effeminate behaviour: as Priscilla persuades him to play the role, he simpers, bashfully puts a finger to his lip and even chews the beret he holds. The power struggle between him and Ollie is resumed when he drops the beret in front of the butler who, humiliated by having to pick it up, proceeds to hold the headgear gingerly between two fingers. That Ollie's proud manner is just an act – as much a pretension as his aristocratic Colonel in *Duck Soup* – is revealed when, out of his mistress's sight, he kicks and chases Stan.

Upstairs, Ollie must prepare Stan for *his* masquerade as the lover by dressing him in 'the Master's clothes'. If the bedroom in *Duck Soup* was the site of Ollie's conversion of Stan from a man into a woman, using the maid's clothes, here his task is to convert Stan from a child-woman into a man, using the clothes of the husband with whom the 'lover' must compete. First, he instructs Stan to wash, but he refuses, so Ollie drags him into the bathroom and tries to remove his clothes. This causes Stan to cry and the butler to end up in the bath (another early Laurel-induced disaster for Hardy). Eventually, Stan gets into the bath fully clothed, whereupon Ollie washes him as if he were an infant – or rather, given his vigorous hoisting and dunking, like a cloth rubbed against a washboard. Ollie has once again reasserted his dominant/parental position.

Later, Priscilla introduces Stan to her husband as 'Lionel Ironsides – the famous writer of fairy stories', a clear reference to the effeminate homosexuality of Stan's character (the chance of a quick laugh overriding the film's internal logic). To prove his narrative prowess, Stan mimes a biblical story, as Chaplin had done in *The Pilgrim* (1923). But whereas The Little Fellow chose David and Goliath, reflecting Chaplin's concern with class struggle, Stan opts for the gender conflict of Samson and Delilah, in which he must play both male and female roles. As he acts out the story of super-masculine hero and seductive femme fatale, such gender archetypes are satirized by exaggeration and drawing attention to their artificiality. Stan depicts the strong man's pectorals by pulling out his clip-on shirt front – a fake item used to fake something else. Delilah's seductive femininity is conveyed by placing one hand on a hip with the other cupped behind the opposite ear (the fact that he makes these gestures dressed as a man creates a stereotypical homosexual image). The irony of this sequence is that Stan, putting on an act within his act, is more convincing as the seductress than as the male suitor he's being paid to play. Paralleling Delilah's domination of Samson, Priscilla, at the end of the story, is compelled to take the upper hand with Stan and remind him to make love to her. He bashfully hides his face, but finally lets her cradle him in her arms. ''Oos baby is 'oo?' he asks her pertinently.

The rest of the film mainly consists of wild chases through the house at night, but this is preceded by Laurel and Hardy's first cinematic appearance in bed together. The sleeping Ollie – presumably instructed to prevent the gigolo's escape – pinions Stan to the (single) bed by stretching an arm across his bedmate's body. Stan tickles Ollie's nose to make him remove his arm. The two-shot of them in bed suggests that, though they may be enemies, Stan is more aptly paired off with Ollie than with the wife, for class (both are in effect servants) if not sexual reasons. Indeed, the final scene juxtaposes the husband and wife's reconciliation (he's wise to her ruse but doesn't let on) with Stan and Ollie's final separation, as the butler, brandishing a gun, chases the intruder out of the very house which earlier he had tried to prevent him entering. In *Slipping Wives* (as in *Duck Soup*) Stan and Ollie interact with, and provide comedic counterpoint to, a heterosexual couple. Both couples have the potential for erotic union, but in the final scene dominant ideology dictates the heterosexual union is lightly affirmed while the homosexual relationship is abandoned.

In their next film, **Love 'Em and Weep**, filmed around January 1927, Laurel plays Romaine Ricketts, ironically introduced as 'a masterful man'. He is still basically a simpering sissy, though less overtly effeminate or childlike than in *Slipping Wives* (he was starting to use more subtle gestures). Again, his character is required to be a sort of gigolo for a sexually charged woman. This time he's chosen by his boss, a married businessman (James Finlayson), to take his place for an appointment with an old flame (Mae Busch), a vampish actress who's trying to blackmail Fin. The latter is unable to keep the appointment because his wife, as threatening in her way as the actress, has arranged a simultaneous dinner party for a judge (Hardy) and his wife. Stan's – and the film's – anxiety about powerful women is revealed when, told his task by Fin, he asks, 'What about *my* wife – who'll control her?' Fin reassures him, 'You have a commanding power over women' – at which point Stan bursts into tears.

No more a 'Laurel and Hardy' picture than *45 Minutes from Hollywood*, this film is nevertheless interesting in being, like *Duck Soup*, a closely followed blueprint for one of the team's sound three-reelers, in this case *Chickens Come Home*. It also holds a sociological fascination, betraying a quite hysterical male anxiety about increasing female independence and power in 1920s America. The title *Love 'Em and Weep*, clearly addressed (in view of the film's action) to a male audience, is both misogynous and masochistic.

Stan's assignation at Mae's flat is a series of humiliations for him – she brusquely discards his flowers, then sarcastically calls him 'Don Juan' (the John Barrymore film about the great lover had opened in August 1926). Things go so badly for him that, on the phone, he warns Fin, 'I'm losing my control.' Mae decides to drive to Fin's home in Stan's car – a double invasion of male domains – and demands that Stan hand over the car key. When he refuses, she floors him and thrusts her hands into his pockets, reversing traditional images of rape as she wrests the phallic object from his person. On a simpler level, her desire to control the car reflects the independence of the many women who learned to drive in 1920s

America. This phenomenon is also suggested earlier in the film when the 'masculinity' and mobility of Fin's wife, violating the privacy of his office, are conveyed when she tells him she's just 'changed a tire'.

Stan's tussle with the vamp has been witnessed by another misogynous creation, a grim-faced gossip dubbed 'Old Lady Scandal' whom, we are informed, has 'worn four inches off her nose – from sticking it into other people's business'. She rushes to tell Stan's wife that he's involved with a 'wild woman' – female emancipation also posed a threat to conservative women.

The film's denouement, in which all the main characters converge on Fin's home, is reproduced with considerable fidelity in the remake, so I will analyse it more fully in the context of that mature Laurel and Hardy film. (In this original, it's the only scene in which Stan and Ollie meet and even then they do not interact, rarely appearing in the same shot.) Suffice to say, the male fear of women out of control is relieved when Mae (rather improbably) faints, and spends several minutes as an inanimate body being hauled around the house by Fin and Stan. (Similar routines appear in other comedies of the period such as Harry Langdon's *The Strong Man* (1926) and Buster Keaton's *Spite Marriage* (1929).) Eventually, they try to expel Mae from the house by placing her (still unconscious) on the back of Fin, who rolls up his trousers and, concealed by her long coat, walks her out, accompanied by Stan, now masquerading as Mae's husband. The ruse fails: Stan and Fin are chased by their respective wives, as Ollie – a spectator – looks on and laughs. For this he's knocked to the ground by *his* wife, a punishment perhaps designed to give the laughter of the film's male spectators a bitter aftertaste.

Why Girls Love Sailors, shot in February 1927, was considered a lost film until 1986. Its rediscovery was important for it brings Laurel and Hardy together again in a scene which, though brief, illustrates their rapport better than any previous film had done. Moreover, it shows them continuing to define their relationship on the gender difference that had been established in *Duck Soup*.

Stan's introductory scene suggests he has regressed almost to a baby since the relatively mature characterization in *Love 'Em and*

Weep. Although he has heterosexual interests, he conveys his love for his girlfriend (Viola Richard) with incredibly coy mannerisms. Arms behind his back, he simpers and swishes his body from side to side as he gazes at her, putting his hand to his mouth in the babyish gesture of Harry Langdon (on whose persona much of this scene appears to be based). When he gives Viola a necklace and pecks her cheek, the experience is so emotionally overwhelming that he bites the bottom of his sweater, falls over a chair, rolls on a bed, plays with a pillow and licks a lollipop – most unsubtle compared to the methods Laurel would later develop to convey the childlike qualities of his character.

Stan's rival is a tough sea captain (Malcolm Waite) who arrives to find the lovebirds together. As if to prove his masculinity and seaworthiness, Stan shows a ship tattoo on his chest to the Captain, who responds by pouring a jug of water down the gap between Stan's jumper and chest. This action, performed slowly, with a close-up of Stan's face registering only mild and gradual awareness of what's happening, is an embryonic tit-for-tat scene, complete with the victim's inspection of the outrage after it has been committed. But instead of exacting immediate revenge, Stan only cries and feels his bulging belly (a gag literally expanded for the end of *Below Zero*). Meanwhile, water dribbles from the bottom of his trousers – an image which, together with his open-legged gait, suggests an infant's pants-wetting: the Captain has proved that his rival is a child, not a man. Stan follows him as he drags the unwilling Viola to his ship, but gets bounced around and thrown into a net like a dead fish.

Undeterred, Stan boards the ship and eventually finds a hiding place in a theatrical trunk containing women's clothes. Since he cannot compete with the Captain as a man, he decides to adopt a new gender, and emerges on to the ship's deck dressed as a woman, complete with curly wig, huge dangling earrings, necklace and purse. The feminine side of Stan's persona is thus separated from the childlike elements of the earlier scenes and, as in *Duck Soup*, it's made more explicit and purposeful through the use of narrative-motivated drag. In his new guise, of course, he's an erotic magnet for every sailor on the ship, particularly when he winks at them. He decides to dispose of the crew one by one by giving them the come-on – waving and beckoning to each in turn – then coshing them out of the others' sight.

Eventually, he sets about seducing the bearded, pipe-smoking Second Mate, a macho creation of Oliver Hardy. Stan begins by tweaking Ollie's beard, so the latter responds with a gentle tug at the 'girl's' chin. The lewd slap and tickle becomes progressively more violent, revealing the dual masculine aggression beneath the apparently heterosexual encounter, until Ollie hits Stan's thigh and Stan slaps Ollie's face. In its depiction of mutual flirtation turning sour, the scene is an embryonic tit-for-tat routine comparable to Stan's scene with Kay Deslys in the later *We Faw Down*, but not quite paralleled in any other film by Laurel and Hardy themselves.

Finally, Stan seduces the Captain, jumping onto his lap and indulging in reciprocal cheek-tugging. But the Captain's wife (Anita Garvin) has boarded the ship, displaying her 'masculine' strength by flooring Ollie, and she now witnesses the erotic play between Stan and her husband. Anita grabs a gun and, when Stan realizes it will be turned on him as well as his enemy, he removes his wig with a theatrical flourish. Wife and husband are reconciled until Stan exposes the real woman – Viola – in the Captain's cabin. Stan and his sweetheart exit, but their outer clothes are blown away by the irate wife's gunfire. Thus, Stan sheds his drag, leaving both himself and Viola dressed only in their panties – which exposes their gender similarity. Moreover, Stan's enjoyment of his role as a girl who loves sailors has been evident enough to give the film's title an ironic edge, while the Captain and crew's unanimous lust for Stan suggests that sailors love girls most when they are really boys.

With Love and Hisses, filmed about a month later, is a much cruder affair. The first of the team's military comedies, it has no plot and often relies on the limited comic potential of unpleasant odours (some of which are animated, cartoon-like, onto the image) or bodily distortions, such as grotesquely swollen feet and bottoms. The film does exploit Laurel and Hardy's rapport in more scenes than any film since *Duck Soup*, though this is mitigated by the lack of appropriate (or even just amusing) material for them. Ollie, as a sergeant, again has authority over Stan, a stupid private whose effeminacy is underlined by his name, Cuthbert Hope, and by contrast with Ollie's burly masculinity.

The title-writer cannot resist reintroducing the wife-hating tone of *Love 'Em and Weep* at the opening ('There were cheers and kisses as the Home Guards left for camp – the married men did the cheering'), making explicit the motivation for removing the men to a single-sex environment. The train sequence is particularly feeble with Stan, and then Ollie, occupying the luxury compartment reserved for their Captain (James Finlayson). The fact that they do this separately betrays the half-heartedness of the teaming at this stage.

The next scene is camp in both senses. One of many privates on parade, Stan makes a mess of everything: he arrives late, copies the others' movements (so he's always behind) and converts the noble stance he's supposed to adopt into a very effeminate hand-on-hip position, complete with swishing torso and coy, knowing smile. After an altercation with the Captain, he shouts, 'I'm mad at you,' and soon begins to cry (which he also does again on at least two occasions later in the film). His homosexuality, or at least his inability to cope in a tough man's world, is also suggested when, on a route march, he rests his hand on Ollie's shoulder (the Sergeant turns and stares at the hand until it's removed). Bodily contact is, however, avoided in the subsequent nude-bathing scene, which must have been thought risqué enough at the time, especially when the soldiers emerge from the water to discover their uniforms have been burned. Vulnerable to the gaze of two ladies passing on horseback (an unwelcome female intrusion), they hide behind an advertisement board. This is used again to get them back to camp, but en route they upset a bees' nest with predictable results.

As in *Why Girls Love Sailors*, the first half of the film concentrates on Stan's childlike qualities (such as his scoffing of Fin's chocolates), with the second half emphasizing his effeminacy. But, without the theatrical drag or heterosexual motivation of the previous film, Stan's 'sissy' character emerges as more explicitly homosexual, particularly when placed in an environment where men are closely bonded and women largely absent.

After their comedy about soldiers, Laurel and Hardy returned to the nautical theme in their next film **Sailors, Beware!**

This and their previous two efforts make an interesting triptych, each featuring a captain who has authority over Ollie (who plays a purser in *Sailors, Beware!*). In *Why Girls* Stan is an intruder on the ship, in *Hisses* he's a raw recruit, and *Sailors, Beware!* combines his previous two roles by casting him as a taxi-driver who gets onto the ship by accident but is forced to work his passage as a steward.

More strongly plotted than *With Love and Hisses*, but (perhaps due to this) giving Laurel and Hardy fewer scenes together, the film centres on Madame Ritz (Anita Garvin), a jewel thief, and her midget husband (Harry Earles) who, a title tells us, 'wore baby clothes to help his wife's career'. The couple specialize in conning steamship passengers, prefiguring Barbara Stanwyck's card-sharper in *The Lady Eve* (1941), while the midget's masquerade as a baby echoes Tod Browning's *The Unholy Three* (1925, remade as a talkie in 1930). Like that film, *Sailors, Beware!* delights in bizarre images of the midget, showing him smoking a cigar as he paces about in baby clothes and later contrasting his 'baby ways' with his 'chest like a bearskin rug' (as another title puts it).

The interrelationship between Stan and the midget is particularly interesting. In one scene, where the two are throwing dice for money, Stan consciously mirrors his adversary's babyish gestures (including a Langdon-like throwing up of his arms), in the way that an adult would put on an act for a baby's benefit. Gradually, as Stan loses his cash, close-up cutaways to his face register his real feeling of growing consternation – and show Laurel, in a slowly paced scene like this, already capable of facial subtleties. When the midget refuses to return his winnings, Stan's acting yields to a genuine childlike despair, and he cries – as he does several times in the film. Although a fully grown adult, Stan is really more babyish than the midget, whose small stature and disguise conceal the fact he's actually a mature toughie. The paradoxical contrast between them is highlighted at the end of the film when Stan boyishly kicks Ollie's rear and runs off. His place is taken by the midget, whose subsequent fight with Ollie leaves the purser bruised and black-eyed.

After the dice game, Stan takes his revenge on the midget by pushing him, inside a pram, down a flight of stairs. A close-up of the careering carriage strongly suggests a deliberate parody of the most famous image in the 'Odessa Steps' sequence of another nautical movie, Eisenstein's *Battleship Potemkin*, which had received its first American public showings in December 1926, just a few months before this comedy was made around April 1927. Similarly, the strange shot of Stan's face reflected but distorted in a tray, after Madame Ritz (a typically aggressive Roach female) has punched him, looks like a send-up of then current German Expressionist techniques.

The name of Stan's character in *Sailors, Beware!* is Chester Chaste, in keeping with his sexless rather than explicitly feminine nature here. Moreover, like a child, he doesn't distinguish between other people's sexes, matter-of-factly slapping Madame Ritz's rear to remind her of the cab fare, and indiscriminately pushing into the ship's swimming pool both a man and a woman who annoy him. By contrast, Ollie (as in their last two films together) is very much a ladies' man, flirting with all the female passengers as they board, but brusquely hurrying on the men between them. Stan's main function, in relation to Ollie, is to ruin his chances of sexual conquest in a variety of ways. But their main scene together simply highlights Stan's childlike traits: he ropes Ollie into a skipping game, then the two throw a medicine ball at each other with increasing violence (reminiscent of a gun-throwing scene between Stan and Fin in *With Love and Hisses*). This is the nearest they come to tit-for-tat, though there's a stronger hint of that ritual when the Captain throws Stan's cap onto the deck and, in retaliation, Stan mirrors the action. Another scene recalls the Laurel and Hardy bathroom scene in *Slipping Wives*: Stan (replaying Ollie's earlier role) has to bathe the midget (Stan's role) but winds up in the bath himself. His character is a rather incoherent combination of childlike dumbness and almost masculine aggression; indeed, he emerges as the 'hero' (according to a title) of the film, exposing the thieves and returning the jewels they've stolen. Although this and other experiments with his character were not in themselves successful, they enabled Laurel to develop the rich complexity that marked his mature movie persona.

Something of that persona, and of Ollie's, is evident a month later when they started work on **Do Detectives Think?** The advancement is partially visual: since they are detectives, they wear suits (though Ollie's is too small) and derbies, the latter used for several gags. In fact, their profession requires them to keep their hats on when they are indoors (though they do remove them in the bedroom), so that their hands are always free. Presumably, the duo's wearing of derbies in most of their later films, when it often became comically incongruous, is rooted in the realism of their detective characterizations here. The boys also have much more rapport because they are now equals – in terms of both authority and screen time – who (the plot dictates) must work together. The rapport is also reflected in the many joint bits of 'business' (not only major gags) that they perform, as they react with apparent spontaneity to each other. Yet the film built around them is mainly another heavy-handed farce – the first of their horror-comedies – with much frantic running around by all.

As in previous films, the boys are assigned silly names: Stan is another Ferdinand (cf. *Slipping Wives*), surname Finkleberry this time; Ollie is Sherlock Pinkham. Surprisingly, Stan is merely 'the second worst detective in the whole world' and it's Ollie who is 'the worst'. This evaluation would surely have been reversed for their later personas, but it is consistent with the denouement of *Detectives* in which Stan (as in *Sailors, Beware!*) gets his man, albeit more by luck then judgement. Nevertheless, the basic joke of the movie is to present two timid, slow-witted, physically inept child-men in another macho role – Ollie, no longer the explicit authority figure of the last three films, now shares Stan's unmanly qualities. In their introductory scene, which has the slow pace necessary to elicit their subtleties, the chief of the detective agency calls them 'babies', an image they are unable to dispel by brandishing cigars (particularly after the cigar-smoking 'baby' of *Sailors, Beware!*).

The plot centres on an escaped killer (Noah Young) who plans to cut the throat of the Judge (James Finlayson) who sentenced him to death. Sent to protect the Judge, the boys pass a graveyard, into which their derbies are blown. Stan, dog-like, is sent to retrieve them by Ollie, who pompously sees himself as the fearless commander ('Get them hats! – I hate a man that's scared!'), though his actions reveal he's as cowardly as Stan. The latter, in trying to rescue the headgear, is frightened by his own shadow, a gag that is repeated later when they are both terrified of a goat's shadow resembling a horned, bearded devil – perhaps another parody of German Expressionism.

Throughout most of the film Stan looks up to Ollie as his paternal protector, often grabbing his suit or hand for safety. At several points when he's suddenly frightened by something, he hurls himself at Ollie, jumping into his arms or onto his back. One telling moment shows Stan and the Judge's wife (Viola Richard), both terrified by a gunshot, clinging to either side of Ollie; this mirroring of Stan with the lady of the house is a relatively subtle way of feminizing him. But the irony is that Ollie is no more a man than he: as Skretvedt notes, they are like 'two little boys lost in a grown-up world' (Skretvedt, 1987, p. 88).

Stan is the more childlike of the two: an infantile tendency displayed here that would become characteristic is his disposition to eat any food that happens to be around. In the Judge's house he stuffs himself with crackers, and is reprimanded by Ollie, after which the 'teacher' hypocritically helps himself to one. But Stan has the last laugh, edging back into the frame to grab another cracker which he holds up to his shoulder with a flourish – the only effeminate gesture he makes in this film. (In the original script, Stan's cracker-eating continued into the night (Skretvedt, 1987, p. 89).) Told to put an apple on his head, to demonstrate Ollie's alleged William Tell-like accuracy with a gun, Stan starts to eat that too.

The film displays other elements that would become typical of Laurel and Hardy, including a scene where they both lie on (though not in) the same bed. More notable are the final scenes. Stan, having arrested the killer (who was posing as the Judge's new butler), locks him inside the closet in which Ollie is hiding. When the latter emerges he bears two black eyes, in petty revenge for which he undercuts Stan's triumphant exit by bashing the front door into his face, giving him two black eyes also – an early example of tit-for-tat at its most precise, and a comic counterpoint to the more violent (but failed) revenge intended for the Judge. Following this, they pick up and put on each other's derbies, a brief reprise of the hat mix-up which appears (outside the graveyard) for the first time in this film. The hat gag complements the Stan and Ollie that emerge in

Detectives, a fitting reminder that they – like the hats – are superficially the same yet quite different.

In most of Finlayson's scenes in *Detectives* the boys are not present; in view of the two movies that followed it, we can see it was little more than chance that he, not Laurel or Hardy, became the odd man out. **Flying Elephants**, filmed in May 1927, has a Stone Age setting (already used by Chaplin in *His Prehistoric Past* (1914) and Keaton in *The Three Ages* (1923)) which is, however, linked to the 1920s through the then popular sexual concept of the macho 'caveman' (compare one of the fantasy sequences in Harold Lloyd's *Girl Shy* (1924)) and through the ideas of gender reversal that enjoyed currency during that decade.

Although Laurel and Hardy do not appear together for the first three-quarters of the film, a contrast between them is implied by placing them towards opposite ends of the gender spectrum. Ollie, brandishing a club, is introduced as 'a mighty giant' who boasts – as 1920s 'cavemen' no doubt did – that he 'can get five women in five minutes', although in practice he is clubbed by a rival whenever he courts a girl. Stan is a 'pansy' named Little Twinkle Star who, when told of the decree that all men must marry, smiles and shakes his head coyly, pointing out, 'I'm too young – my mother hasn't told me everything.' Completing his effete characterization, he twirls and skips along the landscape, declaiming like a Byronic poet about spring, love and romance. On his way, he casually picks flowers and strolls into the middle of a club fight, whose burly participants are, like Ollie, in stark contrast to him. The scene recalls another in Laurel's solo movie *The Soilers* (1923), where a camp cowboy wanders in and out of a brawl; the comparison illustrates how Stan – one of the fighters in the earlier film – has exchanged his go-getting masculine image for a passively 'sissy' one at this stage. He does show heterosexual inclinations, of a high-flown romantic kind, but the girl he courts is carried away on another caveman's shoulder. When he tries to emulate this macho manner with a haughty young woman (Dorothy Coburn), she resists strongly. 'I'm going to carry you to my cave,' he insists, feebly adding, 'Don't you know the rules?' She laughs at him, then, in a prolonged bout of wrestling, floors him several times. The scene is an incisive comment on male fears in the 1920s that women were indeed flouting the 'rules' of sexual conduct, revealing the 'caveman' concept as a sham.

When Stan and Ollie finally do meet, they engage in a friendship ritual of nose-rubbing and (gentle) head-clubbing, then walk off, Ollie with his arm affectionately round Stan. But soon they discover they are in sexual competition for the daughter of James Finlayson. Stan tries to dispose of Ollie by pushing him off a cliff, an act he is too weak to accomplish, but which is conveniently executed for him by a belligerent goat. So, in an unlikely conclusion, Stan gets the girl, though he too is attacked by an animal: like Antigonus in *The Winter's Tale*, he has to 'exit, pursued by a bear'.

At some point in mid-1927 Laurel and Hardy both had supporting roles in a two-reeler called **Now I'll Tell One**, starring another Roach comedian, Charley Chase. Only the second reel is known to be extant, and that was discovered just a few years ago by David Wyatt (see Wyatt, 1990, p. 7). Until then, nobody knew that both Laurel and Hardy were in this film, and indeed it seems that they work separately. In the surviving reel, Ollie appears briefly as a cop in a flashback sequence, and Stan has a larger role as a lawyer in the film's courtroom framework.

Laurel also plays a lawyer in **Sugar Daddies**, shot about June 1927. This was the first film featuring Laurel and Hardy to be released (on 10 September 1927) through MGM, Roach having abandoned his distribution deal with Pathé. But the new alliance did not immediately produce any new thinking about the personas of Stan and Ollie, or the types of situations in which they could be most effectively presented. *Sugar Daddies*, in its opening half particularly, seems like another retrogression to earlier movies. Hardy is back in the butler role of *Slipping Wives* (but now allowed a moustache), bringing to it his appropriate dignity and precision. Laurel, as the inept lawyer, has lost his childlike qualities and (despite the female impersonation of the second half) his effeminacy, but returns to the brash stupidity of his early solo films – he even does a Chaplinesque corner skid. Like *Love 'Em and Weep*, the film really centres on the romantic entanglements of James Finlayson, who again plays another successful businessman who is being blackmailed, this time by the family of a woman he married while in a drunken stupor. Ollie is his butler, Stan his lawyer. They have an amusing bit of business together (recalling their first scene in *Slipping Wives*) as Stan enters Fin's home, clonking Ollie's head with his umbrella, then refusing to let the butler take his derby.

But the film only takes wing as a Laurel and Hardy film (or indeed as a comedy at all) when, in a variation on the finale of *Love 'Em and Weep*, Fin, trying to evade his unwanted relations, rolls up his trouser legs and Stan mounts his back. Donning a female wig, hat and long cape, Stan – looking like an abnormally tall lady with a bandy-legged gait – walks with Ollie, who explains to a suspicious cop, 'She's my little wife.' This single gag sustains the entire second half as Fin's wife, her daughter and burly brother-in-law pursue Fin and his two cohorts through a hotel lobby, a dance hall and the fun house in an amusement park.

Although this is still an All Star film, it signifies a shift from *Love 'Em and Weep* by catering to Laurel's penchant for drag (the tall 'woman' now conceals *two* men) and by positioning Hardy within the masquerade instead of merely observing it from the sidelines. The dance-hall scene, where Stan and Ollie perform a wild tango, anticipates the nightclub sequence of *That's My Wife* with Stan again in drag as Ollie's spouse. The motivation for the masquerade in *Sugar Daddies* does not originate with Stan or Ollie (as it does in *That's My Wife*), yet the second half shows Fin already being relegated to a supporting role – literally! However, the film demonstrates the problem of presenting three stars together: Fin's status means he has to become visible again before the film's end, upsetting Stan's balance and indeed the comedic balance between Laurel and Hardy. Although he would be a very valuable player in many of their later films, *Sugar Daddies* marks the last occasion on which Finlayson was allowed a share of the movie equal to his erstwhile co-stars.

This is apparent in **The Second Hundred Years**, filmed a few weeks later, in which Finlayson has only a small supporting role. Even more than *Do Detectives Think?*, this seems, with hindsight, the first movie in which we see not only the 'real' Stan and Ollie personas but the larger world in which they exist – a fatalistic world. This is partly because it's the first of their prison comedies; much more believable as convicts than they were on the right side of the law in *Detectives*, they are obviously among life's losers, a state with which they would become identified as their personas deepened in later movies. The fact that we are not told of their crimes (a title simply states that, in Stan's case, 'the Judge took one look at him, and instructed the jury') adds to the feeling that, in society's eyes, prison is simply where they belong.

Nevertheless, they try to escape, first of all by digging a tunnel – unfortunately, straight to the warden's office. Their second attempt, masquerading as painters who have been working in the prison yard, does get them past the gates: turning their striped uniforms inside-out so they are dressed all in white, they proceed to paint the town white also, proving their profession and (via colour symbolism) their virtue to a suspicious cop. When he finally catches on, they make their escape by stealing the clothes of two men travelling in a taxi which, in this fatalistic world, turns out to be heading for the prison. Assumed by the prison authorities to be visiting French police chiefs (the men whose place they usurped in the taxi), they must now make, in effect, their third escape attempt through yet another masquerade. After a reception at the mansion of the governor (Finlayson), their cover is blown when, taken to inspect their old cell block, they are recognized by their mates – and the real Frenchmen. With open-armed gestures of resignation, they return to their cell. Gone is the gimmicky wrap-up gag of the end of *Duck Soup*; this is an unvarnished 'narrative of failure' – of three failed escape attempts.

Of course, the film is lightened by humour, but it's a much more slowly paced, naturalistic humour than in their previous films. Above all is the sense that they are a team (they were announced as such on the 1927 press sheet for the movie). It appears that whatever they do they will do it together: the original script even proposes a touching scene in which, confined in separate cells, the duo steal a guard's key, not in order to escape from the prison but simply to be together in one cell (Skretvedt, 1987, p. 97). Yet the film, as released, seems at pains to avoid the homosexual resonances that often come with prison life (in both films and reality). Stan – helped by his butch regulation haircut – has shed almost all his effeminate traits (though he still cries a lot and jumps, childlike, into Ollie's arms when frightened). Moreover, when a French official, believing they are the police chiefs, kisses them on both cheeks, Ollie counters with a homophobically indignant stare. Having been greeted like women, the boys reassert their masculinity by introducing themselves to the female guests with inaptly vigorous handshaking and matey backslapping.

Much of the film's humour depends on the opposition of prison confinement and regimentation with the liberation of movement they experience in the outside world. The opening scene has an appropriately static quality: the pair are sitting at a table in their cell, planning to share a cigarette but (establishing the despairing tone of the film) unable to find a match. Scenes in the prison yard convey an equally tedious sense of disciplined movement: the prisoners drill in single file, each with a hand on the shoulder of the man in front. Physical exercise is similarly regimented, but Stan, a free spirit who cannot be contained, is out of synchronization with the others (as in the team's military films), adding dance-like kicks to the specified movements. This prefigures their escape disguised as painters, where their swirling, rococo motions resemble an improvised ballet, contrasting with the linear marching in the prison yard. As such, the painting sequence also displays the anarchic value that would intensify in their major tit-for-tat movies, namely a wanton vandalism of society's icons: at one point, they slap paint all over a parked car, including its windscreen and engine. Similarly, the reception at the governor's mansion allows Stan and Ollie to transgress the rules of high society. The fact that they are ignorant, rather than contemptuous, of its values and etiquette makes it all the funnier, as does the paradox that, by masquerading as the 'guests of honour', their chances of escape depend on their success at integration.

Before their hair had time to grow back, Laurel and Hardy made a sort of guest appearance in **Call of the Cuckoos**, a two-reeler in Roach's series starring Jewish comedian Max Davidson. Together with James Finlayson, Charley Chase and Charlie Hall, they play Davidson's 'cuckoo' neighbours whose wacky outdoor antics cause Max and his family to agree to a no-questions-asked house exchange with a stranger. The new house is a jerry-built nightmare which, among its features, has reversed gas and water supplies (this gag would be reworked for Laurel and Hardy themselves in *Saps at Sea*). After a disastrous house-warming, Max wonders whether anything else can happen – and indeed it does, for he discovers that the 'cuckoos' have moved next door.

The film is most interesting when considered in its chronological context. Unlike the other 'guest stars', Laurel and Hardy are allowed a brief scene of their own in which they perform a William Tell parody. In effect, Stan takes revenge for the similar scene in *Do Detectives Think?* when Ollie attempted to use a gun to shoot an apple off his partner's head. In the later scene, Stan reverts to a bow and arrow and hits Ollie in the posterior. Allowing them a scene to themselves was no doubt a tiny part of Roach's campaign to familiarize the public with Laurel and Hardy as a team; it also suggests that he regarded them as more important than the other 'guest stars', who are not accorded solo scenes.

With hindsight, Laurel and Hardy's 'characters' in this film resemble their later movie personas taken to extreme. (Their famous theme tune, composed in 1930, is usually known as 'Cuckoo' – spellings vary.) They are outsiders – literally, in that all their scenes are outdoors, while the Davidsons gaze in disbelief at them from inside their home, almost as if they are in a different film (the home-owners and the 'cuckoos' never appear in the same frame). But they are also outsiders in the sense that they (along with the other 'cuckoos') are defined as abnormal, people to be feared and watched by 'normal' bourgeois people, whose main concerns are property values and household appliances. Their childlike natures seem positively child*ish* here as they romp around like infants out to play, using broomsticks as hobby-horses. But of course they are adults, not just dumb adults but actually insane (Stan and Ollie's shaved heads, a legacy of their recent convict roles, intensifies their strangeness). The opening description of the 'cuckoo' residence as a 'training school for radio announcers' is presumably a satirical jibe at the cinema's hated rival ('the quicker they go daffy, the sooner they get a diploma', adds the title gratuitously). And yet, the anarchic spirit of the 'cuckoos' is close to that of Laurel and Hardy in their later extended tit-for-tat sessions. It's easy to share their sense of fun and to delight in their triumph over the bourgeois home-owners.

Tit-for-tat and conflict with home-owners both occur in their next film, **Hats Off**. The only (known) Laurel and Hardy film which is completely missing, it seems to have been an important two-reeler for many reasons. It was a highly popular movie, heavily promoted by Hal Roach who, considering it their best work to date, again used it to familiarize the public with Stan and Ollie. It was in fact the first film in which Laurel and Hardy both used their own names for the characters they played, though this would not become a standard procedure for some time. It was also the first occasion in which Stan appeared with his hair upraised like a fright wig. Moreover, the duo returned to the suits and derbies they had worn in *Do Detectives Think?* – without the professional excuse of that film.

In *Hats Off* (of which the cutting continuity and various stills exist) Stan and Ollie play door-to-door washing-machine salesmen. It has often been remarked that the film is a prototype for *The Music Box*, in which they deliver a piano up a long flight of steps. Here, they laboriously carry the washing-machine up the same steps but, according to the detailed synopsis in *Laurel and Hardy* (McCabe, Kilgore and Bann, 1975, pp. 38–41), they are not merely *delivering* the bulky contraption but attempting to sell it. This, together with an earlier scene (which sounds like a reworking of the labour-exchange sequence in Chaplin's *A Dog's Life*), where they try to sell at a four-door apartment complex – never managing to get the machine to the door that is open – suggests the film is also a prototype for *Big Business*, in which they play Christmas-tree salesmen.

This view is reinforced by the climax, which apparently contains their first extended tit-for-tat sequence, as the duo knock off each other's hats and then those of various male passers-by. A riotous scene evolves, with much destruction of headgear, until the police arrive. The title *Hats Off* suggests that symbols of civilized respectability are stripped away, as the crowd of men descend into savagery. This is of course the genesis for the climactic sequences of several Laurel and Hardy movies, including *Big Business*. But *Hats Off* as a whole, like the later film, locates the duo on the bottom rung of the capitalist ladder, and it's partly from their failure to ascend it (they never sell the washing-machine) that frustration causes anger, which in turn leads to reciprocal destruction. This ultimately includes the demolition of the consumerist status symbol that they were trying to sell: the washing-machine, abandoned in the road, is run over by a steamroller.

Despite the key elements established in *Hats Off*, Laurel and Hardy's personas were still undergoing experimentation. **Putting Pants on Philip**, filmed in August 1927, is a superficially atypical film which nevertheless reinforced a characteristic dimension in their screen partnership. Many of their movies implied a child–parent relationship, explicated in this instance by casting Ollie as the American uncle of Stan, the kilted Scottish visitor (actually named Philip) whose ship he has come to meet. The importance of the relationship is that it's based on power: Ollie is, theoretically, the adult authority figure to whom Stan should submit. But, as *Putting Pants* is the first to demonstrate clearly, this is not borne out in practice.

Ollie plays the epitome of bourgeois respectability, one Piedmont Mumblethunder, 'influential, dignified, proud, a credit to society', as a title tells us. Stan has childlike qualities: he hates being touched by the ship's doctor who tries to give him a medical examination, and we are informed that he 'doesn't believe in Santa Claus but still has faith in Little Jack Horner'. However, his manic woman-chasing – demonstrated repeatedly during the film – makes him more like an oversexed teenager than the sexless infant he came to resemble in later movies. This public display of sexuality offends Ollie's sensibilities: not wishing other citizens to associate him with Stan, he instructs his nephew to walk well behind. A lengthy backward tracking shot reveals how this only attracts the attention of the citizens, who watch Stan as he gradually catches up with his uncle, and grabs his hand like a child. Ollie pompously tells a cop to make the people stop laughing at his nephew, but the cop only joins in the hilarity.

The crowd's fascination centres on Stan's kilt, particularly when he steps over air vents which cause it to billow upwards (a scene which anticipates the famous image of Marilyn Monroe in *The Seven Year Itch* (1955)). When this scene is repeated, after Stan has lost his underwear during a powerful sneeze, some of the crowd faint at the sight with which they are presented. Now the cop does intervene, telling Ollie, 'This dame ain't got no lingerie on.' Part of the kilt's fascination is surely that, in resembling a woman's skirt, it suggests effeminacy to Americans (it evidently does to the cop). Yet in this film, it is also linked to Stan's aggressive heterosexuality, just masking – indeed unmasking – his maleness, and allowing him the bodily freedom to perform an especially spectacular scissors kick whenever he sets off in pursuit of a woman. To complicate the imagery still further, the kilt gives Stan the appearance of a child in short pants.

To return to the plot, Ollie decides the answer to his problem is to put (long) pants on his nephew, thereby Americanizing and masculinizing him. Stan's terror during the tailor's attempts to measure his inside leg has a childlike dimension, but his reaction is also homophobic, confirming that he sees himself as a red-blooded heterosexual man. (His indignant stare recalls Ollie's expression when he is kissed by the Frenchman in *The Second Hundred Years*.) Yet, as the sequence progresses, Stan is increasingly feminized and/or homosexualized. First, he hides behind a curtain from the tailor and Ollie, who are both now trying to measure him; then he runs into an inner room (offscreen), pursued by his uncle. When Stan finally emerges, slowly and sadly, his clothes are disarrayed, he hangs his head in shame. It's a subtle yet effective parody of the deflowered maiden of movie dramas, Laurel resorting to his familiar cry only at the end of the vignette.

Stan eventually manages to escape from the tailor's, rejecting the pants chosen for him and instead pursuing a woman (evidently, *he* sees the pants as emasculatory). Another crowd gathers, from which Ollie pulls him onto a bus. Insisting that Stan relinquish his seat for him, Ollie inadvertently allows his nephew to get away from him again. But, having grabbed the kilt of another Scotsman who happens to be standing nearby, Ollie mistakenly believes Stan is still there. Fixated by the kilt – the signifier of difference – it is all he sees, all he uses to define Stan.

Eventually, his error becomes apparent and, catching up with Stan (and yet another crowd), he attempts to introduce his nephew to the woman he's been chasing throughout the film (Dorothy Coburn). His gallant approach is met with a flicked nose. Stan, with even greater chivalry, lays his kilt over a mud puddle for the woman to step on, but she contemptuously leaps over it. Ollie implicitly feminizes himself by repeating her nose-flicking gesture on Stan and insisting that he use the kilt himself. But as he steps onto it, he falls into the puddle beneath, which turns out to be five feet deep. This time the crowd gathers to observe Ollie's humiliation. Of course, its comedy stems from the poetic justice inherent in pride before a fall, but it's made even more pointed by the incorporation of the kilt. Stan has, in effect, consented to half of his uncle's demand by removing it, and now it lies in the mud Ollie wants to trample on the hated garment. His obsession proves to be his downfall.

Yet the film, one of the richest Laurel and Hardy silents, is most remarkable for the complex characterization of Stan. His effeminate and childlike qualities are not (as in most comedy) linked to homosexuality, except perhaps in the 'rape' scene at the tailor's, but to an aggressive expression of its opposite. (The film may have been inspired partly by Laurel's solo two-reeler *Short Kilts* (1924), in which he also plays a vehemently heterosexual Scotsman.) Although his sexuality (in either direction) would never again be as explicitly stated as in *Putting Pants on Philip*, his persona's containment of ambivalent identities would become a regular feature.

Their next film, **The Battle of the Century** is, like *Hats Off*, a more obviously typical two-reeler. Unfortunately, it is another that has not survived – at least not completely. Despite its recent 'restoration', about half of the film remains missing, including some of the celebrated pie fight which forms its climax. The extant version of the sequence starts abruptly and builds far too quickly, lacking the motivational force present in Laurel and Hardy's later tit-for-tat battles, while the end of the film is also missing.

The title *The Battle of the Century* might be used with some justification to describe the pie-throwing climax, but it also refers, more ironically, to the film's opening third, a boxing match between Stan and his tough opponent (Noah Young), which appears to parody the controversial 'long count' in the Tunney–Dempsey fight of 22 September 1927. Stan's character is called 'Canvasback' Clump, better known, a title tells us, as 'The Human Mop' – which, incidentally, was Buster Keaton's sobriquet as a child star in vaudeville (Keaton and Samuels, 1960, p. 3). This fight sequence (long lost, but rediscovered in the 1970s) finds Laurel in Harry Langdon mode, avoiding the simplistic 'sissy' characterization he would probably have used only a few months earlier. Slow, sleepy and totally dumb, he cries in the ring, is afraid to punch the other boxer, but does fight the referee. Eventually, he's knocked out, the blow causing Ollie, his manager, to faint too, suggesting the empathetic closeness of their relationship. (In *Tit for Tat* Charlie Hall warns Ollie in Stan's presence, 'I'll hit you so hard that *he'll* feel it.') When he regains consciousness, Ollie finds Stan still lying in the ring, sleeping like a baby.

The film's middle third (still missing) concerns Ollie taking out an insurance policy on Stan, and his attempt to cause a lucrative injury with a banana skin thrown in his inept fighter's path. This sequence, which characterizes Ollie as rather villainous, was not reworked until the 1943 Fox feature *The Dancing Masters*. It does, however, serve as a starting point for the climactic 'battle', when pie delivery man Charlie Hall slips on the skin intended for Stan.

Even judging from the mutilated version of the pie fight that survives, it does seem to be carefully constructed, influenced perhaps by Soviet montage techniques in its linking of disparate elements. Stray pies draw various bystanders into the fray, including a dental patient, a postman and an elegant young woman (Anita Garvin) who slips on a pie thrown on the pavement. Having sat squarely on it, she rises gingerly and delicately shakes her right leg. The film was obviously conceived not only as the ultimate pie-throwing comedy but as a variation on the riotous tit-for-tat climax of *Hats Off*. It also appears to parody slapstick conventions, partly through exaggeration (nothing approaching this number of pies had been thrown in a single film before) and partly by combining the pie-in-the-face routine with another stand-by, the banana-skin fall, in the same sequence. Moreover, the end of the picture suggests an ironic detachment, as Stan and Ollie, having moved to the edge of the battlefield, are asked by a cop if they started the pie fight. 'What pie fight?' asks Ollie innocently.

Battle continues the trend of placing Ollie in a role of authority over Stan, who nevertheless manages to get his minder into trouble (in the middle section, Ollie's face is coated in ink from a fountain pen). And of course it reinforces the childlike qualities, not only of Stan in the boxing sequence but of both in the climactic throwing of food. It's also interesting to note that money is the root of their troubles: a dialogue title makes it clear that Stan will get only five dollars if he loses his fight (as opposed to one hundred if he wins), and it's presumably this financial set-back that precipitates Ollie's drastic plan, which in turn leads to the pie fight. Money would be increasingly important as a motivator for their characters.

Leave 'Em Laughing, filmed in October 1927, is, like *Battle*, a two-reeler divided into three parts. A slowly paced film, it contains in its first two-thirds some of Laurel and Hardy's most subtle work to date, and is one of the best early examples of their implicit child–parent relationship. It is also the first of the movies in which we find them living together in a seedy boarding-house. Although it was still officially one of Roach's All Star films, it seems obvious, at least in retrospect, that by now Laurel and Hardy deserved their own series (for which, however, they had to wait another five films).

Leave 'Em Laughing opens with the duo sleeping in the same bed, each making a little star 'entrance' by separately pulling the blanket away from their faces. The first third concerns their attempts to sleep despite Stan's toothache. His appearance in a baggy, nappy-like nightshirt, with a bandage around his jaw tied in a bow on top of his head, is positively babyish: the bandage looks like a bib fixed too high and the huge bow is like a hair ribbon – or a rabbit's ears – which flaps when Ollie prods his aching teeth.

Forced into the role of comforting parent, Ollie goes to fetch a hot-water bottle, and in the process is hit (twice) by the swinging door of the bathroom cabinet and stands (twice) on the same tack that he's thrown back on the floor. He does not learn from the pain of experience. Eventually, Stan rests his swollen jaw on the bottle – which leaks. In one of those remarkable long-held close-ups, an extension of his camera-look, Hardy displays his gift – as great as Harry Langdon's – for subtle facial pantomime, conveying his belief (mixed with disbelief) that the warm liquid is coming directly from Stan. This fleeting suggestion of bed-wetting is obviously a further component of Laurel's infant imagery. For a moment Ollie becomes the punishing parent, telling Stan to 'go and ache in the corner'. The naughty child obeys.

But soon Ollie decides to pull out Stan's aching teeth with a piece of string (a method surely most suitable for a child's loose milk teeth). Looking for something to which to attach the free end, he absent-mindedly leads his charge around the room like a dog on a leash. Naturally, all attempts end in disaster, and their noise arouses the wrath of their landlord (Charlie Hall) who tells them they must move out tomorrow. A session of reciprocal bottom-kicking follows and, after the landlord leaves, the boys continue fighting each other. But when Ollie socks Stan's jaw, it knocks him out, and the child is literally dragged into bed by the long-suffering parent. The final indignity for Ollie comes when he steps on the hot-water bottle, lying abandoned on the floor (like the tack earlier), and the remaining contents squirt up his legs. His countenance does not obey the imperative we can just see in a frame on the wall behind him: 'Keep Smiling'.

The next day finds the two in the dentist's waiting-room. Ollie assumes the role of reassuring father, but Stan is so frightened that he faints, and has to be carried into the surgery like a babe in arms. His childlike tendency to sleep, or somehow to become suddenly unconscious, would become a regular feature of his persona. Yet here he strongly resists being rendered unconscious by the gas which the dentist applies: in a long close-up, with the mask held over his face, Laurel conveys his mounting terror by acting with his eyes alone. Ollie takes charge once again and, sending the dentist away, calmly demonstrates how Stan should sit in the chair and relax. But before he's finished his performance, the nerve-racked dentist has instructed his assistant to extract teeth from the patient in the chair – and this is what happens, with Stan dumbly standing by. When Ollie revives, close-ups of his face provide another opportunity for subtle pantomime as his tongue searches for the missing teeth.

Each having spent part of the dentist sequence unconscious, Stan and Ollie now veer to the other emotional extreme, as both accidentally become overdosed with laughing gas. Outside, in their car, they display a childlike capacity for helpless laughter when they carelessly bump into other vehicles. This intensifies when they seize opportunities to undermine adult authority, personified here by a humourless traffic cop (Edgar Kennedy). The gags in this final third are not very inventive, however, and the sequence, based on a single joke, needs sound for the laughter to become really infectious, as similar routines in their talkies would prove.

Yet the laughing sequence is a fitting climax to this film, which for me is the first that *feels* like a typical Laurel and Hardy. This is perhaps due to the naturalism of the first two-thirds at least: there are no spectacular gags, tit-for-tat is scaled down and subtly integrated, the locations are as ordinary as the characters – it's just 'a day in the life of' Stan and Ollie. The final third shows that, despite their inter-generational relationship at the start, both of them are children at heart – and that, despite their troubles, they are ultimately able to do more than 'Keep Smiling'. It's as if the gas has penetrated their inhibitions, releasing the *joie de vivre* which was always there, but had been restrained by adult propriety. And, of course, Laurel and Hardy act as laughing gas to the audience, so we enter their anarchic world, a child's dream of deregulation come true.

Chapter three

Work and Women: The Mature Silents (1927–29)

THE 'Stan' and 'Ollie' personas and their interrelationship having been established in the last few films, a decision seems to have been made that they should now be put to work. **The Finishing Touch**, made towards the end of 1927, is the first of two consecutive films which present the boys in unlikely jobs, and prioritize gags over plot or character development. Relatively conventional, their chief interest is that they show the team refining – putting the 'finishing touch' to – long-established slapstick routines. Evidently based on Laurel's solo film *Smithy* (1924), in which he is mistakenly put in charge of completing a half-built house, *The Finishing Touch* casts Stan and Ollie as 'professional finishers' who are deliberately engaged to perform a similar task for 500 dollars. Several gags are filched from the earlier movie, such as tiles sticking to clothing, Stan sawing a plank on which a man is standing and, for the climax, the sudden collapse of the completed house. But in every case the later film elongates the gag, adding comic suspense and milking it for all it's worth until the final pay-off.

Care is also evident in the setting up of the final gag at the start of the film. The brakes on Stan and Ollie's truck are faulty, so when they park it on top of an incline (the half-built house is situated at the bottom), they place a rock under a back wheel. Near the end, a dispute with the home-owner – concerning the 500 dollars he paid them before the house began to collapse – descends into reciprocal brick-throwing. Their search for the largest missile leads them to the rock: they remove it, and the truck rolls down the hill, demolishing the house they were contracted to complete. This is another 'narrative of failure', where a portent of the ultimate catastrophe is established right at the beginning of the film.

Structure (albeit not much sturdier than that of the house) is also imposed on the film by the use of repetition: Ollie accidentally swallowing a mouthful of nails and his fall from a bridging plank at the front of the house are gags which (with variations) are each used three times. Similarly, external characters are repeatedly brought into the film. Edgar Kennedy, as in *Leave 'Em Laughing*, plays a grim-faced cop whose authority and dignity are undermined. He, Stan and Ollie are all punched at some point in the film by a nurse (Dorothy Coburn) from a nearby hospital. An early example of the aggressive female in Laurel and Hardy pictures, her violence is given an ironic edge by her caring profession. Like other women in their world, she uses a conventionally masculine weapon (her fists), which may explain why Stan does not usually distinguish between the sexes in the type of assault he uses against them. In this case, however, he retaliates by tearing a piece of sandpaper in two as the nurse bends over; highly embarrassed, she departs. (As she does, Stan makes a quick gesture of triumph, raising each leg in turn as he brings the opposite arm across his chest; the same action can be seen in the army section of *Smithy*.)

The paper-tearing gag really needs sound, as do other scenes in this film where the nurse's wrath is repeatedly aroused by the noise the boys are making. When the cop tells them, 'If you must make a noise, make it quietly,' they obey to extreme, walking on tiptoe and conversing in sign language. It seems likely that these gags were intended as a satirical comment on the battle between sound and silence that was currently raging within the film industry: *The Jazz Singer* had opened in October 1927, just a month or two before *The Finishing Touch* was made. With hindsight, it is tempting to see Laurel and Hardy – who would embrace the new medium so successfully – as symbolizing the talkie, while the nurse represents the ailing silent movie.

Having portrayed butch builders, Laurel and Hardy were now cast as wimpish waiters at a dinner party hosted by a *nouveau riche* couple (Tiny Sandford and Anita Garvin) who have no more sense of etiquette than the boys. As such, **From Soup to Nuts** is to some extent a social satire, reflecting the increased sophistication of Hal Roach comedies, but mixed, in this case, with some very traditional slapstick. Two clichés of the genre – the banana-skin fall and the pie-in-the-face – are resurrected and combined, as they had been in *The Battle of the Century*. Here, the banana skin is initially dropped by a dog and the pie becomes an enormous cake which Ollie proudly carries into the dining-room. After he falls into it, he's allowed a particularly long solo spot for camera-looks and the punctilious removal of cream from his face. As in *The Finishing Touch*, repetition is used to structure the film and to build on initial laughs. Thus, Ollie, after inspecting the banana skin which caused his downfall, throws it back on the floor. Stan is the next to slip on it, but, like his partner, he tosses it back. But when he sees that Ollie, by now carrying another cake, is about to step on the skin, instead of warning him, Stan merely covers his eyes – and Ollie is covered in cake again. At this point, Stan displays an uncharacteristic burst of anger (reminiscent of his belligerent persona before the official teaming), accusing Ollie of falling down on purpose and shooing him away with a scissors kick. His temper is then turned on the startled guests; ranting at them, he pushes their chairs up to the table. Curiously, Laurel doesn't seem quite sure of his character even at this stage, whereas Ollie, adding new detail to his earlier pompous butler roles, appears entirely comfortable with his.

Equally uncharacteristic, especially for Stan, is the boys' fascination with Anita's wiggly walk. Such explicit signs of heterosexuality (as opposed to merely romantic love) are rare in their mature work. More suited to their style is the element of sexual innuendo which occurs when Stan is asked to serve the salad 'undressed'. He relates this request to the household's pretty young maid. 'I always serve it that way,' she replies, to which Stan enquires, 'What kind of a party is this?' By connection with the maid, whom he believes routinely displays her body for guests, Stan is implicitly feminized as he re-enters the dining-room carrying a bowl of salad, dressed only in his underwear. When Anita eventually sees him, she turns away in shock. At this point, the preview print included a scene (of which a still survives) where Ollie, looking for something to cover his colleague, removes Anita's long dress in the belief it's merely a shawl (Skretvedt, 1987, p. 116). But perhaps this was thought too risqué, for the final cut simply opts for Anita pushing Ollie into his third cake. The film ends there; despite the title, it has barely exceeded the soup course.

You're Darn Tootin', filmed in January 1928, has more plot and structure than the previous two films. A two-reeler divided into three parts of unequal length, it opens with another work situation. Stan plays the clarinet and Ollie the French horn in a military band but, as in their army comedies, they have no sense of military precision, being totally out of synchronization with the other players even before the music commences: when the others sit, they stand, and vice versa. After missing several entrances and losing their music, they accidentally produce a domino effect knocking over all the band's music stands.

The second and shortest section is set in the dining-room of their boarding-house. Here we learn, from the landlady's note, that they are already behind with their rent and, incidentally, that they got their jobs in the band only recently. Now, the landlady's son, who was present at the disastrous concert, reveals to his mother that they were fired that afternoon. Consequently, she immediately evicts them, literally putting them on the street where they try to earn a living as buskers.

This forms the third and longest part of the film, where their unsuccessful efforts are compounded when a cop demands to see their licence, not to mention an abundance of manholes into which they and their instruments repeatedly fall. Ollie blames Stan for their troubles and breaks his clarinet in two, so in retaliation Stan destroys his partner's horn. This leads to a bout of belly-punching (by Ollie) and shin-kicking (by Stan), interspersed with the tearing of small items of each other's clothing. When Stan gets a taste of his own medicine – a kick in the shin from Ollie – he retaliates by extending the clothes-tearing to ripping off his pal's pants. By now, many passers-by – significantly, all male – are embroiled in the fray; their kicked shins make them (literally) hopping mad and they 'dance' wildly. More trousers, even those of the intervening cop, are torn off until everyone is semi-naked. In this scene, more than in most Laurel and Hardy, the liberation and vitality that can result from destruction is very apparent. The pants-ripping is of course a *removal* from the body (as opposed to the application of pies in *The Battle of the Century*), a partial shedding of civilization and a reversion to the more primitive masculinity also suggested by the savage shin-kicking and the resulting 'dance'.

The film's final shot is of Stan and Ollie escaping the riot and the law by walking away, one behind the other, both inside the same huge pair of pants they've torn off a fat man. The image could be read homosexually, but it more readily suggests a sense of unity – the duo, after their cathartic conflict, are now 'in step' with each other. It's a brief moment of consolation at the end of a film which charts a downward spiral of catastrophes with the detail and tragic force of a nineteenth-century novel. The connection between each misfortune is highlighted with due regard to its social and psychological consequences. Having lost their jobs, Stan and Ollie lose their home, which in effect forces them to beg on the street. The climactic violence thus seems to erupt logically from frustration at their personal misfortunes. Defeated by the world, they turn on each other, and then on anyone who crosses their path. This may seem an excessively dour reading of a slapstick two-reeler, but it is important to remember that Laurel and Hardy's comedy in this and many other instances was based on the contemporary realities of everyday life in the United States, where no national social security schemes existed to assist the poor and the unemployed.

Having made several films which centred on the world of work, Laurel and Hardy now made their first major foray into the world of women, which also means that **Their Purple Moment** has much more plot. Disregarding the primitive *Love 'Em and Weep* (in which Hardy had a very minor role), this is the first film in which both are married. The opening title – 'Dedicated to husbands who "hold out" part of the pay envelope on their wives – and live to tell about it' – indicates where the film's sympathies lie. Both Stan's wife, actually called Mrs Pincher (Fay Holderness), and Ollie's (Lyle Tayo) are portrayed as money-grabbing shrews who force their spouses to hand over every dollar they earn.

Love appears to play no part in these marriages. When Stan returns from work, he gives his wife's cheek a ritualistic peck, and her response is to hold out her hand, fingers itching for his wage (a gesture repeated, incidentally, by a cigarette girl later in the film). A title tells us, 'The boldest thing he ever did was to whistle in the back yard,' but this is not quite true. Stan has hidden a few dollars under his collar, which he transfers to a wallet (containing previous savings) secreted in a large photograph of a top-hatted gent hanging in the hall. When Hardy ('Just another husband') and his wife arrive, the sexes pair off and Ollie tells Stan that the money will enable them to enjoy themselves, to 'be men among men'. The sense of male bonding is intensified by the fact that the money has been secreted 'inside' another man, whose photograph projects a vision of the masculine affluence to which they aspire. But the vision is illusory: the inanimate man hanging on the wall really represents Stan's vulnerability. The spying Mrs Pincher has, unbeknown to her husband, extracted the cash from inside the photograph and substituted worthless coupons (*her* savings) – an act symbolically suggestive of castration.

The boys claim to be heading for the bowling alley, but their real intentions are conveyed in a marvellous single shot involving a long view of Stan's home with the pavement in the foreground. The boys walk out of the frame's right edge, at which point Stan's wife appears in the background, opening the door for a gossipy female friend who has come to visit. Two young ladies walk into the frame from the right, quickly followed by Stan and Ollie, who, suddenly noticing the watchful women in the distance, reverse to exit as before. The shot brilliantly exploits the comic potential of a static frame, and the interplay between foreground and background action, in much the same style that Jacques Tati would develop in his comedies several decades later.

Mrs Pincher's visitor, simply called 'The Gossip', is a middle-aged woman whose sole business seems to be telling tales on husbands. When Stan and Ollie pick up a couple of flappers (Anita Garvin and Kay Deslys) and, unaware that the wallet contains no money, take them to an expensive restaurant, The Gossip runs to inform their wives. She has witnessed Stan accidentally falling on top of Kay, an image that parodies copulation, particularly (when it happens a second time) during Stan's strenuous efforts to get up. But the basic innocence of the boys is conveyed – to the audience at least – by their coy immaturity on meeting Anita and Kay, as they simper and shyly look away – acting more like girls themselves. The flappers, however, are not so innocent, since both carry weapons, smaller versions of those traditionally used by men: one brandishes a stiletto, the other conceals a pistol in her purse.

In the restaurant the boys order more and more food, running up a huge bill which they only belatedly realize they can't pay. Their escape attempts cause a waiter to fall head first into a cake: the gag was executed with more aplomb by Hardy in *From Soup to Nuts* and, here performed no fewer than four times, it becomes decidedly tiresome. The final occasion takes place in the restaurant's kitchen during a brief tit-for-tat sequence involving some of the staff and the recently arrived wives. A row breaks out between Stan and Ollie and they throw pies in the faces of each other's spouses, who therefore become 'whipping girls' for their husbands. It's the film's way of punishing the wives (The Gossip, having ganged up with them en route to the restaurant, has already fallen into a mud-hole). Moreover, they are not allowed to retaliate: in this relatively early film, physical aggression by women is limited to threats.

It's a great pity that the film's original ending did not survive previews; as extant stills show, and Randy Skretvedt explains (Skretvedt, 1987, p. 119), the sequence showed Stan and Ollie trying to escape the irate wives and restaurant staff by masquerading as female midgets (a troupe of midgets had provided the floor show at the restaurant). In this guise, Stan even flirted with a cop played by Edgar Kennedy. Perhaps preview audiences found it all too bizarre or tasteless. Or maybe the film's very misogynous theme required the substituted ending and precluded the depiction of Stan and Ollie as 'belittled' women themselves.

Should Married Men Go Home?, the first film in Roach's official Laurel and Hardy Series, appears to continue this misogynous theme, albeit from a masochistic viewpoint. The opening title runs: 'Question: What is the surest way to keep a husband at home? Answer: Break both his legs.' However, the first shots project a scene of marital bliss at the Hardy home (in contrast to the opening scene at the Laurel household in *Their Purple Moment*). Ollie, in his dressing-gown, cuddles up to his wife (Kay Deslys) on the sofa. But their dream world is shattered by Stan, apparently a bachelor, knocking on the door with a golf club – an icon of manly leisure here wielded as a weapon, it pounds ominously on the ramparts of the heterosexual home. An amusing scene of social satire (developed more effectively with sound in *Come Clean*) follows: trying to avoid an open confrontation, the Hardys pretend they are not at home, but even Stan cottons on when, after he pushes a note under their door, Ollie removes – and then replaces – it.

This is the first film in which Stan invades the Hardys' domesticity, threatening their marriage by competing with the wife for Ollie's attention and affection. Having gained entrance, he positions himself on the sofa, but Ollie hastily sends him to a chair so he can resume his place with his wife. A shot, held for twenty seconds, of the static trio subtly conveys the 'three's a crowd' tension in the situation. But this is the calm before the storm: several household objects are accidentally destroyed and eventually Mrs Hardy tells the men to go and play golf, which appears to have been Ollie's intention all the time, since under his dressing-gown he's already wearing golfing gear. And so the married man leaves home with his similarly attired male friend. As he does, Ollie, seeing his wife looking out of the window, attempts to display his virility and independence by leaping over the garden fence – boundary of the marital home – as bachelor Stan has just done. The fence collapses – and Ollie falls with it.

At the golf club, Stan and Ollie have to pair up with two young women (Edna Marian and Viola Richard), since only groups of four are allowed to play. A scene of coy flirtation follows, very similar to that in *Their Purple Moment*. Before going on the course, the boys try to buy sodas for their partners, but they haven't quite got enough money (recalling again the previous film) so Ollie attempts, with difficulty, to persuade Stan to refuse when offered a drink. As in the opening scene, the film satirizes the complex social games people play rather than admit the truth.

The rather feeble finale is located on the golf-course itself. After routines reminiscent of W. C. Fields's famous golfing sketch, a tit-for-tat battle develops that is obviously modelled on the climaxes of earlier films, particularly *The Battle of the Century*. Here, the pies which are thrown are made of mud and the golfers end up covered in it, imagery which suggests the primeval state to which the participants of the civilized game have degenerated. The film visualizes for us the literal, ugly truth of 'mudslinging'.

Their next movie, **Early to Bed**, is a pure two-hander which extricates Stan and Ollie from the worlds of work and women. An unusual Laurel and Hardy film, it nevertheless contains typical features and reinforces aspects of their relationship. It opens, like several of their other films, with the pair seated on a park bench, in this case accompanied by a pet dog, Buster. Ollie opens a letter which informs him he has inherited a fortune. When Stan, crying, asks what will become of him, Ollie decides to make him his butler. Thus, the pair's egalitarian friendship is severed, and the master–servant relationship, hitherto implicit in many of their films, or in the case of *Duck Soup* merely play-acted, is made explicit and real through an inequality in wealth.

The next section of the film, henceforth set in 'Hardy Manor', concerns an inebriated Ollie arriving home late and trying to persuade Stan to 'play' with him. Evidently, he misses his friend and would like him, at least for the moment, to step out of his butler role. Stan, prim and proper, resents his master's playfulness and noise; he's more concerned with the dog, whom he has just put to bed. 'S-s-h, Buster's asleep,' he warns, as if the dog were his (or their) child. Indeed, in an intriguing reversal of their usual roles, Stan is also a parent figure to Ollie's unruly child. 'You're going to bed,' commands Stan, but Ollie snaps at the pointed finger like a dog (Buster is now seated beside the master, highlighting the similarities between the two). 'I don't want to go to bed – I want to play,' persists Ollie.

The 'play' turns out to be highly physical: he repeatedly musses Stan's hair and 'walks' his fingers up the reluctant playmate's chest until he reaches the tie, which he unravels. When Ollie announces, 'I'll go to bed – but you've got to catch me first,' it could be taken as further evidence of the child in him, or as a bedtime come-on. A chase around (and briefly on) the bed ensues, ending with the pair wrestling on the floor, their bodies interlocked. There is a dissolve – a traditional cinematic device often used to indicate sexual intercourse – and next we see Ollie 'counting out' Stan, who's lying flat on his back. In this mock-erotic scene (during which Ollie's bed is visible in the background) the parody of cinematic sexual imagery continues, with Stan shamefaced and crying in much the same way he was after Ollie 'raped' him in *Putting Pants on Philip*. Modern gay viewers can certainly find amusement in the dialogue title where Stan tells his pal, 'You've worn me pink!'

Stan goes to bed, but Ollie interrupts his sleep. 'Take a look at my new Spring outfit,' he insists, like an excited wife (as so often, the boys interchange masculine and feminine roles). Stan gives notice, but Ollie is too attached to him (in whatever way) to accept the resignation: 'You can't leave – I won't let you.' Frustrated, Stan begins to kick the furniture, eventually knocking over a table by accident. 'Be careful – you might break something,' warns Ollie. This gives Stan an idea and the film goes into a variation on tit-for-tat as he tries to get himself fired by destroying various objects. Casually, he pushes a lamp, a potted plant and valuable vases onto the floor. Ollie's efforts to restrain him only result in the destruction of more items, and together they wreck much of the house.

At one point, Stan falls headlong into a birthday cake which he had baked (before the drunken homecoming) for Ollie and accompanied with a touching note – evidence that he still has feelings for his old friend beyond that of a butler (he anticipates Erich von Stroheim's butler/husband in *Sunset Boulevard* (1950)). Now, Stan falls face first into the cake which, together with his uncharacteristic behaviour, leads Ollie to think he's rabid. 'You're frothing at the mouth!' he exclaims. In appearance, Stan has metamorphosed into a mad dog, effectively displacing Buster who ran away at his owner's first display of (dis)temper. Of course, Stan is (more or less) putting on an act, perhaps having finally discovered a sense of play, so he behaves in a way which appears to verify his alleged insanity. Terrified, Ollie conceals himself within his most decadent possession, a fountain ornamented with various gargoyles each modelled on his head. He replaces one of them with his own, emitting a jet of water in imitation of the imitation. Stan, suspecting this, repeatedly hits the heads with a fly-swatter to test their efficiency at spewing water (and therefore which is real). Ollie eventually breaks up, rises laughing and, in a moving scene of reconciliation, the pair muss each other's hair – they begin to play.

This ending suggests that warmth and spontaneity – presumably a part of their relationship before the inheritance – can only be restored once Hardy's possessions and home, symbols of his new-found wealth, have been destroyed. This erodes the master–servant relationship which inhibits play: only when Stan matches the power of Ollie's wealth with a display of his own power, through anger and destruction, can the duo find the equal footing which permits it again. Ollie's discovery that he prefers the equality of play to the power of wealth is reached through his drunkenness. Liquor is a liberating force which brings about the same 'loss of control and the gaining of vitality' that Robin Wood notes is induced by the rejuvenation drug in Hawks's *Monkey Business* (Wood, 1968, p. 84); see also Chapter 1. Most crucially, in the final sequence, Ollie must substitute the artifice of the fountain with his real self in order to reclaim what he genuinely wants. This scene is, however, ambiguous enough to imply that, initially, by hiding in the fountain and literally becoming a part of his property, Ollie is still attempting to preserve his position, cocooning himself within a display of his wealth – until his true self, accompanied by liberating laughter, breaks out.

Their next film, **Two Tars**, is among the most famous of Laurel and Hardy's silents. It's remembered chiefly for the tit-for-tat riot which forms not merely its climax but the main body of the film. Yet its first third is equally interesting, albeit for different reasons. After stirring documentary footage of the US Navy, the film proper opens with a continuation of the male bonding seen at the end of *Early to Bed*: the boys – sailors on shore leave – are in a rented car, Ollie with his arm round driver Stan. Talking face to face, they are so absorbed in each other that the car crashes into a telegraph pole. Even when Ollie takes over the driving, they remain equally engrossed and hit a lamppost.

However, they are soon distracted from each other by two young ladies (Thelma Hill and Ruby Blaine) in trouble with a gum machine outside a shop. The two couples gaze at each other, flirting bashfully in a manner that recalls *Their Purple Moment* and *Should Married Men Go Home?* The boys fancy themselves as gallant rescuers of ladies in distress, even fighting each other for the privilege of performing the mock-heroic deed of extracting gum from the recalcitrant dispenser. But they only succeed in destroying the machine, which spills its contents onto the pavement. Stan and the girls retreat to the car while Ollie, stuffing gum-balls down his sailor shirt like a greedy child, is caught red-handed by the shopkeeper (Charlie Hall). The latter, though diminutive, easily defeats Ollie who doesn't even attempt to retaliate. Stan leaps out of the car but, repeatedly falling on the gum balls, cannot stand up long enough to hit Hall. Vengeance is left to the ladies, who order the sailors into the car. They obey, and watch passively as Thelma and Ruby take control of the situation, giving Hall the hammering which the 'two tough tars' (the film's working title) were unable to do.

This role reversal is underlined by the foursome's appearance when we next see them. Altogether in the car, the girls are sporting the sailors' headgear, while Stan and Ollie wear the females' flowery hats – and keep them on for the rest of the film! The wounding of their male pride in the encounter with Hall surely contributes to their belligerence when they hit a traffic jam. Indeed, one of the girls incites Ollie to commit the first deliberate assault: when the motorist behind (Edgar Kennedy) accidentally hits their vehicle, she queries, 'Are you gonna let that bozo bump our car?' Ollie, determined not to be humiliated again by the fair sex, is quick to respond with a retaliatory bump. Having proved to be ineffectual at fisticuffs, Stan and Ollie now fashion weapons out of, and redirect their aggression on, automobiles – perhaps the most coveted of status symbols in the consumer-crazy 1920s.

This tit-for-tat is a form of movement that arises as a response to the frustrating stillness of the jam: although the reciprocal destruction proceeds slowly and logically, the other motorists do seem to be itching for a fight. The film demonstrates the need (shared by participants and movie audience alike) for variation during tit-for-tat, especially when the same type of object is being destroyed. At one point, a driver accidentally opens his door in Ollie's face; Stan moves forward to pull off the door – the most logical retribution – but Ollie, apparently recalling that they've already done that to another car, stops him and they proceed to pull up two fenders. As another variation, Thelma and Ruby get into their own private fight with another woman (Kennedy's wife) – no surprise after their earlier display of aggression.

Although some violence is inflicted on human bodies – mainly through the application of fruit, oil and cement to heads and faces – most of it is reserved for cars. The close-up of an irate motorist using a penknife to slash a tyre on Stan and Ollie's vehicle does, however, strongly suggest a potential for similar injury to humans, as the knife digs into the fleshy rubber and produces a huge swelling from the inner tube, which explodes.

Eventually, a motorcycle cop arrives and literally blows the whistle on the riot. At this point Thelma and Ruby disappear for, once the riot is finished, their main function of cheerleading the violent male game has ended. All the motorists quickly return to their vehicles and, when asked who started it, they point to the sailors. If the film suggests that humans can quickly degenerate into savages, it also indicates that they are even quicker to pretend they are law-abiding citizens. Stan and Ollie are different in this respect for, as soon as the cop's back is turned, they laugh about the disturbance they have caused – accidentally, perhaps, but their attitude to the events is genuinely anarchic. It's an attitude evidently shared by the film, for a truck flattens the cop's bike, effectively removing his power and mobility. Stan and Ollie drive away, and in order to pursue his quarry the cop is forced to try hitching a lift in one of the wrecked cars. Unsuccessful even in this, he also degenerates – into a raving lunatic, wildly tearing out his hair.

A lunatic, in the form of a potty professor, motivates the narrative of **Habeas Corpus**, filmed in July 1928. A throwback to the team's over-plotted and frenetic Pathé comedies – and to the graveyard scene of *Do Detectives Think?*, in particular – it's perhaps the weakest of Laurel and Hardy's mature silent films. The feebleness of this horror-comedy is clear from the opening, when the mad scientist (Richard Carle) engages Stan and Ollie to steal a corpse from a graveyard. His dotty behaviour forces the duo into the roles of straight men; it's no wonder that in the finished film – though not the original version (see Skretvedt, 1987, pp. 131–32) – he's whisked away by the police before he can make the movie as unbalanced as he is.

As a modern Burke and Hare, Stan and Ollie are predictably incompetent. The best scenes depict their laborious efforts to perform simple tasks, notably scaling the cemetery wall. This extended gag, mainly shot in long takes, has an improvised quality: Stan and Ollie employ no props, except each other's bodies, and the result has the comic purity of a mimed stage performance. In stark contrast are the scenes which resort to the contrived paraphernalia of horror-comedy: a bat, a black cat, a lamp on top of a moving tortoise(!), a detective who inexplicably wraps himself, ghost-like, in a white sheet – apparitions which send Stan and Ollie into fits of shaking and frenzied mugging, reminiscent of their early co-appearances.

Habeas Corpus was the team's first film to be issued with a synchronized music and effects track (there's an attempt at a sound gag when the detective scares them by clapping in the graveyard). But, like so much else in this disappointing effort, it is an extraneous gimmick that has little to do with Stan and Ollie's characters. The film's most 'real' moment – when the hungry pair arrive at the professor's home, asking for a piece of buttered toast – is nullified in most TV and video copies by the removal of the dialogue title. Some even fail to include the one that relays the scientist's offer of 500 dollars for a corpse, thus effectively removing the monetary motivator that is so crucial in this and many other Laurel and Hardy films.

The boys appear to be relatively well off in **We Faw Down,** the first film since *Their Purple Moment* in which both are married. Here, the wives (Bess Flowers and Vivien Oakland) are much prettier – if no less threatening – than those in the earlier movie. Yet the opening scene clearly separates them from their husbands: they play cards at a table while the boys sit on a sofa in another part of the room. Stan and Ollie would prefer to be playing cards with men and a phone call renews the invitation to a poker game they have arranged to attend. Lying that they have to meet their boss, they go out to the game but en route rescue a young lady's hat and end up almost literally being picked up – out of a wet gutter – by the owner and her girlfriend (Kay Deslys and Vera White).

Their passivity in relation to the opposite sex continues when they go to the girls' apartment to dry off. Kay tries to seduce Stan, putting her arm round his neck. He removes it, explaining, 'I don't want to play.' In a lengthy and delightful scene she goads Stan into playing and, in the process, discovers the nearest he has to erogenous zones: when Kay presses his nose, his right eyebrow rises; poking his adam's apple makes his tongue stick out. Stan retaliates in kind to the 'slap and tickle', his irritation mixed with a childlike enjoyment, but he never seems to share Kay's erotic intentions; indeed, he says he doesn't like her because she's too fat. The scene does not develop into all-out tit-for-tat, but often seems poised to do so: at one point, Stan responds to a little slap by pushing Kay off her chair. It therefore highlights the thin division between play and malice in tit-for-tat, and suggests its erotic element more obviously than could be shown in all-male scenes of reciprocal violence. Significantly, when the boys return to their wives (who have witnessed them jumping half-dressed out of the girls' apartment window) Stan's attempt to play with his spouse by poking her adam's apple is met with icy indifference. In Laurel and Hardy's world, wives are not playful or erotic; their aggression is malicious and purposeful, as in the film's last scene when they chase the boys out of the house with a shotgun.

Before this happens, however, the boys claim they met their boss at the Orpheum Theatre, not knowing (as their wives do) that the Orpheum has just burned down. Determined to prove that they attended the show, Ollie tells the spouses, 'You shall hear all about it!' and Stan edges into the frame with a confirmative nod. With aural hindsight, we do almost hear: the sequence perhaps works better now than it did in 1928 because we can imagine Ollie's confident vocal tones as he describes the show to the simmering wives. However, since this is a silent film, humour is created from Stan's miming of the acts advertised in the newspaper, which he (but not Ollie) can see. In effect, it's a game of charades, with Ollie often misreading the clues and eventually imitating a hula dancer by donning a lampshade and wiggling his body. This is a telling moment for, in his desperation to convince the wives, to make them visualize the act he claims to have seen, Ollie is forced to convert from his role of (alleged) male spectator to that of (pretend) female performer. In a startling role reversal, the man becomes an object of scrutiny for incredulous female spectators.

The women's active role continues to the end of the film, as they pursue their husbands between two blocks of flats from whose windows, at the sound of gunshot, pour many half-dressed men. The image universalizes Stan and Ollie's predicament, suggesting they are typical (married) men. (Earlier, we saw them in the same situation, which is why the gag is effective here but not when repeated in the 1938 feature *Block-Heads*, where it comes out of the blue.)

Liberty, in contrast to *We Faw Down*, is almost plotless and purely visual, its few subtitles barely necessary. Despite this marked difference, it evolved directly from the previous film (see Skretvedt, 1987, p. 137). The boys play escaped convicts who, having changed their prison uniforms for civvies, discover that in their haste they've put on each other's trousers. For most of the film's first half, they are repeatedly trying to find a private place in which to swap them. Originally shot for *We Faw Down*, following the duo's escape from the girls' apartment, this sequence had to be excised because it pushed that film over the two-reel limit. The decision to construct the new movie around it is understandable. Among the sequence's virtues are fine judgement of camera placement and framing: in one shot, the boys – in the lower right corner of the image – attempt to exchange pants in an apparently deserted alley, unaware that a cop lurks round a corner on the left, while a woman pokes her head through a window above them. There is a sense, similar to that in later films noirs, of society crowding and oppressing the individual – of a deprivation of liberty, in fact.

According to the French film critic André S. Labarthe, the sequence 'offers, to anyone who can read, the unequivocal sign of unnatural love' (quoted by Russo, 1981, p. 73). But the key word here is surely 'sign'. Stan and Ollie's secretive behaviour emits homosexual signals – and, paradoxically, the greater their furtiveness (as when they are discovered in the back seat of a parked taxi), the stronger the signals are. But their only intention, as far as we know, is to exchange pants; the joke is that their actions are repeatedly misinterpreted. It would have been even more pointed in *We Faw Down*, since there they would have arrived at their embarrassing predicament from a *hetero*sexual context. Nevertheless, it's interesting that by now Laurel and Hardy felt confident enough with their personas to play with images of homosexuality.

The rest of *Liberty* is more conventional, borrowing heavily from Harold Lloyd in the skyscraper-walking thrill climax after the boys' accidental ascent in a construction-site lift. In addition to this obvious imitation, the unknown presence of a crab in Ollie's pants improves on a similar gag in the amusement-park sequence of Lloyd's *Speedy* (released about six months before *Liberty* was filmed), and Stan's clinging to a rope which gradually unravels, threatening his balance, recalls a gag with a fire-engine hose in the climactic chase of Lloyd's *Girl Shy* (1924).

A more surprising parallel occurs in **Wrong Again**, the team's most surreal film. In a very different two-reeler of the same year (1928), Luis Buñuel's *Un Chien Andalou*, there are images of (dead) mules on a grand piano. In Laurel and Hardy's film a comparable situation arises when, as stable-hands, they believe they have a stolen horse called Blue Boy, though in fact the theft they've heard about refers to the famous painting of the same name (which, incidentally, can be glimpsed inside Hardy Manor in *Early to Bed*). Aware of the 5,000 dollar reward offered by the painting's millionaire owner (Del Henderson), they take the horse to his mansion, where, dressing upstairs, he asks them to bring Blue Boy into the house and place him on the piano.

It's basically a one-joke film which, like Buñuel's contemporaneous classic, defies analysis. However, the joke is a good one if you respond to the surrealist penchant for juxtaposing incongruous images. Moreover, it helps to define the psychology of Stan and Ollie. As so often, they are motivated by money, not only because they want the reward but also because they respect wealthy people. Even they realize the millionaire's apparent requests are very odd but, instead of considering that *they* might have made a mistake, they decide that since he owns the house and the horse, 'we'll do as he says'. Money talks. Ollie explains that millionaires think 'just the reverse' to other people, twisting his hand for visual emphasis. Whatever strange requests or discoveries come to them in the film, they are able to explain them with this gesture. So when Stan encounters a nude Greek statue with the posterior on the same side as the face, he (eventually) twists his hand knowingly. What he doesn't realize is that earlier Ollie has accidentally broken the statue and clumsily rebuilt it with the middle section in reverse (primly covering the offending portion with his jacket during the process). This bizarre alteration to a work of art occurs again in the film's final sequence, when the Blue Boy painting falls onto a detective in such a way that his head penetrates the canvas, replacing that of the boy. These surrealist-like acts suggest that the film is mocking traditional art, though it would also seem to satirize the philistinism of Stan and Ollie who see 'crazy' modernism where it isn't. The end of the film, however, draws us towards their anarchic spirit: when the police arrive with the recovered painting, they realize their error but, instead of leaving apologetically, the duo break into uncontrollable laughter.

That's My Wife, shot in December 1928, presents a logical 'marriage' between the movies in which Stan and Ollie live with each other and those where they have wives. In the opening scene Mrs Hardy (Vivien Oakland) walks out on her husband, never to return, due to (a title tells us) 'a serious misunderstanding'. This concerns Stan who, the wife points out, dropped in for five minutes and stayed with them for two years. He and Ollie seem to find this *ménage à trois* a satisfactory arrangement: when Mrs Hardy tells her husband, 'He leaves – or I leave,' Stan doesn't offer to go and Ollie doesn't encourage him to do so. Only when the wife has left does Stan belatedly and tentatively suggest that maybe he ought to have gone instead – but Ollie shakes his head. Perhaps the latter's 'misunderstanding' with his wife was that she didn't realize until now that he prefers Stan for a partner.

What is clear, however, is that the only loss Mrs Hardy's departure poses to her husband is monetary. The sole argument he uses to persuade his wife to stay is that his Uncle Bernal (William Courtright) won't leave them a dime if she goes. He sees her purely as a financial investment. Her parting shot is 'What do I care for money?' and, as if to prove her contempt for materialism, she smashes two large flowerpots on the way out. This indirectly leads to a minor tit-for-tat session between the boys, which culminates when Stan, already imitating Mrs Hardy, tells Ollie, 'You go – or I'll go!' Reminded that it's Ollie's house, Stan goes upstairs to pack.

Meanwhile, Uncle Bernal pays a surprise visit, hoping to meet Mrs Hardy for the first time and offering to buy 'a fine new home' for Ollie – providing he's happily married. In a scene which recalls the conception of the maid masquerade in *Duck Soup*, Ollie rushes upstairs to convince Stan to play the role of his wife: 'It means thousands to me – you must do it.' Obviously, Ollie is motivated by money and now apparently sees Stan, like his real wife before, as an investment. Perhaps he's also seizing an opportunity to prevent his pal's imminent departure – to lose both partners in one day would be too much! Stan's motives for agreeing to the deception are even less clear (he isn't offered a cut); perhaps he likes the idea of being Ollie's wife, a role which he has already assumed by displacing the real spouse in his friend's affections. It's perfectly fitting that he should now become Mrs Hardy, wearing her clothes and a doll's wig. To suggest a bosom, Ollie gives him a dumb-bell – equipment mainly associated (in 1928) with male body-building, here used to construct a female body.

The 'Hardys' begin to project their illusion of heterosexual harmony in its natural location, the home. Sitting on the sofa with Uncle and Ollie, Stan – not quite willing to play his role to the hilt – rebuffs the 'husband's' petting and makes a few slips, as when he gratefully accepts a cigar intended by Uncle for Ollie. This reversion to masculinity threatens to erode the crucial gender difference (but it is in character, since the opening scene of the film established Stan's cigar-smoking). However, the error is successfully dismissed by Ollie as his wife's 'clowning'.

The going gets tougher when Uncle insists the three go to dinner at The Pink Pup. That Stan's masculinity is struggling to escape from beneath his drag is suggested symbolically when the dumb-bell falls to the floor, removing his bosom and thus part of his femininity. More difficulties arise when a drunk (Jimmy Aubrey) begins to flirt with Stan. Uncle demands that Ollie, apparently unconcerned, assert his patriarchal authority by doing 'something forceful'. In the now-established tradition of Laurel and Hardy pictures, he uses food as a weapon, pouring a bowl of soup over the head of the drunk, who calmly leaves the nightclub.

A further problem arises, however, when a terrified thief disposes of a necklace he's just stolen by dropping it down Stan's back. In a scene which parodies the often bizarre and erotic popular dances of the 1920s, the 'Hardys' attempt to locate the offending object by going onto the dance floor where their jumping, hugging, pawing and other wild movements, designed to extricate the necklace, only succeed in attracting the attention of other patrons, including Uncle. A sequence of vignettes follows, recalling the attempted exchange of pants in *Liberty*, in which the couple are repeatedly discovered in compromising positions, Ollie's hand (fishing for the necklace) well down his 'wife's' back. On the first two occasions, they are caught behind a screen and inside a phone booth; as in *Liberty*, their furtiveness compounds their guilt. The third and fourth discoveries contribute to the film's mockery of heterosexuality. A man and woman are about to enter a curtained private room, traditionally a site for wealthy patrons to make love, but it's already occupied by the 'Hardys' in what appears to be a grotesque sexual manoeuvre. By now, the necklace has been found on the floor and returned to its owner, but Ollie's body search continues. After the cafe's MC announces a stage performance entitled 'The Pageant of Love', the apparently amorous couple are revealed once again in another mock-erotic entanglement, this time witnessed by Uncle Bernal.

Ollie's search for the valuable stolen necklace parallels and destroys his attempt to 'steal' his uncle's money through the masquerade. The game is up, not least because Stan's wig has fallen off. Uncle Bernal decides to leave the café but not his money – at least not to Ollie, who, having lost his wife and fortune, now loses his dignity too, as a bowl of soup is poured over his head, courtesy of the drunk (tit-for-tat with a delayed action). Yet the film closes with Stan and Ollie laughing about their lot, comforted, it seems, by the knowledge that they still have each other. If the early scenes suggested that material comfort depends on presenting an image of heterosexual harmony, the final one implies that emotional comfort is not determined by such conformity, whether actual or apparent.

Big Business, filmed only days after the shooting of *That's My Wife* was completed, is perhaps the best-known of all their silents. As in *Two Tars*, the main body of the movie is a mammoth tit-for-tat session, but this time Stan and Ollie have only one adversary, variety being provided by the range of objects destroyed.

The pair return to their *Hats Off* occupation of door-to-door salesmen, this time trying to sell Christmas trees from their car in a wealthy Californian suburb. They meet considerable sales resistance: one householder (out of sight) clonks Ollie's head with a hammer. This, however, is a mere skirmish compared to the battle that develops when they meet James Finlayson, now working for Roach again after about a year's absence from the studio (he had played a small role as a shopkeeper in *Liberty*).

Fin, who makes his refusal to buy clear from the start, does not appear to be an inherently belligerent man any more than Stan and Ollie. His patience in the early stage of the encounter is in fact more difficult to believe than his later violence – though the suppression of his aggressive feelings during Stan's persistent sales pitch and repeated (if accidental) trapping of the tree and his coat in Fin's door, makes the ferocity with which they later erupt all the more convincing. Fin's first act, cutting the tree to bits with shears, is a fairly mild, reasoned move designed to show his contempt for the item on offer (to cap it all, Stan has asked if he can take his order for *next* Christmas). But once this first act of destruction has been committed, a tit-for-tat battle begins which slowly but surely escalates into total war.

What the film depicts is a kind of trade war, not between rival companies but between the salesman and the customer. Although it would be too much to claim that the film is an allegory of capitalist exploitation, it is worth remembering that much violence was committed in 1920s America in the name of big business. Al Capone, the most notorious racketeer of 'the lawless decade', called himself 'a businessman' (Rosow, 1978, p. 88) and claimed to be supplying 'a public demand' by bootlegging: 'If I break the law,' he said, 'my customers ... are as guilty as I am. The only difference between us is that I sell and they buy.' (Rosow, 1978, p. 95). In *Big Business* the only difference between the boys and Fin, all of whom are guilty, is that they try to sell and he doesn't buy. It's from this conflict of interests (which the gangster salesmen of bootleg beer resolved by holding a gun to their customers' heads) that violence erupts.

However, in *Big Business* it is significant that almost no violence is inflicted on the human body – only on property and merchandise. Both combatants attack each other's possessions, a course of action that would have been particularly shocking in the consumer-crazy America of the 1920s. In the tit-for-tat process, an implicit rule is followed that the appearance and/or value of the property destroyed must be roughly equal – 'an eye for an eye'. Thus, in revenge for Fin's destruction of the tree, Stan strips wood from his front door and breaks the slivers (like the tree) into pieces. Ollie tears out Fin's doorbell in retaliation for the smashing of his watch (both mechanical objects are round). Each side uses a lamp to smash a window. The removal of a door from the boys' car leads to the demolition of Fin's front door. In his garden, trees are axed and shrubs uprooted to avenge the massacre of the Christmas-tree stock. But of course the conflict escalates after each equal 'hit', and by the end of the film Fin's house and its contents, like Stan and Ollie's car and their merchandise, are annihilated. In the world of big business, goods that cannot be sold are destroyed.

'An orgy of destruction' was John Grierson's term for such a tit-for-tat battle (Grierson, 1946, p. 51). The sexual metaphor is apt: the violence builds gradually to an orgasmic climax, intensified by its delay. There is surely also a sado-masochistic enjoyment of the proceedings on the part of the protagonists – and, by extension, the audience – even when, as here, it does not involve bodily pain. As each new outrage is committed, with the refined deliberation of a master torturer, the victims passively look on (like the audience), their silence suggesting consent to the act, which they feel excuses a subsequent and similar one by themselves. The pain of material loss is apparently outweighed by the pleasurable degradation of submitting to violence and then, when the roles have reversed, the exhilaration of perpetrating it.

This enjoyment is confirmed by the final sequence of *Big Business*. A cop (Tiny Sandford), who has also been observing the proceedings for quite some time without intervening (like the authorities who turned a blind eye to gangster activities in the 1920s), eventually enforces a tearful reconciliation between Fin and the boys. But this is no Christmas truce; the salesmen laugh about their experience the moment they are beyond the law's reach. Chased by the cop, Stan and Ollie nevertheless manage to deliver Fin a parting shot: the Christmas present of a cigar which, when he lights it, explodes in his face. This gift is the film's ultimate subversion of the values of Christmas and indeed of Christianity: as the opening title explained it is 'the story of a man who turned the other cheek – and got punched in the nose'. This, together with the film's action, portrays the truth of many people's experience of the season of goodwill. *Big Business* may be the most honest Christmas movie ever made, yet it is not an amoral film. Although the boys have the last laugh, it's also painfully obvious that they've lost their means of transport and of earning a living. This ambivalence is crystallized in the cigar which, like its donors, assaults Fin but, in the process, destroys itself.

Before their next film **Double Whoopee** was shot in February 1929, sound equipment was installed at the Roach studios. Although this film was still silent (the sound facilities were not yet ready), many of its gags suggest that the makers were increasingly considering the comic potential of sound. (Indeed, in 1969 it was dubbed into a talkie by Laurel and Hardy enthusiasts.) The film's release was delayed until the talkie-hungry public had seen, and heard, the team's first proper sound movie, *Unaccustomed As We Are*.

Double Whoopee often seems like a recapitulation of their earlier work. Set in (and just outside) the lobby of a Broadway hotel, it returns to the almost plotless format of *From Soup to Nuts*, with Stan and Ollie in dignified but subservient work roles again – respectively, a footman and doorman, both uniformed. But the film also has unusual aspects, in particular the opening which, instead of introducing the boys, focuses on the snobbish, fawning hotel staff and guests excitedly awaiting the imminent arrival of a Prussian prince (John Peters, parodying Erich von Stroheim in *Foolish Wives* (1921)) and his prime minister. After the two men emerge from their car, it quickly becomes apparent that their behaviour and relationship are exaggerated versions of Stan and Ollie's. Then, as the aide-like PM brushes the haughty Prince's uniform, Stan himself casually strolls into the frame, obscuring our view of the Prussian pair. He is soon followed by Ollie, who stops to examine the Prince then turns to give the camera a conspiratorial glance. This address to the film's audience – who, unlike the people in the lobby, have been awaiting the arrival of Laurel and Hardy – implies an awareness that the Prussians have tried to steal the picture from its true stars, and that tit-for-tat revenge must eventually be exacted. As he leaves the frame, Ollie pointedly extracts his hands from beneath his cape, a gentleman's equivalent of rolling up his sleeves. The function of this scene resembles those early TV shows where the star introduces a play in which she or he will later appear in character. It implies that, while the Stan and Ollie we later see seldom realize the consequences of their actions, there is also a knowing collusion between stars and audience.

In the next scene the boys enter the lobby and are mistaken for the Prussian pair by the hotel staff. Thus, the servants-to-be effectively usurp the VIPs, avenging their usurpation in the opening shots of the film. During protracted attempts to sign the hotel register, Stan begins the assault on the Prince's admirers, accidentally sending ink flying into a vain lady's powder case: she continues to beautify her face, eyes raised, blissfully unaware that now she is smearing ink over it. Eventually, the real VIPs are identified, Stan and Ollie having belatedly produced their credentials from the employment agency.

While the boys are sent upstairs to put on their uniforms, the lobby snobs persuade the Prince to make a speech, elevating further his already high opinion of himself. But it's a case of pride before a fall. A close-up follows of a hand, evidently on an upper floor, pressing the button for the lift. The theatrical flourish attached to the action identifies it as Ollie's, but it could equally be the Hand of Fate – Ollie is unaware that the timing of his action will mean that the pompous Prince tumbles into the lift shaft, the doors of which have remained open. While the subjugated Prussian fumes in the shaft's filthy base, Ollie descends in the lift, then strides out, resplendent in his doorman's uniform and appreciative of the crowd he believes have come to greet him. The Prince is extricated, *his* uniform now blackened. 'This would mean death in my country!' he shouts, then turns to the lift, only to fall again into the dark, dungeon-like base of the shaft – poetic justice for his fascist ranting (and, incidentally, a fate similar to that suffered by von Stroheim in *Foolish Wives*, at the end of which he is dropped into a sewer). This time Stan has called the lift and now descends in it, dressed as a footman. The boys' two descents have each displaced the Prince from the lift and from the film – just as each frame of a film descends into the gate of a movie projector, displacing the previous image. In so doing, they have finally achieved the star entrances – complete with glamorous costumes – which they were denied by the Prussians' arrival at the beginning. It has now been firmly established that this is a Laurel and Hardy picture!

Outside the hotel, Ollie cuts a proud figure in his uniform, like Emil Jannings in Murnau's *The Last Laugh* (1924). But he is still a child and, when he notices a whistle attached to the uniform, he blows it without thinking. A taxi promptly appears. The driver (Charlie Hall) is displeased when he sees there is no customer, but Ollie shifts responsibility for his error to the whistle: 'It blew,' he explains. The impression of children at play is confirmed later in the scene when Ollie steals the quarter Stan has received as a tip. Stan cries and the intervention of a cop (Tiny Sandford) is required to rectify the crime. The cop, moustached and uniformed, is in effect another double of Ollie, but his greater size and darker uniform bereft of the artificial decoration of the doorman's, reinforces his real authority – he's the teacher and Ollie merely the playground bully.

Stan inadvertently takes revenge by blowing Ollie's whistle, which produces the mean-spirited genie of Charlie Hall again. The doorman's attempt to evade responsibility is as unsuccessful as before, though this time he is innocent. The taxi driver crushes the whistle with his foot and proceeds to mutilate Ollie's uniform, removing a button from it, like an officer stripping a disgraced soldier (the scene also recalls Jannings's demotion in *The Last Laugh*). Stan retaliates on his colleague's behalf by attacking Hall's cap, part of *his* uniform. And it doesn't end there, for Hall responds by pulling another button off what he thinks is Ollie's uniform but is in fact the cop's.

Double Whoopee plays with the symbolism of clothing in a variety of ways, which endows the film with a certain subtlety when compared to the straightforward pants-ripping in *You're Darn Tootin'*. The garments which (often falsely) define many of the characters, especially those who wear uniforms, are ruined or removed, exposing the naked truth of their wearers. In the case of Jean Harlow, the back of whose long dress is accidentally trapped in the taxi door by Stan, the removal of her clothing intensifies the glamour she is already deliberately projecting. But even she is disturbed by the loss of her garment, since she's no longer displaying her body in a way that is socially acceptable (at least, not in the context of this hotel). When Ollie, escorting her into the lobby, eventually becomes aware of what has happened, he removes Stan's coat to cover Jean, little realizing that this leaves Stan clad only in *his* underwear – the footman's uniform, including a clip-on shirt-front, is a sham. This gag, a reversal of that intended to conclude *From Soup to Nuts*, implicitly feminizes Stan by comparing him to a woman. But part of the joke is also surely that, while Jean's visible underwear enhances her femininity and sexiness, Stan's appearance in long johns is totally sexless.

The scene with Harlow is almost mirrored by Stan's two altercations with a male guest. In the first he helps him to put on his overcoat but, in so doing, accidentally removes the man's shirt. Later, during a tit-for-tat session in the lobby, the guest returns to bare his breast to Stan, who then removes the man's next layer of 'clothing' – hairs from his chest – which he then stuffs down the victim's low-cut vest. The man tweaks Stan's nose, so the footman now 'clothes' him by attaching a large sticky label to his hairy chest – which the guest painfully removes himself. The tit-for-tat snowballs until many of the staff and guests, including the Prince, are drawn into the fracas, during which the boys furtively retreat upstairs. Once again, the Prince tumbles into the lift shaft, followed by Stan and Ollie's simultaneous descent in the lift. Having relinquished their uniforms, they are back in the clothes they arrived in. As usual, they have failed in the world of work, but not as stars of the film: their final displacement and humiliation of the Prince allows them a triumphant exit – as important to a star as an effective entrance. They are in the last shot and (like Emil Jannings's demoted doorman) get the last laugh.

Exhibition of **Bacon Grabbers**, Laurel and Hardy's penultimate silent film, was delayed until several of their talkies had been released. Superficially, it resembles *Big Business*: Stan and Ollie drive to a suburban home, tangle with the owner and besiege the house until a cop intervenes. In both cases their car is destroyed. But in this film they represent the law themselves, assuming the roles of attachment officers from the sheriff's office who must serve a subpoena on householder Edgar Kennedy and repossess the radio he has not paid for.

The film opens inside the sheriff's office, where we find them sleeping together on a bench – an image that reconciles their unusual professional status with their more typical roles as vagrants. Woken by the sheriff, they walk to his desk but Stan, standing beside it, dozes off again. The duo's protracted attempts to leave the office and set about their task soon dispel any fleeting belief in their competence. The main body of the film, set outside Kennedy's house, comprises a long series of mix-ups: a sandwich being mistaken for the subpoena, a toy dog for a real one, etc. (The latter gag is filched from *Along Came Auntie*, the 1926 Roach–Hardy film discussed in Chapter 1, which, incidentally, also features an attachment officer.)

Eventually, they manage to retrieve the radio with the help of a passing cop, like thwarted children enlisting the aid of teacher – Ollie even pulls a face at Edgar. They carry the radio to the road where they leave it, diverted by a brief bout of reciprocal bottom-kicking with Kennedy. A steamroller runs over it (just as one destroyed the washing-machine they were trying to sell in *Hats Off*). At this point Mrs Kennedy (Jean Harlow) arrives to inform her husband that she's just paid for the radio: 'We own it.' Stan and Ollie laugh triumphantly, but in this film they don't have the last laugh: the steamroller moves on to crush their car. Made in the last year of the consumerist 1920s, this visibly low-budget film is comparatively restrained in its destructiveness, instead voicing concerns about the affordability of luxuries and the uncertainty of ownership. The crushing of the radio and car anticipated the crashing of Wall Street in October 1929 when *Bacon Grabbers* was finally released.

The team's last silent film, **Angora Love**, was completed in March 1929 but shelved until December while priority release was given to their first six two-reel talkies. Perhaps due to its limited commercial potential, this is another low-budget film, but it is entirely suitable for the subject: the viewer can almost smell the poverty – not to mention the runaway goat which precipitates the narrative.

The boys first appear on the street eating doughnuts from a bag. Ollie criticizes Stan's purchase: 'You would spend our last dime for pastry with a hole in it.' But the food attracts a goat, called Penelope, which has escaped from a pet shop. Stan and Ollie, unaware of the goat's sex or name, assume it's male. 'He likes me,' declares Stan, feeding it. Naturally, the goat follows them down the street: a backward tracking shot of the duo pursued by the animal recalls that of Stan walking childlike behind Ollie in *Putting Pants on Philip*, an echo of which film is also provided by the latter's descent into a mud-hole at the end of the sequence.

Eventually, the exhausted pair, still accompanied by the indefatigable goat, return to their home – a seedy room in a boarding-house which, as in *Leave 'Em Laughing*, is run by a tyrannical landlord, this time played by Edgar Kennedy. Paper is peeling off the walls even before the goat starts to strip more of it. The anarchic animal, which also attacks the furniture, could be seen as a projection of Stan and Ollie's usual destructiveness. Their noisy efforts to control it wake Edgar whose room is unfortunately located directly below theirs. Standing in the doorway, the landlord tells them, 'This is a respectable hotel!' – an assertion promptly belied by a sailor's lustful pursuit of a girl on the landing behind him. This is also, I think, the film's subtle way of suggesting that Edgar has mistaken his boarders' noisy behaviour for homosexual activity: when he arrives, they have just managed to conceal the incriminating goat under the bed, and now stand beside it looking very guilty.

This is certainly one of the films which show Stan and Ollie physically involved with each other, though the level of it is more sensual than sexual. In one scene they sit down together, Ollie accidentally picks up Stan's leg instead of his own, removes the shoe and sock, then massages the foot, his eyes closed as his face registers pure bliss. Stan also enjoys the experience, appreciatively watching Ollie and eventually asking him to scratch his back too. If, in the boxing match of *The Battle of the Century*, Ollie felt Stan's pain, here (and when the gag was repeated in *Beau Hunks*) he shares the same physical sensations enjoyed by Stan – the implication being that subconsciously Ollie enjoys pleasuring Stan's body as much as if it were his own. When he realizes what he's been doing, however, he contemptuously throws down his pal's leg.

As I suggested above, the goat's relationship to the duo resembles the one established between Stan and Ollie in *Putting Pants on Philip* – that of a child. This is established early in the film when, realizing that the police know about the apparent theft of the goat, Ollie exclaims, 'We'll get ten years for kidnapping!' As in later movies where they again become involved with anthropomorphic animals, Stan competes with the pet for the role of child. Indeed, he identifies strongly with the goat, taking its hiding place under the bed when the landlord threatens to enter, then sitting in the tub with it when Ollie is about to bathe the odorous animal.

Towards the end of the film, the roles within the trio are subjected to comic fluctuation. As the two parents wash their 'kid', there's a knock at the door; Ollie, believing it's the landlord, quickly substitutes Stan for the goat. In fact, it's only another boarder (Charlie Hall), who has mistakenly come to the wrong room. When he leaves, the animal is returned to the tub, but now Edgar does appear, noticed only by Stan, who belatedly substitutes Ollie. The film ends, after Penelope has been taken away by a cop, with three kids emerging from under Stan and Ollie's bed – in effect, their grandkids. But this image of birth also marked a death: as far as Laurel and Hardy were concerned, their completion of *Angora Love* put silent films to bed for ever.

Chapter four

Silence into Sound: The Early Talkies (1929–30)

BY SPRING 1929, when the installation of sound equipment at the Hal Roach Studio was completed, the new medium had established its supremacy in Hollywood. Even MGM, the last major studio to embrace sound, had made its first all-talking film, the musical *Broadway Melody*, and on 4 May 1929 its distribution wing rushed the first Laurel and Hardy talkie, a two-reeler called **Unaccustomed As We Are,** to the public with great success.

Although the title suggests that the team were tentative about sound, the film itself is just the opposite. Hardy seems to brim with vocal confidence, and if Laurel felt anxious about his voice (see Skretvedt, 1987, p. 157), the plot and script of *Unaccustomed As We Are* conceal and even exploit his timidity. It begins in the hall outside the Hardys' apartment with Ollie verbally in command as he describes to Stan the wonders of his wife's cooking, which he hopes his friend will presently sample. After Ollie has detailed the elaborate menu he envisages, Stan asks, 'Any nuts?' – the laconic bathos of the line perfectly complemented by Stan's childlike nasal whine (which later in the film enhances his cry).

A trivial conversation develops between Ollie and his neighbour (Thelma Todd) from across the hall, the two formally and repeatedly referring to each other as 'Mr Hardy' and 'Mrs Kennedy'. Stan, standing silently between them, uses subtle facial pantomime to comment on the unnecessary words expended by the two chatterboxes – a satirical comment on the verbosity of the early talkies. After the conversation has ended, Ollie explains, 'That was Mrs Kennedy.' Stan replies dumbly (rather than sarcastically), 'I was wondering who it was.' The Mr Hardy/Mrs Kennedy exchanges recur twice later in the film, each time accompanied by a puzzled Stan staring at the audience (a usurpation of Ollie's usual camera-look).

The situation comedy of the film draws on the domestic scenes of such silents as *Should Married Men Go Home?* and *That's My Wife*, in which Stan was cast as a bachelor intruder in the Hardys' home. In this case, Ollie has invited him to dinner, unbeknown to his wife (Mae Busch). Her first scene develops the cold, aggressive characterizations of wives already established in the silents with the addition of a piercing voice, which she uses to rant at the men. Mrs Hardy objects violently to Stan's presence, so she and Ollie engage in an argument where both speak simultaneously, drowning each other's voices; Stan (again) stands as silent observer. If the scene with Mrs Kennedy parodied the theatrical punc-tiliousness with which dialogue was written and delivered in most early talkies, this one exaggerates the incoherence that resulted if such precision was abandoned. As Mrs Hardy gains the aural high ground, Ollie puts on a dance record, the ha-cha-cha rhythm of which gradually dictates his wife's speech patterns. This variation on the misogynous joke about the similarity between a nagging woman and a cracked record is also perhaps a comment on the prevalence of musicals since the advent of sound. Hypocrisy is added to Mrs Hardy's unattractive features when she complains, 'I can't get a word in edgeways with you two.'

Eventually, she decides to leave and Stan obligingly opens the door for her, highlighting that he is the cause of her departure. Ollie, determined that his friend will have the promised dinner, now assumes his wife's role as cook. This is the first of the many films in which the duo are forced to perform 'woman's work' in the absence of a female. Their inadequacy for the task is quickly revealed when they initiate a series of explosions from the gas cooker. In one of these, the dress of Mrs Kennedy (who has come to assist) catches fire and has to be removed, an incident which unfortunately coincides with the arrival of her tough cop husband (Edgar Kennedy).

Bedroom farce ensues when Mrs Hardy also returns, and Ollie tells Mrs Kennedy to hide in a trunk. Understandably, Stan – whose claim to the role of 'the other woman' was established before hers – thinks Ollie is addressing him, so he tries to climb into the trunk first. (The gag is a clever variation on the duo's concealment of the goat in their previous film *Angora Love*.)

Mrs Hardy apologizes for her earlier behaviour – a rather unconvincing turnabout, but perhaps in keeping with the film's parody of the theatrical triangle dramas which were Hollywood's staple diet in the early sound period. This is certainly evident in the dialogue which follows, as her attempt at reconciliation is met with lines like, 'No, Barbara, we are through,' enunciated by Hardy with mock gravity and accompanied by histrionic hand gestures. He declares that he's leaving for South America with Stan – and his trunk. Mrs Hardy's efforts having failed, she now vents her wrath on Stan, confirming his role as her rival for Ollie. 'It's men about town like you that cause all the trouble between man and wife,' she tells him. Stan's childlike passivity (emphasized in this film by his frequent silence) contrasts amusingly with the popular image of a man about town, or the 'wolf in sheep's clothing' she also brands him. But of course the joke is also that these accusations would normally be directed (at least in fictional works of 1929) at a male lover running off with a wife, not a husband!

Mrs Hardy's anger turns to physical violence as Mr Kennedy, alerted by the noise, enters the apartment and receives her side of the story. He calls Stan 'a homebreaker' but, hearing a woman (he doesn't know who) in the trunk, his mood changes to that of heterosexual male camaraderie. 'We married men, we gotta stick together,' he asserts, then goes on to brag about the sexual 'technique' he exercises on his beat. When his wife finally emerges from the trunk (now in the Kennedys' apartment) she retorts, 'You get a bit of my technique, dearie,' and begins to throw household objects at him, recalling Mrs Hardy's earlier assault on Stan.

The Kennedys' marital discord is audible from across the hall in the Hardys' apartment, as the married couple and their guest, all reconciled now, finally sit down to dinner. Stan and Ollie's enjoyment of their meal is severely undermined by their anxiety about the repercussions of the row they are overhearing. Sure enough, the cop enters and, with a whistle, beckons Ollie into the hall where another offscreen scene of violence occurs, after which Mr Hardy returns holding his nose. Kennedy reappears, now whistling and beckoning to Stan, who also follows him into the hall, though not before finishing his cup of coffee – a possible parody of early talkies which critics dubbed 'teacup dramas'. But this time Kennedy is knocked unconscious from a blow with a vase delivered by his still irate wife. Stan nonchalantly re-enters the Hardys' home, unscathed, picks up his hat and leaves. As Ollie follows him into the hall, the apparent victor echoes Kennedy's whistle and points to the policeman lying on the floor. Only we know that the 'masculine' role of the tough cop's conqueror, which Stan assumes, is rightfully Mrs Kennedy's. This reverses the gender confusion earlier in the film when Stan occupied the role of 'the other woman', from which Mrs Kennedy effectively usurped him by hiding in the trunk. Stan's interchangeability with her is finally underlined when he says, 'Goodbye, Mr Hardy,' in a fruity voice which mimics her politeness. But, as always in Laurel and Hardy, it's a case of pride before a fall: Stan plummets head first down the stairs, his offscreen descent charted aurally by a series of bumps.

Unaccustomed As We Are is such a bold and accomplished first talkie that, with hindsight, its title seems to be not merely an acknowledgement that it is a new venture for Laurel and Hardy but a pointer for the audience that the film is *about* the sound medium. The opening of Chaplin's *City Lights* (1931) is renowned for its parody of primitive talkies, with its distorted and muffled speech by pompous officials, but his satire is not nearly as daring, sophisticated or varied. Moreover, in Laurel and Hardy's film sound is not merely used as a medium to convey information but becomes a theme itself which is integrated into the narrative. Before the boys enter the Hardys' home, Ollie tells Stan, 'Now don't make a sound – tiptoe in and surprise her.' The husband's cry of 'Yoo-hoo' backfires as Mrs Hardy, defined by her voice before she even appears, shouts from off-camera, 'What d'ya mean, yoo-hoo?' Later, Mr Kennedy offers to give her husband 'a good talking to' so she'll have 'peace and quiet' – only to meet, seconds later, an explosion of noise from his own wife. Both couples are characterized by the large amount of noise they make (often emphasized by being offscreen), usually accompanied by physical violence. It is therefore poetic justice that Stan, silent and passive through most of the film, emerges as the victor, a role gently underscored by his whistling of 'When Johnny Comes Marching Home' in the final scene.

Although *Unaccustomed As We Are* is as static and stage-bound as any early talkie, the makers successfully exploited their restrictions. Forced by noisy cameras to set the movie indoors (like most early sound efforts), they decided to make it a domestic comedy, developing situations from the silents and establishing new ones which would be reworked for some of the team's finest sound films (in particular, the feature *Block-Heads*). It was also fortuitous that Laurel and Hardy's voices perfectly matched and even enhanced their preconceived personalities, yet also made them more recognizably human and typical. This universality is underlined by the film's ironic opening title: 'The world over – a wife loves to have her husband bring a friend home to dinner – as a surprise.'

Another surprise is that the team's second talkie, **Berth Marks**, is much more tentative in its use of sound. Perhaps this was because the emphasis on dialogue in *Unaccustomed As We Are* had hindered its conversion to a silent for screening in the many cinemas not yet equipped for the new medium. Or maybe it was felt that Laurel and Hardy, having given their first talkie as much novelty value as possible, should now return to the predominantly visual comedy for which they were famous. Whatever the reason, *Berth Marks* is an uncomfortable attempt to add sound to an essentially silent film in which the sight-gags are not very inventive anyway.

Virtually plotless, the two-reeler begins at a railway station (methods were being developed for shooting talkies outdoors, particularly when synchronized sound was not required). Stan and Ollie are a musical vaudeville act en route to their next engagement, but they have difficulty even in finding their way to each other on the platform. Having finally achieved this, their next problem is to identify the correct train. The conductor shouts a list of destinations, but it emerges as gibberish (a gag reworked by Jacques Tati at the start of *Monsieur Hulot's Holiday* (1953)). This, the film's most creative use of sound, is again (as in the scene in Chaplin's *City Lights*) probably a parody of the technical crudity of early talkies.

Eventually, the duo manage to board their train, but in the rush they lose their music (by the end of the film they will also have lost the cello vital for their act). In one of the carriages they are indirectly responsible for starting reciprocal clothes-tearing among the other passengers. But they remain aloof from the tit-for-tat exchanges (evidently based on the pants-ripping of *You're Darn Tootin'*) which, interspersed throughout the rest of the film, lack the necessary continuity, momentum and sense of ritual. These scenes are merely used as counterpoint to the main action involving the duo's protracted efforts to climb into, then undress inside, their upper berth. The initial part of this sequence, reworking the ascent of the graveyard wall in *Habeas Corpus*, at least exploits the potential of sound through their unsuccessful attempts to be quiet as they climb (their noises wake other passengers including a baby). But in the feebly executed six-minute scene inside the cramped berth the repetitious verbal ad libbing distracts from the slight humour in the boys' bodily contortions. These anticipate the mock-eroticism in *Be Big* and other later films, but here the images are too prosaic to be taken at much more than face value.

Their next film, **Men O' War**, set in a park, contains a similarly weak climax, but for its first two-thirds manages to reconcile visual and verbal humour even more effectively than *Unaccustomed As We Are*. Indeed, the central and finest sequence – with impecunious sailors Stan and Ollie entertaining two girls at a soda fountain – is a close reworking of a similar scene in *Should Married Men Go Home?* The silent prototype evidently ensured that visual reactions were maintained in a routine that could have relied too heavily on dialogue if it had been conceived purely as a talkie.

Nevertheless, the soda sequence makes excellent use of dialogue and shows how expressively the team could now deliver it. Sound enables them to add extra nuances to the child–parent dimension of their relationship, Ollie verbally reprimanding Stan to make him realize how badly he's behaved. When financial restrictions force the pair to share a soda, Ollie lets Stan drink his half first but the latter consumes it all. The disappointed father-figure (as much priest as parent) asks softly, 'Do you know what you've done?' Guilt-ridden, Stan looks away and nods. 'What made you do it?' persists Ollie gently, seeking to understand the sinner. 'I couldn't help it,' explains Stan, playing up to the liberal line of enquiry, 'my half was on the bottom.' He cries on Ollie's shoulder, fully aware and ashamed of the enormity of his crime.

As in *Two Tars*, the duo are wearing sailors' uniforms, adding irony to their inept rowing of a small boat on the park's lake. This leads to a tit-for-tat battle in the middle of the lake with water and cushions that improves on *Berth Marks* by pitching the boys into the fray and thus provides a bathetic justification for the title *Men O' War*. However, the sequence does not really work, partly due to the restrictions of primitive sound techniques which result in shots that are too long in terms of both camera placement and time span. Moreover, the events are meaningless because the oars, cushions and boats that are destroyed do not belong to the protagonists – only to proprietor James Finlayson who, like the camera, is forced to observe helplessly from the mooring point. This was Fin's first appearance in a Laurel and Hardy film since *Big Business*, comparison with which only highlights the insipidity of the boating-lake battle.

The following short, **Perfect Day**, successfully locates tit-for-tat within a satire on bourgeois values. Stan and Ollie are going on a Sunday picnic with their wives (Isabelle Keith and Kay Deslys) and uncle (Edgar Kennedy). The atmosphere of domestic bliss is soon shattered when the boys, wearing aprons, enter the living-room with a huge plate of sandwiches that they have prepared and then promptly destroy by using them as missiles directed at each other. When Mrs Laurel reminds them, 'This is the Sabbath, the day of peace,' they hang their heads in shame and fondle their aprons, like naughty sisters being scolded by their mother. Stan and Ollie promise 'no more arguments', but spiritual harmony doesn't reign any longer on this Sabbath than it did during the Christmas preparations of *Big Business*. As the family group get ready to leave, they indulge in small talk with neighbours who, in the manner of suburbia, are relaxing in their gardens. The trivial conversation culminates in an extremely protracted series of reciprocal 'goodbyes' – a sharp satire on the repetitive, meaningless chatter in early talkies (and suburbia) that anticipates the endless 'goodnights' in W. C. Fields's 1933 short *The Fatal Glass of Beer*. Departure is delayed still further by a puncture, the group's hope deflating with the tyre (a close-up of Stan and Ollie shows them sinking physically – and psychologically – as air escapes from the tyre). Soon the mutual goodbyes develop into mutual destruction. A jack is accidentally thrown through a neighbour's window as he waters his lawn; he returns it via the car's windscreen. Stan lobs a brick through a window of the neighbour's house, and the man promptly does as he has been done by. Beneath the ultra-polite surface of suburbia lurks destructive savagery.

Egged on by the wives and Uncle, Stan and Ollie remove their jackets to get down to serious tit-for-tat, when something seen off-camera causes the entire group to rush into the house. The film's incisive critique of bourgeois hypocrisy becomes even clearer when the terrifying apparition proves to be a parson, he who presides over the 'day of peace'. When they re-emerge for their sinful pleasure there are further difficulties with swapped jackets and the car engine. By now the family group is beginning to fracture: Stan's imperative that Ollie 'step on it' brings a violent retort ('I'll step on you in a minute'); the ladies' complaints about the further delay cause Ollie to shout, 'Oh, shut up!' at them – a rare moment of open rebellion against the wives. At the end of the film, following more protracted goodbyes with a whole cluster of neighbours, the car starts, turns a corner and sinks completely with all hands into a mud-hole.

According to John McCabe, 'the greater part of the film was to concern the picnic itself' (McCabe, 1966, p. 107), but it was never shot. If this was the intention, there is a striking parallel with Jean Renoir's *Une Partie de Campagne* (1936), another film about a middle-class family of five who go on a Sunday picnic. Although the *Partie* group reach their destination, an important projected section of that film was also never shot. The sense of 'incompleteness' intensifies the deflated hope shared by both groups of characters, and contributes to each film's success. The relatively static early sound camera in *Perfect Day* also underlines the inability of the characters to leave their insular, repetitive little world. When they finally do so, they cannot survive and are buried in the grave-like black puddle.

In the same month of June 1929 that marked the production of *Perfect Day*, Laurel and Hardy accepted an invitation to appear in MGM's two-hour extravaganza, **The Hollywood Revue of 1929** – a first feature-film appearance which confirmed their status as talkie stars. The movie, as William K. Everson comments, 'seemed to assign most of its stars to do the things that they *didn't* do best' (Everson, 1967, p. 92). In a sense this is also true of Laurel and Hardy, the important difference being that the humour of their six-minute sketch resides in the boys' incompetence as magicians. It is the type of routine that would much later become familiar (at least to British TV viewers) via Tommy Cooper.

The theatricality of their segment, statically filmed on a stage-like set, is underlined by the fact they both acknowledge the presence of the audience, verbally or, in Stan's case, physically. The latter is assistant to master magician Ollie, whose tricks are highly unconvincing even before his partner's greater ineptitude ruins them totally. Stan is dumb in both senses throughout the sequence: he doesn't say a word and, ironically, the only audible sound he makes is to 'shush' Ollie (who later tells his silent partner to 'shut up'). In contrast, Ollie introduces all the tricks with verbal and gestural aplomb. He also whistles in accompaniment to the orchestra's playing of 'The Skaters' Waltz', but when Stan tries to imitate him no sound emerges. Like *Unaccustomed As We Are*, the sketch uses the new medium very creatively, Stan and Ollie's relationship being cast as a conflict between silence and sound.

During the course of their act, both have mishaps with eggs (anticipating their later guest appearance in MGM's *Hollywood Party*) and Ollie reprises his *From Soup to Nuts* gag of stepping on a banana skin and falling head first into a cake, its aftermath now enhanced by sound. Covered in cream, he sits on the floor like an infant defeated in his first attempt at walking, an image reinforced by his monosyllabic comment in a toddler's tones, 'I faw down – and go *blop*!' This regression to childhood in the face of life's misfortunes is startlingly sudden and complete even by Laurel and Hardy's standards.

The duo's next short subject, **They Go Boom**, is another of their boarding-house films. It's basically a two-hander which reworks the first third of *Leave 'Em Laughing*, this time with Ollie as the patient, suffering from 'the sniffles' rather than toothache, and Stan filling the role of carer with predictable ineptitude. The framed motto 'Smile all the While' (instead of the earlier film's 'Keep Smiling') hangs over the bed in and around which they spend most of the two reels. Even the 'bedwetting' gag is reprised from the silent prototype, though this is now effected by a burst water-pipe above the bed.

The arrival of Charlie Hall, playing the authoritarian landlord again, briefly casts the duo in the role of children. Ollie, out of bed, gets all the blame for noise they have both made, while Stan, recumbent, smiles innocently at Hall. When the landlord leaves, Ollie is about to redistribute punishment but Hall pops his head round the door, so Ollie, quickly changing his action and role, paternally tucks in the angelic child.

Like the team's other bed-based movies, *They Go Boom* has a pleasant intimacy and naturalism, creating comedy from the mundane situation of treating a cold. There is no plot, but isolated images are memorable: Stan stirring a cauldron-like foot bath with a broomstick, iconography which brings a suggestion of witchcraft to his cold remedies; Ollie's face fleetingly registering a belief that his friend is a 'shirt-lifter' when Stan tries to retrieve a mustard plaster stuck to the back of his nightshirt; Ollie's belly swelling grotesquely from excessive inhalation of air from the bed's mattress – an early example of freakish bodily distortion in the team's films. The title is explained by the climactic gag in which the mattress is accidentally overfilled with gas, raising its two sleepers to the ceiling, until it explodes. The 'boom' comes with the sudden collapse of the bed, a symbolic premonition of the economic collapse, three months after the film was shot in July 1929, which ended the rather different kind of 'boom' which the United States had enjoyed in the 1920s.

Meanwhile, the team made **The Hoose-gow**, the oddest of their prison comedies in that it takes place almost entirely outdoors. However, there is a strong sense of confinement and constriction (reminiscent of *Berth Marks*) in the image which introduces the boys, who lie entangled on the floor of the patrol wagon which brings them to jail. Unlike their earlier prison film, *The Second Hundred Years*, this one provides a clue about their crime. 'We were only watching the raid,' claims Ollie, a reference, presumably, to a raid on one of the many speakeasies that flourished during Prohibition. The warden (Tiny Sandford) is not impressed by their protestations of innocence, so the boys decide to activate an escape plan by throwing two apples over the prison wall, a signal for comrades on the outside to reciprocate with a rope ladder. But before this can be done the warden approaches, and Stan is forced to conceal one of the apples inside his mouth. A childlike panic grips him as he finds it has inextricably lodged there. He cries anxiously, and Ollie is forced into the role of problem-solving parent, encouraging him to cough it out. Eventually, Stan swallows the apple. The warden throws the remaining one over the wall, causing the ladder to appear. During his investigation of this mystery, the boys are accidentally locked out of the prison, but Stan, feeling excluded, knocks on the gate. By representing Stan's submission to authority in this patently stupid act, the film questions the wisdom of observing the law, a viewpoint with which the millions of Americans who violated Prohibition must have sympathized.

The second half of the film is set in a labour camp. Last to arrive for lunch, the duo find there's no place for them at the prisoners' table, but an old lag directs them to a separate one, in reality the warden's. This is a reworking of the Captain's compartment gag in *With Love and Hisses*, and anticipates the scene in the Dean's quarters in *A Chump at Oxford*; it seems the set-up can be adapted for any hierarchical male community. At the table, Ollie's bowl of soup is rendered inedible when Stan forgets to replace the top of the pepper-pot properly (a routine adapted from *You're Darn Tootin'*). In any case, the warden appears and clears them away from his table. Hungry, the boys go to the cook who offers them food in return for chopping wood – the more wood, the more food. Ollie puts on an impressive display of masculinity by chopping down a tall tree, at the top of which sleeps a lookout guard.

They receive neither food nor punishment due to the sudden arrival of the governor (James Finlayson) and his entourage – two haughty ladies who inspect the prisoners, now digging a ditch, as if watching animals in a zoo. During a scuffle with Stan (perhaps inspired by a scene in Laurel's 1923 mining comedy, *Pick and Shovel*), Ollie throws a pick which damages the radiator of the governor's car, causing it to leak. The boys plug it by filling the radiator with rice. As soon as Fin returns to his car and informs the warden, 'Everything seems quite in order,' chaos erupts as 'rice pudding' spouts from the radiator. Having been short of food, the boys are now confronted by an excess of it, as if in payment for the immoderate amount of wood they've chopped. A tit-for-tat battle, with the rice as weapon, gradually develops between convicts, prison staff and visiting dignitaries – all are reduced to the same level of pettiness, and social status is eradicated by the sticky mush that obscures the clothes which normally distinguish their roles. Although this sequence is less inventive than its silent prototype in *The Battle of the Century*, it's interesting for the location of tit-for-tat's liberating power within a normally confining and hierarchical environment.

In September 1929 Laurel and Hardy were loaned again to MGM for their second appearance in a major feature film, **The Rogue Song**. Although more substantial than their sketch in *The Hollywood Revue of 1929*, their contribution amounted to only eight scenes, most of them very short, and was apparently an afterthought designed to provide comedy relief for the rather sombre musical that had already been made and previewed. Laurel and Hardy were also now successful enough to be used as box-office insurance for an expensive Technicolor feature like *The Rogue Song*.

The film is basically a vehicle for the operatic baritone Lawrence Tibbett, who had shot to fame at the Metropolitan Opera House during the second half of the 1920s. He plays a bandit chief, while Stan and Ollie (actually called Ali-Bek and Murza-Bek) are two of his henchmen. It's difficult to assess their contribution, since only one of their scenes survives in both sound and vision. Although the complete soundtrack has been preserved on disc (a method of reproduction for early talkies), very little footage from the film is known to exist, so its visual aspect can only be surmised from stills and written material.

Fortunately, the extant scene is quintessential Laurel and Hardy. As in *They Go Boom* (and numerous other films), the boys are trying to sleep, but this time their bed is inside a tent which is blown away during a ferocious storm. Seeking alternative shelter, they enter a cave, unaware that a bear has preceded them. The camera remains static, outside the cave, as dialogue alone conveys the fact they are sleeping with the bear – which Ollie mistakes for Stan. 'Where did you get that fur coat?' asks Ollie and, after a protracted exchange in which Stan denies having a fur coat, we hear a roar and the boys exit the cave, presumably 'pursued by bear' (as Stan was in *Flying Elephants*). The scene anticipates a sequence in *The Chimp* when Ollie sleeps with the eponymous primate in the belief it's Stan – as so often in their work, Laurel is interchangeable with an animal.

The preservation of their usual personas and type of material, even when under the control of another studio, was no doubt due to the negotiating power of their boss Hal Roach, who also directed their scenes in the movie. When the team returned to MGM in the 1940s, without Roach's assistance, they were not accorded the same deference. *The Rogue Song* does, however, seem to have influenced Laurel and Hardy's 1930s musical features, particularly *The Devil's Brother* in which they are again cast in the roles of henchmen to a bandit chief. Although that later film would feature a considerable amount of music from Auber's opera *Fra Diavolo*, the singing hero would be subordinated to (and more integrated with) Laurel and Hardy's comedy, inverting the proportions in *The Rogue Song*.

The team's next two-reeler, back at the Roach studio, was **Night Owls** – a dark film in every sense. Made around the time of the Wall Street crash (in which Laurel lost a lot of money) on 24 October 1929, it seems to anticipate Depression movies, and even the films noirs of the 1940s, with its story of a corrupt cop whose devious scheme backfires on him. It begins in a police station where the Chief (Anders Randolph) chastises the cop (Edgar Kennedy) for his inability to catch the very active burglars on his beat. In the next scene, Kennedy finds Stan and Ollie sleeping on a park bench and threatens them with 'ninety days on the rock pile' for their vagrancy unless they rob the Chief's house – so he can take credit for their capture. Reassured that 'Kennedy will fix it' (implying they won't go to prison), they submit to his blackmail.

The main section of the film concerns their inept attempts to break into the house, a more effortful operation than an SAS assault. Much of the comedy derives from the tension between their need to be quiet and the noises they inadvertently make: they tip over dustbins, fall into a glass garden frame, drop their tools and (eventually) their loot. Inside the house, they even manage to start a player-piano which belts out 'Under The Anheuser Bush' (a useful tune since it was equally well known in Britain as 'Down At The Old Bull And Bush'). Attempting to muffle the machine, they stuff a bearskin rug inside it, an image that parodies the dead mules inside the piano in *Un Chien Andalou* more closely than the live horse in *Wrong Again*. The film ends with the cop somehow left holding Stan and Ollie's swag and being told, 'You'll get life for this,' by the irate Chief, while the boys make their escape.

After the expository scenes, *Night Owls* does not contain much dialogue – Laurel commented, 'most of our talk is limited to "shushes"' (quoted in Skretvedt, 1987, p. 184) – but it nevertheless uses the potential of sound with subtle creativity. The film exploits the anticipatory element in Laurel and Hardy's humour with particular regard to the soundtrack, holding the audience in (comic) suspense while the next noise is awaited. The small quantity of dialogue must have eased the production of foreign versions of *Night Owls* – the first Laurel and Hardy for which this was done – in which the team spoke their lines phonetically. In *Ladrones*, the longer and (for Stan and Ollie) bleaker Spanish version, Kennedy goes free and denies knowing the boys, who are therefore arrested and taken to prison – making the film almost suitable as a prequel for their previous two-reeler *The Hoose-gow*.

The most charming element of *Night Owls* is perhaps the duo's masquerade as cats after they crash into the garden frame, thus allaying the suspicions of the Chief and his butler (James Finlayson) inside the house. Crouching behind a bush, the two cat burglars miaow repeatedly until Fin throws slippers at them – one of which Stan, unable to sustain a single identity for long, hurls back at the astonished butler. Even before this scene, Stan's position on his hands and knees on top of a wall – along which a real cat has just passed – has established his felinity. Later, after the slipper episode, he twice reverts to miaowing, once to communicate with Ollie, the second time because he associates it with the crouching position in which he finds himself again. The final shot of the film shows Ollie chasing him down the road behind the house, Stan wedged in a dustbin and running on all fours – more alley cat than night owl.

Blotto, shot in December 1929, was Laurel and Hardy's first three-reeler, though it returns to the two-part structure of the silents, *Their Purple Moment* and *That's My Wife*, in which the first section has a domestic context and the second takes place in a nightclub. In this case, Stan is the married man, while Ollie is apparently a bachelor – the intruder who, by telephone, encourages his friend to come out to the club. Stan is a kind of child-groom whose marriage is characterized as unhappy, at least for him. In order to reach the adult pleasures of the club, he has to ask his wife (Anita Garvin), 'Can I go out?' like an obedient teenager pleading to his mother. As she plays solitaire (suggesting their estrangement), he explains, 'I need fresh air!' Marriage is stifling and belittling. Mrs Laurel pushes Stan into a chair like a naughty infant, telling him, 'Now sit down! Stop annoying me!' The Laurel–Hardy child–parent relationship has been recast between husband and wife, while Stan and Ollie are equals in this film.

When Ollie phones Stan, the latter has to pretend that it's a wrong number because his wife is in the room, indicating the necessary furtiveness of the men's friendship. Mrs Laurel is, however, well aware of it, since she wrests the phone from her husband and exclaims graciously, 'Oh, how are you, Mr Hardy?', then leaves the room, supposedly to allow the men privacy. In fact, she eavesdrops on the extension upstairs. On Ollie's suggestion, Stan pretends that a telegram has arrived, calling him away on 'important business'. He addresses the imaginary messenger boy in patrician tones (similar to the Lord Paddington accent he would assume a decade later in *A Chump at Oxford*): 'That's alright, son, keep the change.' In order to be released from the child world of marriage, Stan must act as an adult in authority, a performance which he evidently relishes for its own sake (there is a parallel here with his enjoyment of drag in other films) – so much so that he momentarily forgets to produce the all-important telegram. Continuing his masterful masquerade, he flicks a speck from his derby and (after a reminder) kisses Mrs Laurel goodbye like an important businessman leaving his homely wife for the office. A hint of the child who has been allowed out by his now liberal but concerned mother remains, however: when Mrs Laurel – wise to the ruse, of course – pats him on the cheek, advising, 'Don't stay out too late,' Stan meekly replies with a compliant, 'I won't.' These are adults acting like children playing 'house'. Since both participants know it's all a sham, the film begs the question, is all such 'adult' behaviour like this?

Another aspect of the Laurels' marital game concerns a bottle of liquor which Stan plans to steal from his wife, who saved it when Prohibition began. Aware of Stan's intention from her eavesdropping, she pours the contents down the sink and substitutes cold tea, spiced with various condiments. (This recalls the wife's substitution of coupons for banknotes in *Their Purple Moment*.) Stan escapes from the house with the bottle stuffed down the front of his pants, an image with phallic overtones, especially when the circumstances are also considered – the bottle, already suggestive of illicit pleasures, is removed from the wife to be shared with a male friend. Even when the boys are in the nightclub, the bottle has to be concealed. Stan's strenuous efforts to uncork it in his lap resemble furtive sexual activity and provoke disapproving looks from other patrons.

The duo are totally fooled by Mrs Laurel's concoction, 'You can certainly tell good liquor when you taste it,' comments Ollie. Their belief in its inebriating power is so strong that they begin to act like drunkards. Ollie gradually turns away from one of the nightclub's acts, a sexy female Spanish dancer, to gaze dreamily at Stan. The next act is a baritone who, standing next to their table, delivers the melancholy ballad 'The Curse of an Aching Heart' to such effect that Stan weeps uncontrollably and Ollie, almost overcome himself, has to comfort him with a manly embrace. The singer's absence from nearly all the shots focuses our attention on Stan and Ollie's reaction to the song of spurned love. The suggestion that they are moved by the lyrics' reflection of their own lives (perhaps Stan 'left' Ollie to get married) is particularly strong, since they are sung by and to members of the same sex. In this scene, Stan's cry is less childlike than feminine, as he reacts in the conventional way of a woman to the romantic song.

In keeping with this role reversal, Mrs Laurel is masculinized by her purchase of a 'big gun' – a double-barrelled shotgun which she brings with her to the club. Meanwhile, the boys, in contrast to their earlier fit of weeping, develop one of their laughing jags, which isn't curtailed even by the sight of Stan's wife staring coldly at them from a nearby table. However, when she tells them that she substituted cold tea for the liquor, a claim Ollie confirms by sniffing the bottle, they become suddenly sober. Her interruption of their orgasmic laughter exposes the two men as impotent in the face of the power of her knowledge and the physical display of her gun: a double phallus that makes their single bottle (whose contents she has emasculated) seem puny by comparison. In the final scene, she chases them out of the club, demolishing the taxi in which they've tried to escape with her gunfire.

My view that Mrs Laurel's anger is provoked by sexual jealousy is supported by comparison with *We Faw Down*, at the end of which Ollie's wife pursued him with a shotgun after his girlfriend turned up with his vest. But by the time of *Blotto*, Stan and Ollie did not need to have the extramarital heterosexual liaisons of silent films such as *We Faw Down* and *Their Purple Moment* to incur wifely wrath. Nor did Stan need to drag up as Ollie's wife, explicitly replacing the real one, as in *That's My Wife*, a film with strong structural similarities to *Blotto*. As the 1930s dawned, Stan and Ollie were becoming all things to each other, their personas and relationship fluid enough to eliminate the need for other characters in their films if they so wished.

Brats, a two-reeler made in January 1930, demonstrates this perfectly. Laurel and Hardy are the only players in this film, the first of three (the others being the much later *Twice Two* and *Our Relations*) in which both have dual roles. It is also the first movie where Stan and Ollie have children, played, of course, by Laurel and Hardy. The fathers and sons all apparently live in the same house, while the wives/mothers have gone out – a situation which makes the all-male foursome seem like a self-contained family unit. Laurel and Hardy have, in effect, assumed the roles of wives as well as those of children.

The use of two identical sets (the childrens' three times the size of the fathers') creates a convincing illusion, reinforced by skilfully chosen camera angles (a low angle for the adults to emphasize their height when they talk to the children, whose smallness is stressed by high angles). The brats not only look like their fathers – except that young Oliver has no moustache – but share their mannerisms, underlined in an early scene where each son responds to his father's distinctive smile (and, in Ollie's case, a wave too) by precisely mirroring it. Other links are made between the brats and the familiar adult characters played by Laurel and Hardy, such as young Oliver's delivery of the plea to Stan (already becoming one of the team's catch-phrases), 'Why don't you do something to help me?'

The absence of other characters emphasizes the sense of mirror images and therefore the basic joke: Stan and Ollie's behaviour as adults is as immature as that of the children they presume to correct. Both pairs are brats. The potential for confusion is highlighted when Stan tries to echo Ollie's sternly paternal warning to the brats:

> **Ollie:** Now listen, if you don't keep quiet,
>   you'll have to go to bed.
> **Stan:** Yes, we'll have to go to bed.
> **Ollie:** Not 'we', the kids!

When the fathers play pool, they argue over whose break it is, just as the sons, playing hide and seek, argue over who is 'it'. Adult games are not much advanced on those of children, at least as practised by Stan and Ollie. As pool-playing fathers, they accidentally shatter a glass display cabinet with their cues. Upstairs, the children indulge in violent antics, such as boxing and shooting a toy gun, that eventually bring down part of the ceiling. Destruction and aggression are the most obvious links between the generations, calling into question both the 'innocence' of children and the 'maturity' of adults. Ollie's method of getting the brats to bed is to threaten 'to break their necks'. Even the absent mothers, we learn from an opening title, have 'gone out to target practice'. Traditionally feminine values are represented in the film, notably by Stan who advises his co-parent to treat the children 'with kindness'. But the promise of a nickel to the first one undressed and in bed only encourages competitiveness tainted with dishonesty and ultimately violence. The fathers' attempts to assume maternal roles are also undercut: Ollie, in response to his son's plea ('Mama always sings us to sleep'), sings a lullaby with a high tessitura, but an off-key accompaniment by Stan wakes the children.

Ollie's singing would be featured in many of their films, including their next two-reeler, **Below Zero**, at the opening of which they are street musicians desperately trying to make a buck in a blizzard. As Ollie plucks a double-bass and Stan pounds a portable organ, the freezing climate seems to symbolize the mixture of indifference and hostility with which passers-by respond to their efforts (the scene reminds me of 'The Organ Grinder', the haunting final song in Schubert's song-cycle *Winterreise*). Their choice of music, 'In the Good Old Summertime', highlights their discordance with the rest of the world, as does the fact they are playing outside a deaf and dumb institute. However, they are no more successful when they find another spot, their only remuneration accompanied by a request that they 'move down a couple of streets'. Stan and Ollie are not wanted, as many American men of employable age were beginning to find with the onset of the Great Depression. The film's bleakness is emphasized by its location in a slum neighbourhood, which, together with the boys' plight, suggests that the introductory title may refer to the economic as well as the meteorological climate in its statement that 'the freezing winter of '29 will long be remembered'. In April 1930, when *Below Zero* was released, America remained unaware that much worse was still to come.

This is also true of Stan and Ollie whose economic survival, as so often, is further jeopardized by a woman – in this case a very tall one (Blanche Payson) who enters a tit-for-tat session with snowballs as the chief weapon. The food splattered in earlier battles is now replaced by a worthless, inedible substance, itself part of the climate which threatens the boys. The woman terminates the fight by breaking the bass over Ollie's head and throwing the organ into the road, where a truck promptly crushes it. As in *You're Darn Tootin'*, the loss of instruments robs them of their only legitimate means of earning a living. However, they discover a bulging wallet, dropped in the snow. Inspecting its contents, they are chased by a tough-looking thug, but are rescued by the intervention of a cop (Frank Holliday).

With their sudden wealth, the duo's bourgeois aspirations resurface (earlier, Stan has referred to a street cleaner – Charlie Hall – as 'one of the lower elements'). Money can buy them not only food but friends commensurate with their supposed status, so they invite the officer to join them for a meal, even linking arms with him to solidify their parity. They treat the humble restaurant to which he takes them as if it were a high-class establishment: Stan hands his coat to a waiter (who immediately dumps it on the floor) and Ollie generally adopts a grand manner, pretentiously ordering as many French-sounding items as possible.

After they've eaten and discussed vacation plans, Ollie insists that he and Stan will pay the bill, as the cop is their 'honoured guest'. Only now do they discover that the wallet in fact belongs to their guest, who must have dropped it in the street before they found it. He, however, believes they are 'a couple of cheap pickpockets'. Stan opens a concertina-type purse, whose many compartments only emphasize the absence of money in any of them. Broke, the boys have to face the wrath of the head waiter (Tiny Sandford). After a scene of violence – conveyed mainly in sound when the restaurant's lights are extinguished – the duo are thrown outside, returned, penniless, to the hostile elements that threatened them at the beginning of the film. In fact, Stan, unconscious, is dumped inside a rain barrel full of icy water, eventually emerging from the now empty receptacle with an enormously swollen belly. Faced with drowning, he has drunk all the water, combating the enemy by consuming it. As he hops from foot to foot, he whispers an urgent request in Ollie's ear, reaffirming their child–parent relationship despite the loss of everything else in their lives.

The following two-reeler, **Hog Wild**, concerning their attempt to erect a rooftop radio aerial, is in some ways a throwback to the very physical comedy of silents such as the house-building film *The Finishing Touch* and the vertiginous climax of *Liberty*. Yet it is also a domestic comedy, reversing the pattern of *Blotto* so that Ollie is the married man, prevented from keeping an appointment with Stan by his wife's insistence that the aerial be erected today.

Although Mrs Hardy (Fay Holderness) is as aggressive as any wife in their films – at one point thumping her husband on the head with a frying pan – the audience is invited to empathize with her in the opening scene as Ollie delivers a tirade about his missing derby, which he fails to realize is already on his head. 'That's the trouble with you wives,' he rants, universalizing his complaint, 'you're always hiding things so we husbands can't find 'em'. It is a clear, if rare, example of the misogyny in Laurel and Hardy movies being cast in an ironic light. Mrs Hardy adopts a sarcastic tone, withholding the vital information and thus allowing Ollie to embarrass himself further by summoning the maid, who giggles at her employer's question about the location of his hat. This provokes Ollie to spout more bourgeois bluster to his spouse: 'How do you expect me to uphold the dignity of my home when you belittle me in front of the servants?' Eventually, he looks in a mirror and realizes he has belittled himself, all the more so since his patriarchal stance has been displayed before two women. However, he continues his performance, hastily removing the derby from his head and then pretending to have discovered it under the bed.

It soon becomes clear that, while Ollie may wear a hat, his wife wears the pants in this household, as she underlines her instruction that the aerial be put up 'right now' by smashing crockery. Ollie submits to this intimidation and gets to work, now a servant himself to the matriarch. Meanwhile, Stan has a brief solo sequence, as he drives to the Hardys' home, unusually distracted by the sight of a woman lifting her skirt to cross a puddle. When he arrives, he offers to help Ollie but of course he proves more of a hindrance, accidentally causing his friend to fall several times from the rooftop. Initially, Ollie's motive for performing his task comes simply from a sense of duty, instilled mainly by fear of the punishment that would otherwise follow. But when his wife – having witnessed the damage inflicted on the house during the still uncompleted operation – suggests that Ollie 'had better let that radio go', he proudly contradicts her: 'I'll get that thing working if it's the last thing I do.' The erection has become a means of demonstrating his masculine potency to his wife, particularly after his humiliation in the opening scene.

Mrs Hardy's apparent obsession with the radio – she wants to hear Japan – exemplifies what was seen as a 'feminine' emphasis on the home during the interwar years when domestic consumer durables (often, though not in this case, labour-saving devices for women) were popularized. Throughout most of the film's long middle section, the opposition between the masculine outdoor world (whose values had been increasingly questioned since the Great War) and the feminine indoor domain is represented by cutting from the men's efforts on the roof to shots of the reclusive wife waiting for her domestic appliance. The men's preference for the outdoor life – or at least one away from the home – is expressed by Ollie's urgent desire to leave with Stan, 'the quicker we get the aerial up, the quicker we get away'. But by submitting to his task, he has unwittingly strengthened the knots that bind him to the home. The impression that Ollie is being absorbed into the woman's interior world is underlined when he tumbles down the chimney, landing in the fireplace near to his wife.

Towards the end of the film, Mrs Hardy's materialism is confirmed. As she comes sobbing to Ollie after another near-fatal accident, he reassures her that he isn't hurt, but she replies, 'I'm not crying over you – the men came and took the radio away.' Masculinity is rejected and, moreover, it has failed; Ollie hasn't completed the erection or even prevented the seizure of her radio. As ever-greater numbers of male breadwinners lost their jobs in the early 1930s, and consumer goods bought on credit in the 1920s were removed from those who could not afford to maintain the payments, men would be increasingly blamed and rejected for their failure to match the masculine ideal or to sustain the domestic lifestyle to which women, especially, had become accustomed. *Hog Wild*, made in March 1930 when the Depression was beginning to bite, seems to reflect this phenomenon, exposing the flaws of patriarchy right from its opening scene.

The team's next movie, a three-reeler called **The Laurel-Hardy Murder Case**, also mirrors the Depression but in a more direct way. The introductory titles inform us that 'Mr Laurel and Mr Hardy decided that they needed a rest – they had been out of work since 1921.' In mid-1930 jokes about unemployment were still permissible, the duration of Stan and Ollie's (throughout the decade of prosperity) no doubt seeming unthinkable to the Americans who had been laid off since the stock-market crash of the previous October. The boys are sitting on the edge of a pier, Ollie asleep while Stan is fishing. After Ollie is woken by his pal's efforts, he chances upon a newspaper notice which invites relatives of the late Ebeneezer Laurel to the reading of his will. The estate is worth three million dollars. 'If I can convince them that you're the heir,' Ollie tells Stan, 'we'll be living in luxury the rest of our lives.' Like the discovery of the wallet in *Below Zero*, the advertisement promises material wealth but, as in that earlier film, it proves to be illusory.

When Stan and Ollie arrive at the Laurel mansion during a thunderstorm, they hear that the will isn't even going to be read. Instead, they find themselves in the middle of a murder investigation, complete with detectives, an assortment of suspects and a sinister butler. Indeed, by this time, the film has gone into a heavy-handed spoof of 'haunted house' mysteries like *The Cat and the Canary* (first filmed in 1927). We are back in the horror-comedy territory of *Habeas Corpus*, the third reel allowing even more of the genre's paraphernalia (white sheets, a black cat, a bat, etc.) to be introduced. Stan and Ollie no longer seem to be living in the real world (quite literally, we discover at the end), with the result that their personas are no longer believable or distinctive. Their reactions to the night's contrived catalogue of frights could be those of any comedians.

The most interesting aspect of the film is its variation on the theme established in *Early to Bed*, where the duo's friendship was severed by Ollie's inheritance. Although Stan never receives any money in *Murder Case*, the prospect of it threatens the boys' relationship from the minute they set foot in the Laurel mansion. 'What a beautiful home and what luxury,' proclaims Ollie, 'and to think it's all ours!' Immediately, Stan retorts, 'Whadya mean "ours"? It's mine!' Ollie – no doubt echoing the view of redundant American workers who had made industrialists like Henry Ford fabulously rich – chastises Stan for 'sitting on top of the world and turning down your best pal, your benefactor'. Disgusted, he turns to depart. For a moment it looks as if Stan, tearfully calling him back, is repentant but, after confirming that Ollie is leaving, he gives his friend their umbrella. This makes Ollie determined to stay: 'I'm going to get half of everything that's coming to you.'

This turns out not to be wealth but death – an appropriately bleak vision for this first year of the Depression. In the film's climax the boys are almost stabbed by an old lady who proves to be a man in disguise; even the gender-bending of the silents has taken a highly sinister turn. Before the fight with the transvestite killer is resolved, the image dissolves to the pier, the boys struggling with each other in their sleep. Yet it's hardly a comforting conclusion: the Great American Dream of wealth has soured into a nightmare.

Made at the time when Laurel, in real life, suffered the tragic loss of his baby son, born two months premature (Skretvedt, 1987, p. 200), *Murder Case* is full of jokes about death, murder and, even before the 'nightmare' sequence, execution by hanging. Possibly the most gruesome moment of all occurs during the climactic fight when we see (fortunately not in close-up) Ollie biting the murderer's knife-wielding hand – and apparently spitting out blood!

With hindsight, this three-reeler, generally agreed to be one of Laurel and Hardy's poorest films, seems not only to reflect Depression pessimism but also to forebode the gradual decline in quality that came with the team's conversion to feature-length pictures. *Murder Case* is the first of their mature comedies which wastes time establishing a plot that does not really concern Stan and Ollie, the extra length apparently weakening the discipline that had to be applied ruthlessly when making two-reelers. As in some of their later features, Laurel and Hardy seem to have wandered into someone else's movie.

Fortunately, **Pardon Us,** the first feature-length film in which the team starred, was carefully built around them, though its episodic structure makes it seem like two or three shorts joined together. Another prison comedy, it resulted partly from MGM's serious contribution to the genre *The Big House*, released in June 1930. This was the month in which Laurel and Hardy began to shoot their movie, initially just another two-reeler, but it was over twelve months before the completed six-reeler was finally released in August 1931. The extra reels were added mainly to justify the high cost of building the prison sets. Roach preferred this to the price-tag MGM had attached to their original agreement with him, that in return for use of the sets from *The Big House* Laurel and Hardy should make a movie for them. Roach and his team must have enjoyed thumbing a nose at the big studio by spoofing their prison melodrama in *Pardon Us* (Laurel was used to making parodies from his solo days when, incidentally, he had been allowed to borrow sets from major Universal pictures – see McCabe, 1966, p. 75).

The film begins with a brief street scene in which Stan and Ollie stand outside a shop discussing the ingredients they need to brew their own beer. This was permitted during Prohibition but, fatally, they decide to sell what they can't drink: as they enter the shop, there's a rapid scene change (almost a dissolve) as, instead, we see them entering the main gates of a jail – a telling juxtaposition indicative of the economic prison in which virtually all traders found themselves during the depths of the Depression. As Andrew Bergman comments, 'The motif of imprisonment and entrapment was a popular one in 1930 and 1931, and an entire cycle centering around prison life reached American screens in the post-Crash days.' (Bergman, 1971, p. 93). The optimistic enterprise culture of *Big Business* has crumbled, the boys' plans failing disastrously almost as soon as the film begins. The 'beer barons' (as Ollie introduces himself and Stan to their cell-mates) have been jailed – made into scapegoats for the social and economic ills which beset America in the early 1930s.

Yet the triviality of Stan and Ollie's crime – not much greater than the 'raid-watching' for which they were imprisoned in *The Hoose-gow* – universalizes them, reflecting the sense of entrapment felt by Depression-hit Americans who supposedly had their liberty. Towards the end of *Pardon Us*, the boys threaten a hunger strike, but a guard entices them into the mess hall with visions of a slap-up meal. When they are dished poor regulation food again, Stan bangs on the table with his tin cup and demands the promised 'turkey dinner'. He might well have been voicing the feelings of American citizens to whom President Hoover had pledged prosperity and 'a chicken in every pot' in his successful 1928 election campaign. Hunger marches were widespread in the early years of the Depression.

The film's prison induction scenes resemble those in *The Big House* quite closely, even down to the layout of the sets. As in MGM's film, the desk sergeant instructs the new prisoners to address him as 'sir', so Stan gives his name as 'Sir Stanley Laurel' – a mockery of authority made all the funnier for Stan's ignorance of his effect. Two authoritative male figures are reproduced from the original: the warden (Wilfred Lucas), who delivers a sternly paternal lecture to the boys in his office; and the tough convict leader (Walter Long as 'The Tiger', replacing Wallace Beery's 'Butch') who takes an instant liking to Stan. This departure from MGM's movie (in which

Stan's counterpart soon makes himself unpopular by informing on cell-mates) hints at the homoerotic butch/femme bonding which is a common feature of real prison life and latter-day movie representations of it.

Stan's strongest bond, however, remains with Ollie, whose top bunk he shares, leading to a protracted scene (longer still in a surviving preview print) reminiscent of *Berth Marks*, in which he tries to get comfortable in the confined space with his pal – a microcosm of their life in jail. Stan's closeness to Ollie is also reflected by his attempt to join his friend when the pair are locked in solitary confinement. After they are incarcerated in individual cells, the film reproduces the scene in *The Big House* where the camera remains static, showing the corridor of cell doors, and dialogue between the convicts continues for over a minute. It's a moving moment, an aural precursor of Jean Genet's silent film, *Un Chant d'Amour* (1950) in its representation of the separated men's lyrical dreams (of farm life in Stan and Ollie's case) and their communication through the walls.

The closest parallel of all with *The Big House* occurs in the climactic scenes, a mass break-out attempt which, in *Pardon Us*, begins in the mess hall. This location is used earlier in MGM's film for a scene in which the camera follows as a knife is passed under the table from one man to the next. There is also a sequence in the prison chapel where a couple of handguns and bullets are surreptitiously transferred. *Pardon Us* conflates both in its mess hall scene, reproducing exactly the under-the-table panning shot of weapons being passed, as a machine gun finds its way into Stan's hands. Bewildered by his acquisition, he shows it to Ollie, whose shriek of terror activates both the gun and the jailbreak. The boys are suddenly embroiled in a noisy, macho world of violence, with which they are unable to cope: neither can control the machine gun, which seems to acquire a life of its own, spewing out bullets at random. Fortunately, this gunfire is interpreted as a deliberate 'warning' by the prison authorities, who pardon Stan and Ollie for their (unintentional) part in preventing the break. In a final scene, which mimics that in *The Big House*, they return to the warden's office for a more optimistic lecture about starting again, which leads Stan – ever alert to big business ideas – to ask the warden if he'll order 'a couple of cases'. In this respect, Laurel and Hardy's film is more realistic about the likely effects of imprisonment than MGM's, which ends with its hero determined to go 'straight'.

The material described so far might have made a decent two- or three-reeler, but there is much more to *Pardon Us*, some of it obvious padding that weakens the movie. This is certainly the case with the classroom scene in which the prison explicitly adopts the features of a school: Stan, Ollie and all the convicts, including The Tiger, are reduced to children seated at their desks. They chorus 'Good morning, playmates' to each other and conduct a Will Hay-like question and answer session, full of puns and other verbal jokes, with gowned teacher James Finlayson, at whom they flick ink pellets. He seems as stupid as his pupils, whom he threatens with a variety of punishments, including standing in the corner and staying after school. It's basically a one-joke scene (and a self-conscious joke at that) – hardened criminals treated like kids. The whole world has become childish, so Laurel and Hardy are merely part of it and make no difference. Another, more successful segment reworks the dentist's surgery scene from *Leave 'Em Laughing*, Stan's childlike nature this time more subtly conveyed by his insistence that Ollie (with whom he links arms) accompany him. There is also an underlining of his feminization in this film, when the dentist's assistant (Charlie Hall) addresses him twice as 'Rosebud'.

But much more time (in the movie's middle section) is devoted to a pastoral interlude, a brief realization of the duo's dream of farm life, in which, after somehow escaping, they put on blackface and go to work on a cotton plantation. Having made pets of the bloodhounds sent to chase them (as usual, they find animals friendlier than people), the boys merge with black cotton-pickers, characterized very much as 'happy darkies' who sing endlessly during their work. If the prison scenes are based on *The Big House*, the plantation sequence clearly imitates another MGM movie, the all-black musical *Hallelujah* (1929).

The singing even extends to their spare time, and leads to the first Laurel and Hardy musical scene which isn't played just for laughs. As in most of the later examples in their work, the number is presented as a natural and spontaneous response to a performance already under way by a group of musicians. Here, Ollie hums the melody of 'Lazy Moon', before launching into the lyrics, which he sings perfectly straight. This is followed by a fast tempo reprise accompanied by Stan's slide dancing, probably based on that of the blackface music-hall star Eugene Stratton. Stan's freedom of movement, emphasized by the fact that the camera follows him, expresses the liberation that the duo feel out of prison (the film remains apparently oblivious to the reminders of slavery suggested by the plantation).

Although Laurel and Hardy's confident embracement of sound had been evident since their first two-reel talkie in 1929, the musical interlude in *Pardon Us* confirmed and extended their skills in a medium which had proved unsuitable for most other silent-film comedians. This six-reeler also heralded their gradual move to feature-length movies which, though ultimately detrimental to the quality of their work, certainly enhanced their prestige. Despite the Depression, Laurel and Hardy's career was perfectly sound.

Chapter five

'Tell Me That Again': Remakes and Variations (1930–32)

DURING the long gestation period of *Pardon Us*, Laurel and Hardy made five shorts, most of them of higher quality than the feature on which so much time and money was expended. The first of these, a three-reeler called **Another Fine Mess**, suggests that they were looking for a relatively easy option while work on the prison movie continued, since it is another version of the music-hall sketch *Home from the Honeymoon* already adapted for their early silent *Duck Soup*.

Some attempt was made to dress up the old warhorse, not least with the gimmick of using two young ladies to read out the credits on camera. Yet the film has a very theatrical feel, complete with percussive sound effects to underline the pratfalls. Even Stan and Ollie's park scene, included in *Duck Soup*, is relayed, stage-like, through dialogue between two policemen who are chasing them shortly after the film begins. One of the cops explains that he caught the two vagrants 'trying to make a hotel out of the city park' – an image which mirrors the 'Hoovervilles' of shanties which the homeless were constructing on spare ground as the Depression deepened. Apparently, Stan and Ollie 'even put a couple of benches together so that they could have twin beds'. But the cop got really angry, he says, when he tried to move them on and 'the little fellow' replied, 'Yes ma'am' – anticipating Stan's gender confusion later in the film.

Meanwhile, the boys hide in the cellar of a nearby mansion, whose owner, Colonel Buckshot (James Finlayson), has left for an African hunting trip. When they try to leave the same way they entered, the duo find they've locked themselves in, prompting Ollie to tell Stan that he's got him into 'another nice mess' – already becoming one of the team's catch-phrases, as evinced by the variant which forms the title of this film. The pair go upstairs to the main part of the house, but wherever they try to exit there seems to be a cop waiting. As in *Pardon Us* and their preceding short, *The Laurel-Hardy Murder Case* (in which the detectives prevented them leaving the Laurel mansion), they are imprisoned by the law.

Before they can escape, a Lord and Lady Plumtree (Charles Gerrard and Thelma Todd) arrive in answer to the Colonel's newspaper advertisement offering his home for rent, including maid and butler service, during his absence. The boys have observed the staff leaving for the weekend, so Stan, at Ollie's insistence, gets into the butler's clothes with the intention of sending the visitors away. He fails to do this, and one masquerade leads to another. Ollie is forced to impersonate Colonel Buckshot, while Stan is required to transform from butler (dubbed 'Hives' by 'Buckshot') to maid. Stan does more than necessary to effect the feminine disguise: he takes the trouble to put on a corset and knickers under the maid's uniform, already suggesting that his transvestism is not merely a ruse but pleasurable for its own sake. Eventually, he emerges as 'Agnes', complete with apron and feather duster.

Stan's ease and enjoyment in drag is particularly evident in the sofa scene, reprised from *Duck Soup*, in which Lady Plumtree questions 'Agnes' about the house and staff. It has a remarkably spontaneous feeling, which conveys the impression that 'Agnes' and the Lady are girlfriends, their giggly banter, punctuated by playful reciprocal nudges and slaps, apparently equalizing them in terms of both sex and class. The image is of course deceptive on both counts: the aristocrat is the prospective employer of the maid, who is in fact a man. But Stan doesn't signal any male discomfort or heterosexual lust to the audience, as most comedians would have done in this kind of situation. Even when the young and pretty Lady Plumtree puts her arm round him, there's no indication that he harbours erotic desire for her; Stan's pleasure is more like the warmth felt by an effeminate gay man for a sisterly female friend.

This equality contrasts strongly with the way he's treated by Ollie who, playing Colonel Buckshot to the hilt, orders Stan about the place. Eventually, the servant rebels by asking, 'What do you think I am?' – a good question – but Ollie pushes him away before he even completes the sentence. When queried about Hives's salary by Lord Plumtree, 'Buckshot' whispers the answer in the aristocrat's ear, demonstrating his power by excluding the butler from the negotiations. It's symptomatic of the distinctive personas Stan and Ollie bring to the film that, while the former enjoys a gender masquerade, the latter's inherent pomposity lends itself to class pretensions. These divergent tendencies sever Stan and Ollie's friendship during the middle of the movie, where playful pokes in the chest between 'Buckshot' and the Lord underline their class-based alliance, and recall the nudges and slaps between 'Agnes' and the Lady which develop their gender-based affection.

When the resemblance between butler and maid is noted, 'Agnes' explains, 'I'm twins,' highlighting the gender ambiguity in Stan's basically constant persona. 'She's been in my service since boyhood – I mean girlhood,' adds Buckshot later in the film, when Stan's gender becomes increasingly confused. Required to reappear as 'Hives', he does so wearing the maid's wig, and when he has to revert to 'Agnes' he appears without it, though in both cases the errors are corrected before the Plumtrees notice. The final transformation involves both Stan and Ollie, when the real Colonel unexpectedly returns and summons the police to arrest the 'burglars' in his home. The boys escape by concealing themselves inside one of Buckshot's animal skins. Apparently restoring life to the dead ibex, they run out of the mansion, pursued by the cops and the Colonel, himself armed with a bow and arrow. They have, in effect, exchanged the costumes of their master and servant masquerades for that of the victimized beast, symbolic of their status – reduced as they are to vagrants again – in relation to the aristocratic hunter. Riding a stolen tandem together, and seemingly united after their charade, they cycle into a tunnel, through which a tram hurtles in the opposite direction. When the boys re-emerge at the other end, both animal skin and tandem have been divided in two, suggesting, like the masquerade section of the film, that their relationship can be severed by external pressure.

By contrast, **Be Big**, also a three-reeler, requires Stan and Ollie to present a united front against their wives. The opening titles define the state of wedlock from the husband's viewpoint: 'Mr Hardy is a man of great care, caution and discretion – Mr Laurel is married too.' Despite this cynical statement, the Hardys, in their exchange of romantic epithets, are initially presented as the embodiment of marital bliss. Stan, too, seems happier than in *Blotto*, the last film in which a Mrs Laurel appeared, though again he's portrayed as a 'child- groom' who, embarking on a holiday with his wife and the Hardys, plans to take a miniature yacht, bucket and spade. 'You'll have to carry them,' commands the maternal Mrs Laurel (Anita Garvin, repeating her *Blotto* role). Stan's toys symbolize the immaturity of marriage, especially when compared to the more adult and erotic delights (unspecified, but presumably female 'dancers') of a stag party floor show promised by Cookie, a member of the boys' all-male club, in a phone call just before the two couples leave for Atlantic City. Encouraged by Cookie's assertion that 'no man is bigger than the excuses he can make to his wife', Ollie devises a ruse – as Stan did in *Blotto* – to enable him to pursue manly pleasures without his spouse's knowledge. He decides to feign illness so that the wives will go on holiday, while he and Stan (remaining as his supposed carer) go to the party.

Ollie's 'illness' takes the form of a fainting spell, during which his voice rises an octave as he dolorously tells his wife (Isabelle Keith) that he's 'as light as a feather', an effeminately swishing hand gesture underlining his simile. Ollie behaves like a swooning stage heroine, his theatrical feminization completed by the application of Mrs Hardy's white powder to his face (to make it look pale) and, later, his unwitting substitution of her fur for the towel he's wrapped around his head. The feminization also embraces Stan who, even before he realizes Ollie's illness is an act, develops sympathy pains for his pal, putting a hand to his own forehead.

However, as soon as the wives leave, symbols of masculine virility replace the pretensions of feminine frailty. The boys get out their club uniforms which, as the image of other members revealed during the phone call, are hunting clothes – notably jodhpurs and riding boots. Ollie insists that they both dress in his apartment. Stan, clad in the butch costume, still retains feminine characteristics: using a reducing machine, its vibrating belt around his waist, he affects the postures of a seductive hula dancer (the background music for this scene is similar to that which displaced Cookie's description of the stag party's show). Meanwhile, Ollie discovers he's wearing Stan's smaller boots, a variation of the team's hat mix-up routine which dominates the rest of the film as together they try to remove the tight-fitting footwear. As Randy Skretvedt has revealed, the sexual overtones of the boot removal scenes were more obvious in the original script, which suggested that Ollie cries out, 'Cut it out! You're hurting me!' as Stan drags him around the room by the foot. A bellboy, passing in the hall, investigates the shouts and, after discovering the two men struggling and groaning in 'a very funny position', he makes an embarrassed and apologetic exit (Skretvedt, 1987, p. 210).

Although this scene was not used, the released version includes images that more subtly convey a mock-erotic dimension to the 'hunting' duo's horseplay, assisted by the fetishistic connotations of riding boots. In an early attempt to extricate the footwear, Stan sits astride Ollie's knee, pulling the boot and foot upwards so that the stiffened limb rises between his legs. Before long, they are both lying on the floor, Stan on top of Ollie, his head inside his partner's pullover. Later still, their bodies, again on the floor, become totally entangled, each one's head near the other's feet. The boot sequence, a sort of comical version of the Kama Sutra, is in fact the film's climax, replacing the stag party's orgy of heterosexuality which would be the high point of a more typical narrative. Instead, Stan and Ollie must be satisfied with – and perhaps prefer – each other. *Be Big* subtly exposes the paradox, or at least the irony, of all-male groups which are formed by men who claim to be exclusively heterosexual. It achieves this largely through the boys' obsession with their club uniforms which express gender sameness rather than difference. Ultimately, the film suggests masculinity's symbols interest them more than its traditional pursuits.

It's appropriate that, when the wives unexpectedly return (having missed their train), Stan and Ollie hide from them in the Hardys' marital bed which folds into the wall, closeting the sexually transgressive men. Their masculinity (as much a pretension as Ollie's feminine fainting spell) is usurped by the women, who pick up two handy shotguns – presumably part of the boys' hunting gear – which they fire at the bed with devastating effect: Stan and Ollie are blown through the building's outside wall. The hunters have become as much the hunted as they were at the end of *Another Fine Mess*.

Women are even more menacing in **Chickens Come Home**, the team's third consecutive three-reeler. A close remake of their early silent *Love 'Em and Weep*, it retains the misogynous tone of that film. Its most threatening woman is a brazen vamp (Mae Busch, repeating her role) who uses her sexuality as a weapon. Waving a long cigarette-holder and an even longer white fur, she comes to Ollie's office (Hardy now takes Finlayson's part) in order to blackmail her ex-lover – now married and running for mayor – with an incriminating photograph in which she is seated on his shoulders, 'riding' him as she is now. Mae, like many women in the team's films, wants money ('Ladies must live!') and threatens to put the photograph on a front page if Ollie doesn't come to her apartment that evening and pay up. She imagines aloud the newspaper headline: 'Wronged woman comes out of the past to accuse leading citizen.' This nightmare scenario is particularly disturbing for Ollie who, as the film opened, was to be seen gloating over a real front page picturing him in formal attire with a tribute to him as 'A Home-lover; a Home-builder.' The entire movie exploits the tension between respectable surfaces and 'dark' sexual undercurrents, a theme struck when Mae entered the office during Ollie's dictation of an acceptance speech about his 'aim to keep our city clean of all vice'. In its exposure of hypocrisy, the film is both a social satire and a comic precursor of film noir, complete with *femme fatale*.

Ollie needs to conceal his past, indeed Mae herself, from his wife (Thelma Todd) when she also visits his office. Both women unexpectedly violate the male domain where Stan, repeating his earlier part, is officially Ollie's 'general manager', though he seems to do the work of a secretary (thus occupying, at least in the context of 1931, a feminine role). Ollie's wife, through her inopportune intrusion, becomes as much a threat to him as his old flame. The parallel between the two women is emphasized by the accidental transference of Mae's fur to Mrs Hardy (Ollie has to pretend it's a gift for her) and the 'apple-cheeked boy' epithet they both use to describe him. Mae also becomes a threat to Stan when Ollie instructs him to go to her flat in his place that evening. The prospective mayor can't keep the appointment (to make 'a final settlement') himself because he's promised his wife to be home for a politically important dinner party. This arrangement brings into play the threatening presence of *Stan*'s wife (or 'Mama' as he calls her), who wants *him* to be home for dinner. When Ollie phones her to say Stan will be working late, she threatens to break her husband's arm if he doesn't come home. Ollie lies to Stan: 'She said as long as you were with me, you could go as far as you like' – an expression, perhaps, of Ollie's fantasy world in which women are replaced by Stan, with whom he can go the limit!

That evening Stan visits Mae and uses physical force in a desperate attempt to prevent her leaving for the Hardys' home, where a judge and other guests are assembled. Stan and Mae get involved in bouts of wrestling that look like wild sexual encounters to onlookers, one of whom is a gossipy friend of Mrs Laurel – and the film's fourth threatening female. Meanwhile, at the Hardys', Ollie is singing 'Your Mama's Gonna Slow You Down' to his wife's (or mama's) piano accompaniment. As Mae arrives, Ollie sings another tune, 'Somebody's Coming to My House', which describes the arrival of a baby, who the father, sharing Ollie's dislike of females, hopes will be a boy. But the domestic bliss conveyed by the words is undermined by Ollie's nervous singing of them as he awaits the visitor to *his* house. When Mae enters with Stan, Ollie tells everyone they are Mr and Mrs Laurel. Matters are further complicated by the fact Stan has brought the incriminating framed photograph with him, which Ollie promptly attempts to hide by sitting on it; the glass splinters as he does so, punishing the sexual transgressor in the presence (though without the knowledge) of the Judge.

The finale is bizarre. When Ollie produces a gun, threatening to shoot Mae then himself, she faints. The most dangerous woman is thus rendered lifeless (metaphorically at least) and placed on Ollie's shoulders – as she was in the photograph. Stan then tries to leave with his boss covered by Mae's long coat, her dopey head above it, Ollie's bare legs below it. A variation (not included in *Love 'Em and Weep*) follows when an axe-wielding Mrs Laurel, informed of Stan's activities and whereabouts by the gossip, arrives: Stan and Ollie change places, but topple over, revealing all.

After the bourgeois farce of *Chickens Come Home*, **Laughing Gravy**, made in February 1931, returned Stan and Ollie to the bleak climate of the Depression. Both their economic hardship and their friendship in the face of adversity are conveyed in the opening titles: 'Mr Laurel and Mr Hardy stuck together through thick and thin – one pocketbook between them – always empty.' Both themes are underlined in the establishing shots which present them sharing a bed in a drab bedsitter while a blizzard rages outside. But another element is quickly introduced – the duo's pet dog – whose importance is reflected in the fact that the film is named after it. A series of shots – Stan hiccuping, the small dog waking with a start, Ollie looking at Stan – is repeated several times, bonding the three but also suggesting that the dog, coming between Stan and Ollie, is a possible threat to their friendship.

Laughing Gravy's barks (which are caused by, and echo, Stan's hiccups) do threaten the permanence of even their meagre accommodation: 'If the landlord finds out we've got a dog here,' explains Ollie, 'he'll throw us out.' Most of the film – clearly a remake of *Angora Love* – concerns their efforts to conceal the outlawed animal from the authority figure. When the dog is discovered and evicted by the landlord (Charlie Hall), a rescue attempt by Ollie succeeds in restoring it to Stan. Cuddling his pet, like an introspective child who has no time for the world of 'grown-ups', Stan shuts the window through which Ollie has passed the animal, forgetting that his freezing friend is still locked outside. A later rescue from the roof echoes this situation: Stan fusses over the safely returned dog, ignoring the fact Ollie is stuck in the chimney until he hears an urgent reminder.

But, like *Angora Love*, the film draws parallels between the boys and their pet, partly through gags reworked from the earlier movie. Again, Stan almost takes one of the animal's hiding places –

the chimney this time – when the landlord is about to enter, and the bathing routine, which interchanges the roles of the three, is reprised from the silent prototype. This time, however, Ollie undergoes the most complete transformation when, during the first rescue, the duo's noisy efforts wake the landlord. To divert attention, Ollie pretends to be the dog, barking behind a bush – a moment reminiscent of the cat metamorphosis in *Night Owls*.

Stan and Ollie identify with cuddly Laughing Gravy much more than with the anarchic goat in *Angora Love*. There is a charming scene with all three on the bed, Stan holding and fondling the baby-like dog, while Ollie waves playfully. One effect of this strong identification is to suggest a correlation between the ways in which the banned animal and the boys are treated: the landlord's ejection of the dog is followed by his threatened, then (as the noisy night wears on) actual, eviction of them too. Trying to avoid both punishments, the boys are forced to conceal their outlawed pet, closeting it in a bedside cabinet and later in a wardrobe. To some viewers of today, especially those who are familiar with J. R. Ackerley's 1960 novel *We Think the World of You* about two male lovers and the dog that links them, Laughing Gravy may embody Stan and Ollie's mutual love, which must also be secreted. This theme, briefly suggested in *Angora Love*, is made slightly more overt by the presence of sound in the remake. When the boys are slithering about on the roof, they wake the landlord with their shrieks, groans and sighs – noises highly suggestive of sexual activity which, incidentally, their rooftop bodily contortions also resemble visually. Most of the homosexual resonances in *Laughing Gravy* were probably unintentional, but there is no doubt that the film's emphasis on secrecy and concealment reflects the lives of most gay men – especially in the 1930s.

The makers were certainly conscious of the almost romantic strength of friendship that had evolved between 'Stan' and 'Ollie'. This is demonstrated in the original third reel of the film (shot, but deleted from the English language version), which returns to the two themes established in the opening titles by testing the boys' friendship with Stan's inheritance of 1,000 dollars – dependent on his severance of all ties with Ollie. This legacy has been willed by Stan's late uncle who considered Ollie to be responsible for his nephew's 'deplorable condition' – a phrase which, just before the solicitor's letter and cheque arrived, Ollie used to describe his own state, blaming it on his association with Stan. There follows a long scene, full of dialogue and almost devoid of gags, in which Ollie tries to wheedle the contents of the letter from Stan, who, not wishing to hurt his old pal's feelings, insists it's private. Ollie even sings (repeatedly), 'You'll be sorry just too late, when our friendship turns to hate.' Eventually, Stan relents and shows him the letter. The scene, hitherto at least partly parodic, now seems to turn to genuine pathos, as Ollie advises his friend to accept the money and leave him, Stan apparently close to real tears in place of his usual cry. As Stan makes to leave with Laughing Gravy in his arms, Ollie insists on keeping the dog ('It's gonna be lonesome enough ...'). After considering the situation, Stan tears up his cheque. 'My pal!' exclaims Ollie. 'And to think you're giving it all up for me!' 'For you?' retorts Stan. 'I didn't want to leave Laughing Gravy.' Ollie, of course, is outraged.

The excision of this third reel is hardly surprising, since it plays awkwardly, and its laborious emphasis on dialogue and pathos seems particularly inappropriate after two reels of almost pure slapstick. The ending finally used – in which a cop quarantines the house before Stan and Ollie can be evicted, driving the landlord to shoot himself – is much more concise and pointed in its mock-gravity (the boys and the cop solemnly remove their hats), the degree of parody more certain (before his suicide, Hall theatrically addresses the audience, 'This is more than I can stand.'). But the third reel – which, happily, survives – is fascinating for its explicit statement of themes that underlie much of Laurel and Hardy's work: the inheritance which threatens their friendship receives heavier treatment than in earlier films, and Stan's love of animals, in preference to either money or Ollie, is clearer than ever before.

Around this time – early in 1931 – Laurel and Hardy made a cameo appearance in **The Stolen Jools**, an all-star two-reeler made independently for charity. A rather tedious collection of blackouts strung together on a thread of narrative about missing jewels, the film features detectives Stan and Ollie in a Model T Ford which suddenly collapses, somewhat belying their Inspector's description of them as 'two of my best men'. Their contribution to the film is a typical Laurel and Hardy 'narrative of failure' in miniature.

In the team's next film for Roach, the two-reeler **Our Wife**, Stan actually plays the best man, put in charge of Ollie's wedding plans which therefore go severely awry. As the film opens, the groom is more like an excited bride, humming the Wedding March and practising his delivery of 'I do' (Ollie's optimism parallels his anticipation of his acceptance speech in *Chickens Come Home*). On the first attempt at the two words, they emerge from his lips in effeminate falsetto, the next try brings a baritonal bark, and only after he sprays his throat does he achieve a happy medium. Gender must be strictly regulated by a man embarking on a heterosexual union. Meanwhile, Stan – despite his best-man status – exhibits predominantly feminine traits as he prepares the wedding feast, his apron and feather duster reminiscent of his 'Agnes' masquerade in *Another Fine Mess*. Later, his wearing of a jacket over the apron, which dangles below it like a skirt, clearly conveys the androgyny intimated in other films (such as *Laughing Gravy*) where his jacket is combined with a long, baggy nightshirt.

A phone call from Ollie's bride Dulcy (Jean London) brings the news that her father (James Finlayson) plans to prevent their marriage, so the two lovers – of matching girth – decide to elope at midnight. As Ollie ends the phone conversation, Stan, listening on the extension, echoes his goodbye to Dulcy. Stan's interception of the betrothed, together with his gender fluidity, foreshadows the confusion in the film's final scene.

Before that, however, there's a sequence which recalls the nocturnal activities of *Night Owls* as, burglar-like, the duo steal the bride from her father. The procedure is complicated by Stan's announcement of the elopement to Finlayson's butler and by his choice of wedding car, a baby Austin, which leads to a scene of constriction reminiscent of *Berth Marks* as Stan and the large lovers cram themselves into the tiny vehicle. When they arrive at the home of a JP, they are first met by his wife (Blanche Payson). Her irritability at being woken during the night leads to outright aggression as she socks Stan's jaw, aligning her – much more than Dulcy – with the wives typically seen in Laurel and Hardy films.

Her momentary violence might be forgiven, since her patience has been severely tested by Stan's laboriously literal relay of the bride and groom's wishes. When he tells her, 'We want to get married,' Ollie, pointing to himself and Dulcy, corrects him: 'Not "we" – us!' But Stan merely repeats his friend's last words to the woman, suggesting that it's he and Ollie who want to marry. This is another premonition of the mix-up during the ceremony, eventually conducted by the JP who (played by Ben Turpin, a famous Mack Sennett comedian of the silent days) proves to be cross-eyed. The whole ceremony is a mockery of marriage as the JP mumbles the prescribed words, emphasizing their meaninglessness, then congratulates Stan. Finally, he turns to 'kiss the bride', but bypasses Dulcy and instead delightedly deposits a smacker on Ollie. Dulcy faints and literally disappears from the final shots which show us the newlyweds, Stan crying and Ollie highly indignant.

Although their legal union is nominally the cross-eyed JP's error, it's also prefigured, as noted above, by Stan's behaviour earlier in the film. Moreover, from the perspective of an age when same-sex wedding ceremonies are commonplace, the JP seems politically clear-sighted. Racily but inaptly titled, *Our Wife* presents the logical outcome of Stan and Ollie's relationship as developed in the films they had made to date.

Having completed their first starring feature, *Pardon Us*, by mid-1931, Laurel and Hardy seemed less inclined simply to remake their silent films, though they continued to refine both general patterns and specific scenes from their earlier movies. This can be seen in **Come Clean**, a two-reeler made in May 1931, which begins with a reworking of the opening of the silent, *Should Married Men Go Home?* The Hardys are enjoying a quiet evening indoors with 'nothing to mar [their] happiness'. At the exact moment they are about to seal their marital bliss with a kiss across the dining-table, Stan intrudes on the heterosexual love scene by knocking at the door. No longer a bachelor, he brings his wife (Linda Loredo), despite the fact that she 'didn't want to come'. The Hardys – whose happiness has instantly been soured by an argument about the visitors – don't want to see their friends either, so they pretend they're not at home. After a repeat of the note-under-the-door gag from the silent prototype, with each couple positioned mirror-like on either side of the barrier, Stan opens the door's viewing panel. Seeing him, Mrs Hardy (Gertrude Astor) flutters her eyelids and affects a false smile which suddenly turns to fierce teeth-gritting as Ollie opens the door. Then, she relaxes again to greet Mrs Laurel, embracing her with a kiss and cooing, 'Darling, I'm so glad to see you.' Like *Perfect Day*, the scene is a most incisive little critique of social hypocrisy.

The women having paired off instantly, the boys are left together to enact their child–parent relationship. Stan develops a craving for ice-cream, which Ollie must satisfy by taking him to a shop, where his awkward charge upsets a container of straws and wants a flavour that's sold out. Ultimately, Ollie negotiates the complex transaction on behalf of the baffled child.

But roles and priorities constantly change during this incident-packed short. On their way home, they encounter a *femme fatale* played by Mae Busch – who, when she isn't playing Hardy's wife, often brings a sexual threat connected with money and potential death, as in *Chickens Come Home* and the later *Oliver the Eighth*. Here, she's not so much a vamp as a floozie, who is about to jump off a bridge into a river. It's typical of Depression black comedy that the film mocks suicide. As Mae shouts, 'Goodbye, old world,' Stan chirpily echoes, 'Goodbye' (recalling the pointless politeness of *Perfect Day*). Then, when Ollie, frantically preparing to rescue her, explains she's committing suicide, Stan asks, 'What for?' But we never learn her motive: although Mae is successfully retrieved from the river – and Ollie almost drowned in the process – she tells the boys, 'You've got a lot of nerve, buttin' into other people's affairs ... well, now that you've saved me, you can take care of me.'

When they refuse and try to return to their wives, she blackmails them by screaming and threatening to 'tell the world that you pushed me in the water, that you tried to murder me'. But she's willing to keep quiet 'for a consideration'. The boys' good turn backfires, a motif that recurs in several films of this period. For a while, Ollie thinks they've evaded her: 'It takes me to handle these dumb dames,' he proclaims smugly, like a macho movie hero. But Mae follows them back to the Hardys' apartment, where, in the wives' presence, frantic bedroom (and bathroom) farce ensues.

When she switches on the radio in Ollie's bedroom, they sing loudly, banging kitchenware in time to the music they are trying to cover. Mrs Hardy tells Ollie: 'Just because you have the mind of a four-year-old child, you don't need to display it!' But display is exactly what is required here, Mae's presence forcing Stan and Ollie to act even more like children than they really are. In the Hardy home, Mae becomes a woman to be concealed, pushed about, disposed of, as in the finale of *Chickens Come Home*. Perhaps to compensate for the loss of her fur to Ollie's wife in that film, she tries to appropriate a replacement from this Mrs Hardy's wardrobe. But, atypically for a Laurel and Hardy film, the law saves the day: Mae is wanted by the police and Stan, blamed by Ollie in front of their wives for bringing her to the apartment, is told to collect a reward of 1,000 dollars. The 'bad' woman is redeemed – in the financial sense.

The boys' economic status has worsened considerably by the next film, **One Good Turn**. Its opening title establishes a bleakly ironic tone: 'Seeing America: Mr Laurel and Mr Hardy have cast off all financial worries.' The next title outlines their 'total assets' which, apart from their clothes, are a 1911 Ford and an even older tent. By the end of this two-reeler they will have lost even these.

The stripping of their assets begins in the first sequence where Stan, preparing soup on a campfire, accidentally sets their tent ablaze. Having run out of water to extinguish the flames, he tips the soup onto it. In Laurel and Hardy's world even the basic necessities of life – heat, shelter, food – become agents of mutual destruction. Their spare clothes are also rendered useless when, hanging out to dry after washing, they shrink to an infant's size. Ollie reflects on their predicament: 'Our earthly possessions are slowly getting less and less – no place to sleep and no food.' When he tells Stan, 'We're going to humiliate ourselves by begging for food,' the latter undercuts his pathos by replying, 'What, again?' In mid-1931, when this film was made, the United States was entering the darkest period of the Depression; many householders found less fortunate people begging for food at their back doors.

The boys call on an old lady (Mary Carr) to whom Ollie describes himself and Stan as 'victims of the Depression – we haven't tasted food for three whole days'. Again, Stan ruins his pathetic performance by adding, 'Yesterday, today and tomorrow.' Ollie asks humbly for buttered toast (as in *Habeas Corpus*), to which Stan boldly requests the addition of ham. The old lady agrees, and in repayment for her kindness, Ollie asks if there's anything they can do – 'We're willing to work, you know.' However, he's indignant (privately) when Stan suggests they chop wood, an idea which their benefactress thinks 'splendid'. The scene steers a fine line between a sympathetic presentation (through Ollie) of the plight of Depression victims and a gentle mockery (through Stan's guileless honesty) of this particular case.

When the meal is served Stan appropriates nearly all the sandwiches like a greedy child. Both regress to infants in a tit-for-tat routine with coffee and milk, in which they waste much of the sustenance they have so eagerly sought. But their attention is diverted to the lady's living-room, from which they hear what appears to be her wicked landlord (James Finlayson) threatening to foreclose on her mortgage. During this period of widespread evictions, this would be as likely as the boys' own predicament – so, empathizing with a fellow Depression victim, they believe it's all for real. In fact, they've merely overheard the rehearsal of a community play, complete with the old lady's discovery that she's been robbed of one hundred dollars with which she intended to settle the mortgage. Ironically – in view of the duo's own tendency to play roles – Ollie is taken in by the performance, which has far less basis in reality than the one he enacted earlier on the doorstep. Since 'one good turn deserves another', he resolves to sell the car, their only remaining asset, to raise 100 dollars for the lady.

The street auction of their car reflects the desperate measures to which the newly poor were driven during the Depression. Here, it's all in vain and the car totally collapses anyway. A new plot twist develops when Ollie discovers in Stan's pocket a wallet which a drunk misplaced during the auction. Ollie thinks his 'one-time friend' has robbed their benefactress and, after hurling a stream of abuse at Stan, he roughly escorts him back to the house. The old lady reveals the truth, proving Stan's innocence. But the latter is enraged and, in a startling role reversal, he pokes, kicks and punches Ollie who runs to hide in the woodshed from his axe-wielding pal, cowering and blubbering like a naughty child who won't accept his punishment. As in so many of their movies, the acquisition of money ruins Stan and Ollie's friendship.

The film is unusual in their oeuvre for its sympathetic female. Mary Carr was the archetypal grey-haired grandma, a passive victim (parodied in the play within the film) far removed from the aggressive wives and girlfriends that populate the team's movies. The boys' stereotypical perception of women makes it easy for them to believe in her portrayal of a stock figure of melodrama – just as in *Come Clean* Ollie's over-confidence about his ability to handle 'dumb dames' exacerbated his difficulties with a 'sexual' woman.

The plot of **Beau Hunks** is entirely motivated by a woman, though she appears only as a close-up in a photograph. This four-reeler (neither short nor feature) begins with the boys together at home. The opening shot of an enraptured Ollie playing the piano and singing, 'I love you – you are the ideal of my dreams' is followed by one of Stan who, in the absence of any other information, appears to be the object of Ollie's devotion. After the song Ollie reveals that he's going to be married. When Stan asks to whom, he replies, 'Why, a woman, of course.' To Ollie it doesn't matter which woman. 'Did you ever hear of anybody marrying a man?' he asks Stan. In Ollie's male-centred world 'anybody' means any man. Stan's literal mind interprets it differently: he answers, 'Sure ... my sister'.

A letter arrives from Ollie's beloved, explaining that she's breaking the engagement. At the end of the sequence, the destruction of Ollie's romantic ideals will be symbolized when he falls on top of the piano, which collapses under the weight of his inflated expectations. But before that, the jilted lover goes into the 'feminine' fainting spell feigned in *Be Big*, this time for real. Ollie musters enough strength, however, to tear up the photograph of his 'ideal', 'Jeanie-Weenie' (actually a portrait of Jean Harlow, who had appeared in some of the team's late silents and was now a major MGM star). Addressing the photograph, he shouts, 'You vampire! You wrecker of men's happiness! And I learned about women from you ... ' Clearly, this misogynous tirade is presented with some irony, signalling the film's parodic mode for the remaining three reels.

The film being a spoof of all those movies about the Foreign Legion, Ollie joins up 'to forget', insisting that Stan comes with him.

It's an action typical of the duo's concerted retreat from the world of women into the relative security of an all-male community, populated in this case by uniformed 'beau hunks' – most of whom have also been jilted by Jeanie. In this environment, which consciously excludes women, Stan effectively replaces Ollie's intended bride. So much so, that in one scene their bodies actually combine into a single entity: after a long march, as both are seated on a bunk, Ollie cossets his delighted mate's foot in the belief that it's his own. The gag's mock-eroticism, latent when first used in *Angora Love*, is here more pronounced, as the camera lingers on close-ups of Ollie massaging Stan's toes individually and blowing between them.

'We're buddies,' Ollie tells the Commandant (Charles Middleton), whose stern authority the pair repeatedly, if unwittingly, subvert. Stan addresses him as 'ma'am' and, asked for his number in the squad of new recruits, he obliges by giving his telephone number. His bourgeois concerns are also represented when, unhappy in the barracks, he asks Ollie if they can get a room of their own. Before long, they both go to the Commandant 'to rectify a small mistake' – that of joining up – and to leave a forwarding address for mail. Their rational, democratic approach is met with an autocratic lecture on the rigours of life in the Legion, climaxed by wild laughter from the Commandant – the laughter of insanity, not liberation.

Much of the film's humour rests on the opposition between the Legion's rugged masculinity and Stan and Ollie's bourgeois femininity. (In the scripted but abandoned ending, Stan seems to parody Marlene Dietrich in the final scene of *Morocco* (1930) as he scampers across the desert, like her, to catch up with the Legion (Skretvedt, 1987, p. 223).) When the Commandant orders a route march for the next day – a Thursday – Stan asks if he could make it Friday to give him time to recover from the last one. As they set out, Stan's long johns are visible, since he was unable to find his uniform trousers. Later he gets his rifle tangled with the underwear, symbolizing the incompatibility of his cosy domestic world with the outdoor military one. This dislocation is exploited, however, by the duo's ultimate defeat of the barefoot Arab enemy by sprinkling tacks on the ground; the die-hard legionnaires would never have thought of converting household objects into weapons but, as evinced in some of their tit-for-tat sessions, Stan and Ollie are adept at this. It provided a way of reconciling the boys' personalities with the conventions of longer films which, unlike the 'narratives of failure' permissible for shorts, usually dictated that the boys had to 'make good', even if by accident.

After a tiny guest appearance as unlikely would-be suitors at the end of **On the Loose**, an entry in Roach's series of ZaSu Pitts–Thelma Todd two-reelers, Laurel and Hardy made **Helpmates**, generally considered to be one of their finest shorts. The clever slapstick that dominates the long middle section of the film – a catalogue of disasters as the duo clean Ollie's house after a wild party – is less interesting, however, than the opening and closing scenes. In the shot which introduces Ollie, he faces the camera, the audience and apparently another man, whom he reprimands for idiotic behaviour in his wife's absence. 'Now aren't you ashamed of yourself?' he chides. However, as he continues, 'There were times when I had high hopes for you but that time is past,' the camera pulls back to reveal him addressing his reflection (the image we saw) in a large mirror. This neat variation on Hardy's usual camera-look explicitly splits Ollie's persona into two, presenting the respectable married man as the obverse of the previous night's partying hedonist, whom he is now forced to confront in the mirror – just as his upwardly mobile businessman in *Chickens Come Home* was shamed by viewing the incriminating photograph from his 'primrose days'.

As in *Beau Hunks*, Ollie receives a missive bringing bad news, this time a telegram from his wife (Blanche Payson) announcing that she'll be home at noon that day – much earlier than Ollie expected, judging from the party remnants which litter the house. He phones Stan, whose delay in answering prompts Ollie to ask where he's been. Stan's reply, 'I was here with me,' establishes a verbal parallel with Ollie's dual personality in the mirror scene (and a near-echo of his own 'I'm twins' statement in *Another Fine Mess*). Ollie asks his pal to rush over to help him clean the house before noon. Stan, in pyjamas, agrees and, parodying the cinematic convention of time-compression, arrives fully dressed after only a few seconds. Ollie explains the situation, underlining its gravity by showing Stan his wedding photograph in which Mrs Hardy is scowling formidably. Having put on an apron, which he wears for most of the film, Stan washes the dishes and cleans the house, in effect occupying the role of Mrs Hardy (who scarcely appears in the film). His feminization is underlined when, after receiving a brusque order from Ollie, he rebels: 'Say, what d'ya think I am – Cinderella? If I had any sense, I'd walk out on you.'

Stan's loyalty is a mixed blessing, since the accidents he causes with flour, soot and water ruin all of Ollie's suits. 'It's enough to make a man burst out crying,' he tells Stan who, more accustomed to that display of emotion, immediately does the crying for him. A savage phone call from Mrs Hardy, waiting impatiently for Ollie at the railway station, causes the harassed husband to dig out a flamboyant Admiral's outfit, complete with sword and feathered hat (presumably a lodge uniform, it's very similar to that worn by Harry Langdon in *The Chaser*). One hour after leaving in this impressive display of masculine pride, Ollie returns from the station alone – 'sadder, wiser and dizzier', a title tells us. He sports a black eye, while his sword, dangling by his leg, is bent backwards, a telling symbol of the emasculatory powers of women in Laurel and Hardy's world.

Worse is to come, however, when he enters the house, which Stan has accidentally burned down in his efforts to light a fire for the Hardys' homecoming. 'I guess there's nothing else I can do,' says the helpmate as he starts to leave the charred ruins. Ollie asks him to close the door: 'I'd like to be alone,' he explains, Garbo-like. But, sitting in his now roofless home, Ollie is exposed to the elements: rain pours down on him, adding to his earlier dousings. Preserving a vestige of dignity by removing a tiny foreign object from his trousers, Ollie looks into the camera as the film fades out. The symmetry with his introductory shot is undercut only by the fact that this camera-look is genuine, emphasizing the objective reality of the disasters that have now befallen him, in contrast to the ruin he only imagined when gazing into the mirror. The merely untidy house of the opening, which reflected the spiritual decay Ollie perceived in himself, seems trivial in comparison with the devastation that now surrounds him, expressing the total ruination of his life. Even Stan can no longer comfort Ollie; in the film's scripted ending the boys were supposed to link arms and smile at misfortune, but this was abandoned in favour of what Randy Skretvedt feels is 'probably the most poignant scene in any of the team's films' (Skretvedt, 1987, p. 225). *Helpmates* is an extreme example of Stan as the unwitting destroyer of Ollie's home and marriage, yet it's the film in which ultimately he has to relinquish his role as Ollie's surrogate spouse.

Their next film, **Any Old Port**, in which the boys play sailors on shore leave, underwent post-production cutting from three reels to two. The deleted scenes included one of Stan's most eccentric animal associations – a pet ostrich (Skretvedt, 1987, p. 228). However, the final cut fortunately did include a lengthy attempt to sign a hotel register, adapted from *Double Whoopee*. Irony is added here by the fact that the 'hotel' is a seedy establishment wholly unworthy of Ollie's pompous preparations and requests for such niceties as a floor plan and a room with a southern exposure.

The hotel's tough landlord (Walter Long) attempts to coerce his young female employee into marrying him. The scenes that establish this plot element are played seriously, echoing films by Chaplin and Griffith, but contrasting with *One Good Turn* which, through the community play rehearsal, presented Victorian 'wicked landlord' melodrama with parody and ironic detachment. Although the brutalized employee is as sympathetic as the old lady of the earlier film, she plays a much smaller part and suddenly vanishes from the narrative when she's served the purpose of bringing the boys into conflict with Long.

Stan and Ollie's rescue of her, after she solicits their protection, does allow them to parody the image of movie he-men who rush to the defence of ladies. Primarily concerned (as in *Be Big*) with the protocol of masculinity, they waste time removing their hats and jackets, then carefully roll up their shirtsleeves, before launching their attack on the villain. Stan, whose arms are bare anyway, nevertheless rolls up imaginary sleeves, emphasizing the vacuous rhetoric of the gesture. Moreover, when the boys see that Long doesn't even feel the billiard balls they hurl at his head, they make the ungentlemanly decision to leave. The sequence continues, however, with a wild chase after a key (anticipating the pursuit of the deed in *Way Out West*) and their eventual defeat of the landlord.

More parody of masculinity occurs in the final sequence, a boxing match which Ollie has forced Stan to enter. In fact, the duo's relationship here mirrors that of the landlord and his female employee, Ollie assuming the role of manager while Stan, the fighter, must suffer the blows (his opponent turns out to be the vengeful landlord himself). Told by his trainer to 'hold him in the clinches, and don't let go', Stan embraces his enemy fervently, subverting the macho sport by apparently making love not war. More by luck than judgement, Stan knocks out his opponent, but the difference between a typical comedy – which might end on this happy if unlikely note – and a Laurel and Hardy 'narrative of failure' is illustrated by Ollie's subsequent loss of all the money he received from the fight promoter. 'I bet on you to lose,' he tells Stan.

Although the film ends here, the significance of this impoverishment is suggested earlier when, after a previous cash loss, Ollie comments that they are 'without a dime and on the verge of starvation'. When Stan adds that 'it looks like a tough winter', Ollie replies, 'Tough? If we don't get something to eat we won't *live* till winter.' In the winter of 1931–32 when *Any Old Port* was made and released, life in Depression-hit America was tough indeed.

By the time of **The Music Box**, a three-reeler which won an Academy Award, the duo have 'decided to reorganize and resupervise their entire financial structure', according to an opening title, which adds, 'so they took the $3.80 and went into business'. They have set up a delivery service, using the somewhat antique conveyance of a horse-drawn cart, on which an advertising sign reads 'foundered 1931' – their unintentional slip, but one which nevertheless reveals the truth about so many businesses of the period.

As a concession to sound, the washing-machine of the film's silent prototype *Hats Off* is superseded by a player piano, bought by a lady as a surprise birthday present for her husband (Billy Gilbert). Music from the piano cuts into the 'cuckoo' theme over the opening credits and, during Stan and Ollie's repeated attempts to carry the crated machine up a long flight of steps to the buyer's home, its jangling replaces the dance music that was now normally used on the soundtracks of the team's films.

After the piano's first descent to the bottom of the steps, an innocuous-looking nursemaid, pushing a pram, laughs derisively at the boys. As she bends over to tuck in the baby, Stan treats her like a man by kicking her ('right in the middle of my daily duties', she later tells a cop – a startling double entendre). In retaliation for the kick, the maid maintains the 'masculinity' Stan conferred on her and punches him in the face. Meanwhile, Ollie has been echoing her earlier laughter; for this, she smashes the baby's bottle of milk over his head. The violence may provoke the viewer's laughter, but it's equally true in this scene that laughter provokes violence. Like the hospital nurse in *The Finishing Touch*, the uniformed maid has a 'caring' image which is quickly belied by her bursts of aggression.

When the piano has finally been delivered, and much of the house wrecked in the process, Stan and Ollie switch on the machine while they clean up the mess they've made. As 'Turkey in the Straw' plays, they perform an eccentric dance to the music, repeatedly picking up, then dropping, the same pieces of debris, so that they never make any progress with their task. More interested in the dance than their work, they even join hands for a graceful minuet, while at another point Ollie imitates the strutting of a turkey. The scene highlights the priority given to spectacle over narrative in their films generally, and in this one – which climaxes with Billy Gilbert chopping his birthday present to bits – more than most. Besides winning an Oscar, it also received the tribute of an imitation by Disney in the Mickey Mouse cartoon *Moving Day* (1936), which prominently features a similarly recalcitrant piano.

If *The Music Box* is one of Laurel and Hardy's most highly rated shorts, **The Chimp**, also a three-reeler, is among their most undervalued. It opens in a seedy circus whose attractions are displayed in a public parade. We are introduced to Destructo, a strong man clad only in a loincloth, whose image of super-masculinity is eventually followed by one of super-femininity, Lady Godiva, naked except for her long hair. 'Something for men only!' proclaims the ringmaster (James Finlayson), as she rides past on her horse and Peeping Tom gazes at her through a huge portable keyhole. These images, which exaggerate conventional depictions of gender and sexuality to the point of parody, are, however, separated by a much more ambiguous attraction – Ethel, 'the Human

Chimpanzee', who is driving a car. Not only is Ethel poised somewhere between the human and animal kingdoms, but she is also perceived as androgynous, being referred to at different points in the film as 'he', 'she' and 'it'. (Both ambiguities are crystallized in the fact – extra-textual but easily surmised – that the chimp with a female name is played by a human male, Charles Gemora.)

During the parade, the horse – which looks even less real than the chimp – bolts at the sound of gunfire, knocking Lady Godiva to the ground. Outside the ring, we discover that Stan and Ollie constitute the horse, recalling their wearing of the animal skin at the climax of *Another Fine Mess*. Ollie resolves never to play the rear end again, but Stan counters, 'You look better in that end than I do.' The theme of the interrelationship of humans and animals is thus developed: Ethel imitates human behaviour for the circus, while Stan and Ollie's role within it is to imitate an animal.

They also double as prop men. Having toppled Lady Godiva and her display of femininity, they now inadvertently ruin the display of masculinity by Destructo, 'the Cannon Ball King' (Tiny Sandford) who bares his huge, muscular body. Sandford had played the Head Property Man in Chaplin's *The Circus* (1928), a film which apparently influenced *The Chimp*. Like Chaplin's Tramp in the earlier movie, Stan and Ollie play prop men who unwittingly become clowns in the process of performing their duties to the best of their ability. In contrast to the mighty Destructo, Stan can hardly carry the cannon-ball used in his act, while Ollie is terrified when crouching on top of a tower of tables also featured in it. By overfilling the cannon with gunpowder and lighting its fuse too early, the duo not only destroy Destructo's act but the entire tent too.

Quite apart from this disaster, the circus, like so many entertainment outlets during the Depression, does little business. The manager (blaming bad weather!) declares himself 'flat broke' and invites the redundant performers to draw lots for the show's assets, to be given in lieu of their accrued wages. Stan gets the flea circus while Ollie draws Ethel, whom he plans to pack in a crate and sell to a zoo. The chimp, understandably, dislikes her new owner. As Ethel, wearing a tutu, hurls a bucket at Ollie, a parallel with the aggressive wives in the team's films becomes evident. The boys' relationship with other human females is recalled when Stan strikes an immediate but unspoken friendship with Ethel: the editing and composition of the close-ups in which he and the chimp wink, nod and smile at each other are very similar to those of the boys-meet-girls scenes in several silents (starting with *Their Purple Moment*) and the early talkie, *Men O' War*. The difference is that Ollie is excluded from this flirtation. 'Maybe she likes you better than she does me,' he observes jealously.

Despite Stan's assistance, Ollie is nailed inside the crate by Ethel – the first of several occasions when man and beast reverse roles in the film. Pursued by the circus lion (dubbed 'MGM' by Stan), the three are forced to leave without the crate. On the street that night, Stan maintains his bond with Ethel by holding hands – a splendidly ambiguous gesture equally suggestive of lovers, two children or a child with parent. If the latter relationship applies, it becomes clear that Ethel is the protective parent figure, threatening Ollie whenever he hits Stan. The trio decide to look for a room. When Ollie says that he 'can't sleep with the monkey', Stan replies, 'Oh, she won't mind,' though he takes the trouble to confirm his belief – with Ethel.

The chosen boarding-house is run by the neurotic Joe (Billy Gilbert), who is convinced that his absent wife is cheating on him. When Ollie rings the bell, the landlord roughly drags him inside, then apologizes – 'I thought you were my wife,' he explains. This, the film's first mistaken identity, involves gender confusion, paving the way for even more complex role reversals and mix-ups. The second of these is precipitated by Joe's refusal of entry to the chimp. Ollie devises a ruse where he swaps clothes with Ethel: she is masculinized and humanized by donning his suit and derby (in order to deceive the landlord!), while he is feminized by her tutu. Ollie's wearing of the skirt is somewhat superfluous, since Stan is supposed to throw down his clothes from the window of their room. This plan, however, goes awry. Having made the alternative arrangement of putting Ethel in a box outside, the boys fall asleep together. During the night Stan moves to another bed, only to be replaced by Ethel who has crept in and wants to kiss and make up with Ollie. In a scene reminiscent of the bear encounter in *The Rogue Song*, Ollie – his back to the chimp – believes Stan is cuddling up to him ('How many times have I told you to trim your toenails?'), though he looks incredulous when a sloppy kiss is planted on his neck. Eventually realizing the truth, he forces Ethel (like her contemporaneous cousin King Kong, an embodiment of unacceptably rampant sexuality) into the closet. She takes revenge by stealing Ollie's blanket, which forces him into Stan's bed – also occupied by the flea circus.

The film's themes of mistaken identity, sexual jealousy, gender confusion and human/animal interrelation all begin to converge when Ethel, back in her tutu, starts to dance around the bedroom. When she insists that Stan joins her, Ollie shouts, 'Ethel, will you stop that and come to bed?' We now discover that Joe's wife, who has still not returned, is also called Ethel. In the original script, Ollie was supposed to have delivered more risqué double entendres, suggesting to the jealous landlord that the boys are sharing his wife's sexual favours and climaxing with the sound of squeaky bedsprings as they tussle with Ethel (Skretvedt, 1987, p. 233). But the few lines that remain are enough to bring Joe, toting a gun, up to the duo's room. As the landlord pounds on the door, they conceal the chimp under the blanket of a bed in an adjacent room, but Joe finds her. Addressing the covered figure, he delivers a pathetic speech to the 'deceitful trifler' whom he loves 'more than life itself'. When he calls Ethel the bearer of his name and the mother of his children, Stan and Ollie are perplexed. Even when Joe's wife enters, and the other Ethel is uncovered, they cannot understand the situation. 'You said you loved her,' Ollie reminds the now fuming landlord. The chimp, too, has had enough: irately, she removes her tutu and starts firing the gun at random, proving that she's capable of human failings as well as achievements.

Superficially a silly film, *The Chimp* is actually one of Laurel and Hardy's most complex explorations of shifting roles and relationships. Even the foregoing detailed analysis does not exhaust its riches. It contains many subtle parallels between chimp and human behaviour: Stan and Ethel are equated by their use (at different points in the film) of the same dismissive hand gesture, and in one scene Ollie unwittingly mirrors the chimp's action of slapping Stan's bottom. Humans and animals, like males and females, imitate each other, calling into question the rigid classifications of biology.

Gender confusion recurs briefly in the opening sequence of the two-reeler, **County Hospital**. Stan, attempting to find his hospitalized friend, sees a nurse emerging with a baby from the room he believes is Ollie's – a moment which anticipates Hardy's 'motherhood' three films later in *Their First Mistake*. Stan heaves a sigh of relief when the nurse informs him that he's got the wrong floor.

Most of the film concerns Stan's violation of hospital protocol, starting with the loud noises made by his car as he parks it near to a sign demanding 'Quiet'. Whistling then knocking loudly on the door of Ollie's room, Stan possesses none of the ideal visitor's tact and sympathy. He tells Ollie that he decided to call only because he 'didn't have anything else to do'. Moreover, he hasn't brought a box of candy this time because 'they cost too much' and he hasn't been paid for the last box. Ollie refuses the proffered alternative of hard-boiled eggs and nuts, on which Stan gorges himself, ignoring the patient. Matters only deteriorate with the arrival of the doctor (the excitable Billy Gilbert again), so much so that both patient and visitor are ordered to leave.

Before they do, however, Stan accidentally sits on a syringe containing a strong sedative. As he drives Ollie home, he becomes increasingly tired, his loss of consciousness and control causing a series of near-collisions that forms the film's climax, much criticized for its blurry back-projection. However, it's possible that a parody of that common technique was intended (just as *Helpmates* parodied cinematic time-compression): the car pivots smoothly through almost 360 degrees, underscoring the dislocation between foreground and background. The gliding of the vehicle (more like a low-flying magic carpet than a car) contributes to the surrealist quality of the sequence, in which the fuzzily nightmarish images around Stan ultimately seem less like back-projection than a reflection of his drugged mind. When he finally crashes, the resulting image is an appropriate metaphor for a typical Laurel and Hardy narrative: the car is bent at a ninety-degree angle, causing it to move in an endless circle, like a dog chasing its tail.

In May 1932 shooting began on **Pack Up Your Troubles**, the team's second feature film. Made during the international wave of pacifist reflection on The Great War that produced films like *All*

Quiet on the Western Front (1930) and Broken Lullaby (1932), it opens in April 1917 with a sequence, adapted from the early silent Duck Soup, which mocks notions of patriotic duty. The boys are seated on a park bench, reading a newspaper bearing the headline, 'War Declared!' Ollie, looking skyward, declares, 'Gee, I wish I could go!' Stan undercuts his noble sentiment by asking, 'Go where?' Although Ollie claims that his flat feet prevent him from going to war, he is as disturbed as Stan by the approach of a recruiting sergeant. Close-ups of the sergeant's menacing face as he advances towards them invite empathy with the duo's fear. Having seen a disabled veteran being excused further service by the sergeant, they conceal their right arms underneath their jackets: when the sergeant accuses them of being 'slackers', Ollie retorts, 'You should be ashamed of yourself', and both proudly brandish their empty sleeves. They even shame the sergeant into giving them money for cups of coffee – but Stan receives his coin by producing his supposedly lost limb. They fall in.

As soon as they enter the army camp, Stan almost walks into a group of soldiers drilling on the parade ground. By the next scene they are part of a squad of hopeless raw recruits being drilled by a tough sergeant. They have no sense of direction or military precision, and Stan, shocked by the sergeant's shout of 'Attention!', drops his gun on Ollie's foot. This is all stock army comedy stuff – and the other recruits aren't much better than them – but the sequence ends more subversively as Stan links his arm with Ollie's so he'll know which way to go. Friendship, physically displayed to suggest love, undermines military machismo and discipline.

This is also apparent at the start of the front-line sequence when Stan and Ollie are discovered together in the same bunk, their bodies entwined and their feet sharing a hot-water bottle. The fact that they wear nightshirts (familiar from their boarding-house films) over their uniforms indicates that they prize domestic comfort over military convention. This is underlined by various gags: Stan screens himself while he removes his nightshirt, which he hangs up carefully; he washes, then meticulously combs his hair before going out to do battle; Ollie tries to cook and Stan makes the bed while a noisy, violent raid goes on above them. Their values are feminine and domestic rather than masculine and outdoor but, unlike the 'sissies' of most army comedies (including their own primitive effort *With Love and Hisses*), they retain their dignity. Moreover, the film's attitude to military discipline is ironic: when Stan and Ollie obey a cook's (sarcastic) order to take the garbage to the General, they get into trouble; but when they are too cowardly to obey an order to take a German prisoner, and hide in a tank instead, they accidentally round up an entire trench of enemy soldiers.

Even more loosely structured than their first feature, *Pack Up Your Troubles* stops being an army comedy half-way through to enter the Chaplinesque world of sentimental Victorian melodrama, peopled by wicked guardians and orphanage officials. Stan and Ollie informally adopt a little girl (oddly, never named) because her father Eddie, a wartime buddy of theirs, has been killed in action. It's explained early in the film that Eddie's wife has deserted him – an act of typical female selfishness in Laurel and Hardy films. Although the duo call themselves the girl's 'uncles', the role they occupy is more (in 1932 terms) the absent mother's than the dead father's. This is particularly true of Ollie, feminized much more than Stan in this film. Wearing an apron and stooped over a washboard, he scrubs the girl's clothes, pausing to examine his worn fingernails and to massage his aching back – an image that calls attention to the drudgery of overworked housewives, and even more to the humiliation and inadequacy of men in their role. Later, he tells Stan, 'You take care of the baby a while – I've got my ironing to do!' To this chore, he brings a feminine daintiness, gently sprinkling drops of water on the garment, then moving the iron along its seams with an elegant wiggle. However, this gracefulness is constantly threatened by masculine clumsiness, as he burns his fingers and finally falls on the ironing board, which collapses under his weight.

Stan, meanwhile, regresses to a child's role, settling down in an armchair to have 'a new bedtime story' told *to* him by the infant. The story is 'Goldilocks and the Three Bears' which, with its account of a bear family invaded by a girl, somewhat parallels and adds an extra parodic edge to the unconventional family scene we are witnessing. It is a lovely touch that, at the precise moment in the story when Goldilocks falls asleep on Baby Bear's bed, Stan finally nods off in the armchair. Just as Goldilocks and Baby Bear seem interchangeable (the porridge, chair and bed of the tale suit both), so are Stan and 'Eddie's baby'. But the latter has assumed the role of parental storyteller, sat upright on Stan's knee as he reclines lower and lower; they are not merely both children, they have totally reversed their roles. Indeed, the girl likes to play all the available roles, demonstrated by the conviction with which she impersonates the three bears, adopting a distinctive voice for each. It is quite common for young children to act like adults: earlier in the film, when the girl is staying with wicked guardians, we see her relating the story of 'Cinderella' to her doll, which she then puts to bed in a motherly manner. It is less usual to find an adult who behaves in quite such a childlike manner as Stan. Towards the film's end, as welfare officials and police try to enter the duo's flat, Stan climbs into the child's cot, nonchalantly holding her doll. The parallel with the girl's earlier scene is striking, but whereas she uses the doll to assert her 'adulthood', Stan employs it to complete his 'disguise' as a child.

Although the duo's aim is to restore the girl to Eddie's parents, the film invites considerable sympathy for the sense of family created by the 'uncles'. When Ollie tells her that Stan is out looking for her grandparents, she cuddles up to him and replies, 'I hope he doesn't find them,' a sentiment probably echoed by the audience, partly because we know that when they are found the film will be over. However, it is also true that a sense of aptness and belonging is highlighted by the scenes in which the girl imitates her 'uncles', notably Stan's typical gesture of head scratching and Ollie's smile and twiddly wave of the hand. The home they provide for her is shown as infinitely preferable to the orphanage into which the grimly caricatured welfare officials wish to put her. And it is undoubtedly superior to that provided by the guardians with whom Stan and Ollie find her, where the tale of Cinderella, alienated from her family of 'stepfather and ugly sisters', parallels the girl's own situation. (By contrast, that of Goldilocks, told in the security of Stan and Ollie's apartment, begins with the heroine living 'at home with her mummy and daddy'.) Brought up by her guardians in an atmosphere of poverty and wife-beating, the child, looking at a photograph of her father, pleads with him, 'take me away from here' – and, as if in miraculous response to her prayer, Stan and Ollie knock at the door and announce, 'We've come to take her away.' A fairy tale indeed.

The duo's search for the girl's grandparents is complicated by the fact that their information is limited to the family's surname – Smith (one of the candidates, prompted by a newspaper headline, is Alfred E. Smith, the Democrat who had been defeated by Hoover in the 1928 presidential election). Their investigation takes them to a mansion where a high-society wedding ceremony is under way, which they unwittingly disrupt with the news that they've got 'Eddie's baby'. They've also got the wrong family but, since the name of the groom happens to be Eddie, the wedding is abandoned and the guests sent away. Like *Our Wife*, this sequence mocks matrimony, as Stan again passively assumes the role of groom, and the grateful bride, not yet aware of the error, kisses him on the lips. After she has gone, a spark of heterosexuality ignites within him, but Ollie preserves *his* 'marriage' by preventing Stan from pursuing her.

The wedding sequence satirizes the rich and their family values – the groom's father, bride and prospective in-laws are very quick to believe the unsubstantiated claim about him. But dominant ideology asserts itself in the film's final scene where Stan and Ollie succeed (by accident) in delivering the child to her kindly – and wealthy – grandparents, a concession much more likely to be required in a relatively expensive feature than in a short. In Laurel and Hardy's second foray into the world of feature-film respectability, the plot is still constructed around them, but the movie's splodges of sentimentality and dreary drama forebode the blandness evident in some of their later features.

One of the sharper elements of *Pack Up Your Troubles* is the revenge sub-plot, which involves a knife-wielding army cook who finally catches up with the boys (who 'snitched' on him) at the grandparents' home, and prevents the end of the film from being too soppy. The idea of delayed retribution also figured in their next movie, the last to be made before the team embarked on a European tour in the summer of 1932. A two-reeler called **Scram!**, it begins in a courtroom with the pair on a vagrancy charge – as so often, they've been sleeping on a park bench. The role of the ill-tempered Judge is taken by Rychard Cramer, who played the wife-beater in *Pack Up*

Your Troubles and the sadistic killer in the 1939 film *Saps at Sea*, demonstrating the interchangeability of authority and criminal figures in Laurel and Hardy's world. Here, Cramer gives a formidable display of hammer-waving and teeth-baring as – since 'the jail is full' – he allows the boys just one hour to leave town. Stan and Ollie, as the film's terse title emphasizes, are unwanted and forced to live on the periphery of society.

The next scene takes place in a rainstorm at night: the boys help a drunk (Arthur Housman) to find his car key and, after they tell him they 'have no home', he offers to put them up for the night. Unfortunately, he takes them not to his home but to that of the Judge, a fatalistic coincidence which punishes the pair for their good turn. Ollie's self-congratulation, as they sample the Judge's luxurious bedroom (still believing it is the drunk's), rubs it in: 'You see what a little kindness'll do – now if we hadn't stopped to help him, we wouldn't be in a spot like this.'

They compound their 'crime' by accidentally inebriating the Judge's wife (Vivien Oakland): when she finds them in her home, she faints and they revive her with gin that the drunk (now gone) has substituted for water in a pitcher. The 'water' has a liberating effect, making the wife – then the boys – laugh hysterically. Like Ethel in *The Chimp*, she insists on dancing with them. Although the wife is merely playful, the boys evidently feel threatened by her active sexuality: Ollie pleads, 'I don't like to dance,' and when she pokes Stan's adam's apple (like his girlfriend in *We Faw Down*) he shouts, 'Don't do that!' But eventually all three end up laughing and lying on the bed – at which point the Judge, having smelled gin in the pitcher, enters. Stan extinguishes the light and the film ends in darkness and violence, conveyed only by screams and bangs.

Although *Scram!* is hardly an example of one of the 1930s overt social-protest films, a number of its elements are subversive. The Judge, looking more like a stereotypical tough criminal, is merciless towards the homeless. His capacity for violence, strongly implied in the opening and closing sequences, is contrasted with the boys' compassion for the drunk and for the Judge's wife when she faints. Their poverty and vagrancy are juxtaposed with the luxury of his home. The Judge's grim-faced sobriety – we learn that 'he detests people who drink', emphasizing his representation of the law (Prohibition was still in force) – is contrasted with his wife's anarchic, gin-induced laughter. The film recognizes, however briefly, the problems of vagrancy, homelessness and overcrowded jails. This social awareness, together with the film's emphasis on fate and its visual style – notably in the night scenes of a rain-washed street – prefigure film noir in much the same way as *I Am a Fugitive from a Chain-Gang*, the Warner Bros. social-protest movie also released in 1932. In that film's final shot, Paul Muni's vagrant hero, forced by society to become a thief, disappears into the shadows. *Scram!* ends in total darkness too.

Chapter six

Shorts into Features: The Last Two-Reelers (1932–35)

LAUREL and Hardy's growing prestige was confirmed by several events in the second half of 1932. *Pack Up Your Troubles*, their second feature film, was released in September. Two months later, *The Music Box* won an Academy Award as Best Short Subject (Comedy) at the Oscar ceremony. But the most direct evidence of the team's huge popularity came with the phenomenal success of their visit to Britain during July and August, where they were mobbed by huge crowds.

On their return from Europe, the comedians started work on the next two-reeler, **Their First Mistake.** Perhaps the most audacious and complex of all their films, it was also the last short to feature that remnant of the silent era, an introductory title: 'Mr Hardy was married – Mr Laurel was also unhappy.' These two statements are more connected than they first appear, since Ollie's marriage is the cause of both men's unhappiness. His wife (Mae Busch), given the ironically feminine name of Arabella, is as formidably aggressive as the last Mrs Hardy was in *Helpmates*. As in that film, Stan is the bachelor intruder whose threat to his friend's marriage is emphasized here by his proximity: he lives in an apartment directly opposite the Hardys.

The film opens with a scene of marital blitz at the Hardys' breakfast table. When Ollie greets his wife, she snaps, 'Don't "good morning" me!' and immediately launches an investigation into Ollie's whereabouts of the previous evening. He explains sheepishly that he went to a Punch and Judy show with Stan. This choice is amusing for its obvious childishness, but also for the irony that Ollie has been to see a representation of marriage in which the husband (Mr Punch) traditionally beats the wife. As we soon see, the reverse is the case in the Hardy household. Meanwhile, Ollie's admission fuels Mrs Hardy's jealousy of Stan, with whom her husband evidently spends most of his evenings. 'I'm getting sick and tired of this – it's Stan here, Stan there,' she rants. 'Why, you ought to be ashamed to even be seen on the street with him!' – a statement indicative of her desire for social respectability.

Ollie plays up to his wife's social pretensions when Stan phones to propose another night out. Asked who the caller was, he pretends to her that his new boss Mr Jones has requested his attendance at an important business meeting, where he will meet 'big, influential men – just the kind of men that you want me to associate with'. He conceals his preference for Stan by demonstrating an interest in her values of professional and social status, goals that a husband is supposed to pursue. Mrs Hardy is very pleased: 'At last you're beginning to get some place.' But when Stan arrives in person to explain to Ollie that he was in fact the caller, not Mr Jones (which Ollie, as part of the ruse, had called him), there's a scene of apocalyptic domestic violence as Mrs Hardy attacks her husband – and then Stan too – with a chair and a broom.

The two men escape to Stan's apartment, locking the door behind them. The sexual dimension of Mrs Hardy's jealousy is strongly suggested when she shouts through the door to Ollie: 'You go out with that Laurel again, and I'm through!' A delightful scene follows, statically shot in one continuous two-minute take, of the two men lying across Stan's bed, the camera positioned far enough back to show them in relation to each other and the bed. As they fidget and restlessly adjust their bodily positions, the dialogue proceeds:

Stan: Well, what's the matter with her anyway?
Ollie: Oh, I don't know. She says I think more of
    you than I do of her.
Stan: Well, you do, don't ya?
Ollie: Well, we won't go into that.

The homosexual implications are clear, especially when accompanied by the physical movements which suggest repressed erotic longings – slightly later in the shot, Stan even raises his legs above his head. But the conversation is also important for what is *not* said; it hints at the subject matter which the dialogue 'won't go into', and alerts us to the more implicit, symbolic course that censorship forces the film to take.

Stan suggests that the Hardys need a baby in order to keep the wife's mind occupied while he goes out with Ollie. His garbled statements about 'all the happiness in a home' being derived from a baby are a splendid parody of the ideology of family values reinforced by most Hollywood films of the time, especially those of Roach's distributor, MGM. The idea of the baby thus having been conceived – on a bed – by the two men, the next scene presents them returning to the Hardys' apartment with an adopted infant. Their parental roles are already defined: Ollie, carrying the baby, is 'mother'; Stan, offering a cigar to a neighbour, is 'father'. On discovering that Mrs Hardy has departed, they are forced to maintain these roles. A process server arrives with the news that Ollie's wife is suing him for divorce and Stan 'for the alienation of Mr Hardy's affections'. He concludes grimly, 'She'll take you hook, line and sinker.'

Now there is the problem of the baby (the 'mistake', presumably, of the title), which Stan intends to leave Ollie holding – literally. 'You're just as much responsible for it as I am,' insists Ollie. 'You were the one that wanted me to have the baby,' he chides, clarifying Stan's role as 'father' and his own as unwed mother. 'Now that you've got me into this trouble you want to walk out and leave me flat,' he continues. 'What will my friends say? Why, I'll be ostracized!' Stan replies, 'Well, I'm going to lose my hook, line and sinker' – an image that, in the circumstances, suggests the wife's emasculatory powers. The parody of a common theme of movie drama continues when Stan explains his refusal 'to get mixed up in this thing' by the fact that he has his 'career to think of'. As in the breakfast scene, the film satirizes the values of professional and social status and their conflict with unconventional sexuality. Ollie forces him to stay and, as its first reel ends, the film prepares us for Stan's gradual regression in the second: upset about the situation in which he's trapped, he begins to cry, causing the real baby to cry also.

However, the next role Stan adopts, during the night, is that of 'mother'. Ollie tells him to hold the baby for a while since he's 'all fagged out' (another sub-textual clue, perhaps). Deciding it needs some milk, Stan unbuttons his nightshirt (massive double take by Ollie) and produces . . . a feeding bottle. However, he cannot resist taking swigs of milk for himself, a repeated image that leads to the film's final scene in which the two men and the baby all lie together in bed.

Half-asleep, Ollie tries to feed the crying infant, apparently unaware that Stan, not the baby, is beside him. So he puts his arm round his friend's neck and brings the bottle to his mouth. One writer has commented that 'the prolonged ecstatic sucking that follows is worthy of Cocteau or Buñuel' (Howes, 1993, p. 837). The sexual overtones of this image – Stan greedily drawing the white fluid from the bottle held by his friend – are unmistakable, especially in the context of the film's first half. It is also worth noting that the phallic properties of the bottle and its rubber teat (which Stan chews and swallows) seem to be established by a brief scene earlier in the second reel when Ollie places the bottle between his legs as he tries to pull out the teat, but in doing so spills the milk in his lap. The latter image is also echoed in the film's final moment as Ollie, discovering his error, sits up and snatches the bottle from Stan's mouth. As he starts to reprimand his friend for drinking the baby's milk, he holds the teatless bottle between his legs and the liquid pours out, flooding the bedclothes. Incidentally, the milk symbolism was even more strongly stated in the original script, which proposed an opening sequence in which Ollie goes out for the morning milk as an excuse to see Stan (Skretvedt, 1987, p. 247).

Fluidity of one kind or another is the key to *Their First Mistake*, a subtle Utopian fantasy of personal relationships, in which Ollie's desire for a male friend/lover, a wife and a child are all satisfied by one person – Stan. As originally shot, the film ended with Arabella Hardy returning to the apartment with adopted twins, but this scene was scrapped (see Skretvedt, 1987, p. 248). Although the final version concludes abruptly – even by Laurel and Hardy standards – Arabella's absence from the ending focuses attention on the Stan–Ollie relationship, which lies at the heart of this movie more than any other. It is a remarkable film for its refusal to present that relationship as fixed in any way; instead, it charts Stan's metamorphosis from the 'lover' of the opening scenes, to the 'father' who returns with the baby, to the 'mother' who feeds it and finally to the 'baby' who displaces the real infant. As such, the movie is a summation of the team's most interesting work to date, fusing the 'bachelor intruder' films with those in which Stan is a child to Ollie's parent and those which feminize one or both of them.

Their next two-reeler, **Towed in a Hole**, opens with the duo riding along in their car as Stan conceives the idea of eliminating the middleman in their fish-selling business. But as in *Their First Mistake*, when he attempts to repeat the plan for Ollie, it re-emerges in a severely garbled form. Here, the gag is pointed after Stan's exposition by Ollie's (first) use of the imperative that would become a catch-phrase, 'Tell me that again!'

The bulk of the film concerns their attempts to repair a second-hand boat they've purchased in order to effect their plan of catching the fish themselves. Of course, the refurbishment is hindered by various disasters caused by Stan. On one of these occasions, when Ollie's face has been covered in paint, the childlike miscreant hides from him, moving round the sides of the boat but peeping through gaps in the wood at the strange, war-painted face. A little later, drenched in water after another accident, the belligerence on Ollie's face, cleansed of any other emotion, is conveyed by a startlingly full and sharply defined close-up as he ominously orders, 'Come here.' He does this twice, each shot followed and contrasted by one of Stan's sheepish face viewed through a porthole, emphasizing the latter's vulnerability and submission to punishment from the parent figure. The punishment, however, develops into a tit-for-tat routine, in which the pair pour buckets of water over each other. Eventually, Ollie stops the fight and, with the voice of rational adulthood, he gently pleads, 'Isn't this silly? Here we are, two grown-up men, acting like a couple of children!' Like the moment in *Come Clean* when Ollie's wife compares him to a 'four-year-old child', it is an unusually explicit reference to the infantile aspect of their personalities. But irony is added here when a new conflict immediately erupts over who started the water fight!

After Stan causes yet another accident, he is confined below deck by Ollie, who refuses to speak to him. In the cabin Stan sits alone, sporting a black eye which has apparently been inflicted between scenes by Ollie, a chalk drawing of whom Stan pokes in the eye – the nearest he can get to 'eye for an eye' revenge. Beside the drawing of Ollie lies another he has completed of a boat in full sail, representing an innocent faith in the success of their project. Bored, Stan plays noughts and crosses with himself, a visual indication of the divided personality he usually suggests verbally, then he accidentally traps his head between the bulkhead and the bottom of the mast. This leads to a typically childlike scene of panic, relieved only when he uses a nearby saw to cut through the mast, the head of which Ollie is painting . . . The next sequence opens with Stan tied to a barrel, which, when removed by Ollie, reveals a second black eye.

The film is another succinct 'narrative of failure', all the more poignant for the (literally) sunny optimism of the opening in which Ollie, driving the car, proclaims, 'For the first time in our lives, we're a success – a nice little fish business and making money.' It is their capitalistic greed – Stan's idea is to make 'a lot more money' – which results in the annihilation of both their main assets in the final scene when the boat crashes into their car.

Following this conventional film, Laurel and Hardy returned to the gender-bending of *Their First Mistake* with **Twice Two**, a two-reeler in which they adopt dual roles as their usual personas and each other's wives. This attempt to push the feminization of Stan and Ollie to its logical limits has great curiosity value, yet it emerges as one of their weakest films. Part of its failure can be ascribed to a poor overall structure and to unusually feeble gags that allow scenes to fizzle out. Unlike *Brats*, their previous double-identity film, *Twice Two* seems self-conscious about its technical feats, which include the dubbing of the wives' voices, a practice that exacerbates the artificiality of the conception.

The film's sub-text is intimated in the opening sequence, set in the duo's offices, when Ollie says to Stan, 'Today is our anniversary.' He is confirming Laurel's observation that it's a year since they married each other's sisters but, spoken in the male world of work which excludes the wives, 'our anniversary' seems to refer to a marriage between the two men. This alerts us to the fact that the two 'heterosexual' marriages, linked by family ties, in *Twice Two* merely re-characterize the usual close relationship between the boys. The incestuousness of the set-up is intensified by the implication that (as in *Brats*) the foursome all live in the same house!

The introductory scenes intercut the men at the office with the domesticated women who, wearing aprons, are preparing the anniversary dinner. As in (but to a lesser extent than) *Brats*, the two pairs – here superficially differentiated by gender rather than age – exhibit each other's characteristics. The boys betray their effeminacy when, after Ollie reminds Stan that their home phone number is (aptly) '22', they both affect high-pitched voices as they exclaim 'Too-too!' and wave goodbye to each other. Meanwhile, the ladies behave exactly like the Stan and Ollie we know, notably when Mrs Hardy manages to drop a huge cake on Mrs Laurel's head, the candled centre remaining on top like a crown while the outer part hangs round her neck like an Elizabethan ruff. Stan points to a portrait (which just happens to be on the wall) of the Virgin Queen herself, underlining the visual pun and perhaps suggesting a verbal double entendre – Ollie, feminized twice over, is a 'queen' in the homosexual sense too.

Indeed, Mrs Laurel's convincing appropriation, throughout the film, of Ollie's punctilious mannerisms highlights the effeminacy that resides within Hardy's normal male persona, both in gesture and speech. (The gender ambiguity in the latter is assisted by the use of a deep female voice reminiscent of Hermione Gingold.) By contrast, Laurel – benefiting perhaps from his wider experience of drag roles – makes Mrs Hardy a more original creation. With a squeaky voice like Betty Boop, she talks quickly and is generally much more animated than her brother, though she can suddenly become just as confused as him.

The ladies are also of interest for their absorption of the traits – mainly aggressive – associated with the wives played by women in previous films. Mrs Laurel takes almost all Stan's money from him (recalling his money-grubbing wife in the silent, *Their Purple Moment*), leaving him only 15 cents with which she instructs him to go out and buy ice-cream. When Ollie greets his wife with 'Hello, baby,' she replies, 'Don't "baby" me, you big lunk!' – an exchange which closely parallels that between the Hardys at the opening of *Their First Mistake*. And at different points in *Twice Two*, each lady breaks crockery on her husband's head. In earlier films the humour of the wives' violent dominance derived largely from its 'masculinity'. But here, when two men play the roles, the joke is negated, though its complexity is amusingly acknowledged by an exchange during the anniversary dinner about who 'wears the pants' in each marriage. Despite this and the other moments of ambiguity detailed above, the film cannot escape the problem of its basic conception which, by separating Stan and Ollie's masculinity and femininity, inhibits the gender fluidity that characterizes their best work.

In early 1933 the team began to shoot their third starring feature, **The Devil's Brother**, adapted from Auber's comic opera *Fra Diavolo* about banditry in nineteenth-century Italy. The subject-matter draws parallels with the gangsters that had flourished in the United States for a decade, and whose success stories (the only credible ones during the Depression) were told in a cycle of movies in the early 1930s. But, as Andrew Bergman notes, censorship had reduced the number of such films by 1932, and the success drive resurfaced in the musicals of 1933 (see Bergman, 1971, p. 16). *The Devil's Brother*, a musical of that year, allows its charismatic 'robber-chieftain' Fra Diavolo to succeed in escaping scot-free (though not with his loot) at the end – along with his two servants Stanlio and Ollio.

The duo begin the film as honest and successful citizens who have worked hard in order to save enough money to live on for the rest of their lives. But at the very moment Ollie rejoices in their 'reward' the two bags containing all their savings are stolen by a bandit. Suddenly impoverished, like victims of the Wall Street crash, they decide, as many people did in the Depression, that crime is the only profitable line of business, so they become bandits themselves. But their efforts are no more successful than their attempt to become 'beer barons' in *Pardon Us*. Here, they don't fall foul of the law but of other tricksters and bandits. They hold up a woodcutter who pleads poverty, shaming them into a fit of weeping as they hand over *their* remaining cash, which he promptly deposits in a bulging money bag. In the next attempt Ollie pretends to be Fra Diavolo to scare their chosen victim – who unfortunately proves to be the real Diavolo (Dennis King).

One of the film's chief interests is the breadth of emotion displayed by both of them, but especially Stan. Their weeping in response to the deceitful miser's sob story is followed much later by a laughing jag, induced by alcohol like the one in *Scram!* Between these two scenes of contrasting but equally strong emotions, Stan is rendered more dopey than usual, first by a sleeping powder, then by excessive wine. Much of the film's humour derives from the very marked regression to these primary emotions – weeping, laughing, sleepiness – which are often displayed by children but usually held in check by adults. Stan's childlike quality is also conveyed by his tendency to imbibe anything that's put in front of him (recalling his babyish milk-drinking in *Their First Mistake*), and by his fondness for two games played with his hands – 'kneesie-earsie-nosie' and 'finger-wiggle'.

In one scene Stan is forced by Diavolo to hang Ollie. Before he does so, he confesses that he once prevented his pal's marriage by pretending to be his son – an explicit verbal acknowledgement of the child–parent relationship that exists between the two. Ollie's sarcastic cry, 'My son!' at the end of this scene (Stan having bungled the execution) is echoed, without sarcasm, near the film's conclusion by the innkeeper in approval of his daughter Zerlina's marriage to her soldier lover. The latter is not actually the innkeeper's son (except 'in-law') any more than Stan is Ollie's, but the film's repetition of these words suggests a parallel: in one case, the claim of a paternal relationship validates a marriage (the innkeeper has hitherto opposed the union); in the other, the claim of a filial one prevented matrimony.

Mirroring and repetition are important in this film which, as noted above, contains two games and two extensions of Stan's natural dopiness. There are also two scenes of failed executions and two in which the boys are chased by a bull – the second in the final moments when the rampaging beast scatters the firing squad which they and Diavolo are facing. But the most interesting use of repetition occurs during the laughing jag in which earlier scenes – including Ollie's cry of 'My son!' and the two hand games – are rapidly recapitulated by the two, fuelling their mounting hysteria. The scene, which appears near the end of the film, reminds the audience of its highlights (like stills under the closing credits of American TV sitcoms), but it also locates Stan and Ollie as an audience to themselves, as if they had been viewing the film with us. The effect is, simultaneously, to involve us in their laughter (especially in a cinema context) and to distance us from it by equating the boys' observational position with our own.

The laughing jag seems unrelated to the main plot (Diavolo's attempt to rob wealthy aristocrats), which is carried by other actors. Like the musical numbers, and the scenes in which Ollie and the innkeeper unsuccessfully try to imitate Stan's little games, it appears to be a moment of pure spectacle, divorced from the narrative. But as Stan's hysteria grows, he holds the side of his body with a hand-on-hip gesture that gradually transmutes into an effeminate pose, which underscores his imitation (in a suitably high voice) of Zerlina's mirror song. (He had witnessed her performance the previous night, when he and Ollie accompanied Diavolo during his attempted robbery.) Zerlina, overhearing Stan's imitation, connects him with Diavolo, so the laughing jag reactivates the main plot. Such links between the comedy scenes and the rest of the film are, however, rare – Stan and Ollie don't even have much to do with their old foil James Finlayson, playing Diavolo's intended victim. While *The Devil's Brother* is probably the best of Laurel and Hardy's operetta-style vehicles, its frequent pauses for music and sentimental drama in which they are seldom involved tend to dilute their contribution, anticipating MGM's treatment of the Marx Brothers a few years later.

Stan's confession in *The Devil's Brother* that he prevented Ollie's marriage by pretending to be his son may have provided the pattern for their next short, **Me and My Pal**. The title's play on the contemporaneous movie hit, *Me and My Gal*, is interesting, but in the film Stan is not so much a pal, or even a gal, as a child in relation to Ollie's father-figure. The opening establishes Ollie as adult, heterosexual, materialistic and fully in control of his life as he prepares to marry the daughter of an oil magnate that very day. The arrival of Stan, his best man, presents a clash of values, the catalyst being the wedding present he brings – a jigsaw puzzle which Stan suggests will provide 'something for us to play with' when Ollie is married. The groom retorts, 'My playing days are over,' adding that the jigsaw is 'childish falderdash' on which he cannot waste his valuable time.

However, the rest of the film chronicles Ollie's gradual regression under Stan's influence, as the completion of the 'childish' puzzle takes precedence over the wedding, for which the guests are already assembled at the bride's home. Eventually, her father (James Finlayson) comes to Ollie's home, brandishing a wreath which Stan has sent to the wedding. Although the choice is presumably a product of Stan's ignorance, its equation of marriage with death is in keeping with his gradual if accidental erosion of Ollie's matrimonial plans. This is of course another variation on the 'bachelor intruder' theme, though Stan, as in *Our Wife* (in which he was also the best man), threatens Ollie's marriage before it has even taken place.

By the film's conclusion, Ollie has lost not only his fiancée but also his career – which came with the bride – and his investments. (His ruination echoes that in *Helpmates*, especially when Stan comments, 'I understand, you want to be alone with your thoughts.') Earlier, when a telegram arrived, advising him to sell his stock for two million dollars' profit, he was too obsessed with the puzzle to read it. Now, as he sits covered in soot in the fireplace (having hidden from Fin in the chimney), he learns from a radio bulletin that the same stock, after its sensational rise, has totally crashed. Dispossessed, Ollie is reduced to the state of a child with nothing – except Stan. As at the end of *Early to Bed*, the boys are equalized and thus free to 'play' together again.

The stock-market gag's parallel with the Wall Street crash is highlighted when Stan tells Ollie not to worry because 'prosperity's just around the corner' – a satirical echo of President Hoover who came to power in 1929, the year of the crash, on the strength of such promises. Perhaps Americans thought they could laugh about the past because, by the time *Me and My Pal* was made in March 1933, Hoover had been replaced by Franklin D. Roosevelt, whose New Deal programme of reforms commenced in that month. The optimism about increased employment is reflected in the fact that the team's next three shorts are all located in the world of work.

The first of these, **The Midnight Patrol,** casts the boys as policemen. Just as the cycle of gangster films was gradually being replaced in the mid-1930s by a series of movies which portrayed similar events from the cops' viewpoint, Stan and Ollie here eschew their usual roles as vagrants (or bandits in *The Devil's Brother*) for representatives of the law. The opening scenes explicitly imitate those of MGM's *The Beast of the City*, a 1932 film dedicated to 'the glorification of policemen', through the monotonous tones of the radio operator calling their patrol car. But of course *The Midnight Patrol* is a parody, the boys placed in this position of authority in order to mock the fashion for cop movies, and by extension the profession it portrayed.

In 1933 it was a very masculine profession. As in the team's military films, much of the humour arises from their inability to live up to the movie image of the tough cop. Concerned as ever with domestic comforts, they use the police call-box as a fridge in which to keep their sandwiches and milk. When the radio operator announces that the spare tyre of their patrol car is being stolen as they sit in it, Stan gets out to chastise the two thieves. 'If you come back here again, I'll arrest you,' he threatens feebly. Asked, 'Who will?' he points to Ollie in the car and replies, 'We will!' This reference to his partner provokes one of the thieves (Charlie Hall) to mock the wimpish cop by answering, complete with a hand-on-hip gesture and a stamp of the foot, 'Oh, is that so?' – a moment of 'sissy' humour rare in the team's mature movies.

More of their childlike and effeminate approach to crime control follows when they stumble across a safe-cracker busily working in a jewellers. Stan first ignores, then even assists, the burglar whom he assumes is the owner of the shop. Ollie has the sense to realize the man is a criminal but, issuing him a ticket to appear in court, he treats the break-in as if it were a trivial offence. 'I'll teach you a lesson,' he says, punctiliously preparing his pencil, like a school prefect smugly inflicting detention on a younger boy.

But his dominance is merely the obverse of his submissiveness. When the burglar makes excuses that prevent his appearance in court that week, Ollie is absurdly accommodating. 'How would a week from Tuesday be?' he enquires humbly, after a bout of marital-like bickering with Stan about their own availability.

Like *Scram!* – also set at night – the film has a grim conclusion. The boys are called to investigate a domestic burglary and eventually arrest the 'intruder', but only after their own break-in destroys much of the property they were sent to protect. The 'intruder' turns out to be the Chief of Police (Frank Brownlee) who has been locked out of his home – though the initial withholding of this information from the audience invests the authority figure with a criminal-like appearance, a touch that anticipates film noir. Moral ambiguity is extended by the black comedy of the ending (reminiscent in tone of *Laughing Gravy*) when the irate Chief shoots Stan and Ollie offscreen and exclaims, 'Send for the coroner!' as the other cops solemnly doff their caps. This retribution is a demonstration of the ultimate tit-for-tat. The original ending, filmed but scrapped, featured violence with sexual overtones, as Ollie accidentally shoots the Chief's butler in a region which causes his voice to emerge 'in a high falsetto' (see Skretvedt, 1987, p. 262).

Another projected gag with a strong hint of sexual violence never made it to the released version of their next two-reeler, **Busy Bodies**, set in a sawmill. At one point the script suggests that Ollie applies glue to his pal's bare behind, 'ending up with a violent dig with the brush into Stan's fanny' (quoted in Skretvedt, 1987, p. 264). It is a pity, if hardly surprising, that this astonishingly mock-erotic moment never reached the screen, though the finished film delights in the comic sadism of Ollie's bottom being spanked by an automatic paddle and Stan shaving his pal's face with a specially sharpened plane. The opening scene recalls that of *Towed in a Hole* as the boys drive along in sunshine. Brimming with New Deal optimism, Ollie exclaims, 'What a beautiful morning! ... Gee, it's great to have a good job to go to, it just makes the whole world brighter!' At the sawmill the gags – including tit-for-tat with a colleague (Charlie Hall) and with each other – are so visual and physical that both Stan and Ollie are speechless for long periods. The film is a throwback to *The Finishing Touch* and the other work-centred silents they made before the Wall Street crash in 1929. However, the climactic sequence in which Ollie is sucked into a waste duct anticipates the factory scenes of Chaplin's 1936 *Modern Times*.

The last of the 1933 trio of work-based shorts was in fact called **Dirty Work**, the title referring both to the boys' occupation as chimney sweeps and to the bizarre experiments of their customer, a potty professor (Lucien Littlefield). A link between the two is also established in the opening scene when a cuckoo clock provides both a comment on the professor's mental state and an announcement (by allusion to their signature tune) of the boys' arrival at the front door of his home. Throughout the film, the two types of 'dirty work' under way in the house are intercut.

Like *Busy Bodies*, this two-reeler revives the slapstick of the silent days during the duo's inept efforts to sweep the chimney, which result in a predictable catalogue of destruction. The sparing use of dialogue is highlighted by Ollie's repeated statement to Stan, 'I have nothing to say.' When the latter mimics Ollie's pompous delivery of the line, he receives a blow on the head with a shovel, a punishment which, the second time around, he not only accepts but even assists by removing his derby and handing Ollie the shovel again. This stoicism bordering on masochism echoes an earlier moment when Ollie, having tumbled down the chimney, sits at its foot, waiting silently for a succession of bricks to fall on his head.

In the film's final sequence the mad scientist, excitedly crowing like a cock (perhaps a parody of Emil Jannings in the 1930 film *The Blue Angel*), presents the fruit of his experiments to the boys – a rejuvenation formula, a few drops of which, when put into a tank with the subject, turn a duck into a duckling and then into an egg! As he prepares to make his butler thirty years younger, the duo attempt their own experiment. This goes spectacularly awry when Ollie falls into the tank with all of the formula, eventually emerging as a bowler-wearing chimpanzee who tells Stan, via the dubbing of Hardy's voice, 'I have nothing to say.'

Perhaps the team's cameo appearance as babies in **Wild Poses** was inspired by the rejuvenation theme in *Dirty Work* (both films were made in August 1933). This entry in Roach's Our Gang series is the only example, other than *Brats*, in which Stan and Ollie literally regress to children, rather than merely behave like them. As such, the ten-second cameo is by far the most interesting of their several guest appearances in other Roach films. Clearly, for such a brief appearance to have any impact or value, the boys had to be immediately identifiable; it was evidently thought no obstacle, and presumably an aid, to recognition that they should appear dressed and behaving as infants. Indeed, their nightshirts are like those frequently worn by their adult personas, while their bonnets relate to their usual feminine traits. The bottle of milk they fight over recalls that in *Their First Mistake*: Stan's greedy drinking from it in that film is repeated here.

Identification of the boys is also aided by Ollie's wave to the camera and Stan's typical head-scratching gesture, confirming that a primary function of the appearance is, like that of the average home movie, to solicit recognition of someone already familiar to the viewer. Yet, just as a home movie provides the pleasure of seeing a person in a different way, there is also pleasure in seeing Laurel and Hardy as babies. The tension between the familiar and the unfamiliar is emphasized by the use of a perverted version of their 'Cuckoo' theme (previously used in *The Devil's Brother* to express Stan's drunkenness). Although the cameo was evidently intended to bolster the prestige of Our Gang, it was not linked to the real children of the film.

Laurel and Hardy's own prestige was enhanced by their next feature, which became one of 1934's ten top-grossing movies. Aesthetically too, **Sons of the Desert** was a great success; it is arguably the finest of all their features, since the comedy arises naturally from the narrative development. There is no feeling of gag set pieces and the film's subtle dramatic and musical elements are interwoven with the comedy. This achievement is all the more remarkable in view of the fact that *Sons* borrows heavily from the team's previous essays in marital discord, notably *Be Big* and *We Faw Down*, in both of which the boys devised elaborate ruses to deceive their wives.

The opening scenes juxtapose the male bonding of the eponymous social fraternity (a meeting of which Stan and Ollie attend) with the female world of the home to which they return afterwards. On the way home, they discuss the likely responses of their spouses when they tell them about the Sons' annual convention in Chicago the following week. The fraternity's Exalted Ruler – perhaps intended as a comic Roosevelt figure – has told them to 'face the situation with determination', but Stan doubts that his wife will allow him to go. In contrast, Ollie brags, 'I go places and do things and *then* tell my wife. Every man should be the king in his own castle.' This view of his marriage seems to be confirmed by a close-up of the nameplate beside the Hardys' front door: 'Mr Oliver Hardy and Wife'. This traditional patriarchy is, however, reversed by the words on the adjacent nameplate: 'Mrs and Mr Stanley Laurel'. But, as the film develops, the matriarchal nature of both households becomes evident. Towards the end, the boys' marginalization in their own homes (and their preference for each other) will be symbolized by their need to spend a night together, hiding from their wives, in the attic shared between the two houses, and then by their further displacement onto the roof.

As the duo prepare to enter their homes, Ollie tells Stan to 'be a man', but Mrs Laurel's usurpation of her husband's masculinity is highlighted by the discovery that she has gone duck-hunting. In the Hardys' neighbouring house, where Stan waits for her, various pleasantries exchanged between husband and wife initially suggest marital harmony, the couple's togetherness parodied by their door number '2222' (compare the phone number '22' in *Twice Two*). Then Ollie, incongruously wearing the fraternity's fez in the living-room, broaches the subject of the convention to Mrs Hardy (Mae Busch): he plays the career card (as in *Their First Mistake*), claiming that the trip will be 'good ... in a business way'. But he's trumped by his wife who, brandishing one of the knives she's polishing, launches into a formidable tirade in which she lays down the law: Ollie will not go to the convention but instead will accompany her to a mountain resort which offers games of bridge and lectures on art. Presumably, the type of climbing she envisages in the mountains is of a social nature. She justifies her need for this holiday by describing how she's been 'slaving day after day, washing and ironing until my fingers bleed'. But her proto-feminist speech is rendered unsympathetic by Busch's grating, rapid-fire delivery and by the fact we only *hear* about her servitude, leading us to suspect exaggeration (in *Pack Up Your Troubles* Ollie's washing and ironing was visualized for us).

Mrs Hardy's supremacy is confirmed when she interrupts Ollie's attempt to assert his authority by smashing a vase over his head, an action that literally speaks louder than his words and reveals him as all mouth. A parallel to this occurs when Mrs Laurel (Dorothy Christie), in hunting gear and carrying a shotgun, returns in time to overhear Stan's claim that, 'I certainly wouldn't allow my wife to wear any pants.' Unlike the men who merely masqueraded as hunters in *Be Big*, she brings evidence (a brace of ducks) of her skill at the masculine pursuit. As in that earlier film, Ollie feigns a nervous breakdown, this time getting Stan to persuade a doctor to prescribe a trip to Honolulu, so that they can secretly go to the Chicago convention. The ruse works, even though Stan has engaged a vet who examines the patient as if he were an animal, administering a horse tablet and tapping his nose to make him swallow – a relatively subtle example of metamorphosis.

The convention scenes are the movie's only weak section, except for the number 'Honolulu Baby', a splendidly tacky parody of contemporaneous Warner Bros. musicals. But the practical jokes played by Charley Chase are presented with insufficient irony (perhaps Laurel, an enthusiastic practical joker in real life, found them funnier), and the revelation that Chase is Mrs Hardy's long-lost brother is not only dramatically pointless but seems too far-fetched in a movie that is otherwise quite plausible, at least by Laurel and Hardy standards.

However, the movie regains its stride with the wives' discovery that the steamship on which the boys were supposedly returning from Honolulu has sunk. 'We've got to face the situation with determination,' says Mrs Laurel, echoing the earlier words of the Exalted Ruler – a link which reminds us that the film's main theme is the conflict between the female world and the male one represented by the fraternity. The women's genuine concern for their husbands' safety contrasts with Ollie's selfishness when, ignorant of the disaster, he complains to Stan that his wife isn't waiting to greet him (she's gone to the shipping line's offices to find out if he's survived the wreck). However, the wives' grief is also subjected to irony: Mrs Hardy says, 'I wish now I'd let him go to the convention', but when she discovers that he did, this wish is replaced by a desire for retribution, combined with a contest between the two women over whose husband will admit the lie.

In the final scene Ollie is bombarded with kitchenware, as Mrs Hardy casts off her role of domestic servitude by destroying its tools. Stan, however, is pampered by his wife because he came clean while Ollie breezily elaborated on the original fib, initially persuading Stan to do the same by threatening to tell his wife that he caught him smoking. As in *One Good Turn*, the tell-tale's scheme backfires. Ollie may have more confidence and cunning than Stan, but this proves to be his downfall when he's found out.

The battle of the sexes continued in **Hollywood Party**, an MGM extravaganza featuring Laurel and Hardy as guest stars. Their main scene takes place at a bar with Lupe Velez who, as they meet her, is already displaying her aggressive nature when she is refused a drink. She screams like a cat and kicks her feet so violently that a shoe falls off. Ollie gallantly returns the shoe, but is rewarded by a clunk on the head with its high heel. Stan removes his shoe to retaliate in kind, but Lupe seizes an egg from a nearby bowl and breaks it into the shoe. Eggs alone are used in the ensuing three-minute sequence, their gooey contents emptied and smeared onto bodies and clothing. The slowness and near-silence (despite the potential for sound) with which this is conducted – each new outrage being carefully inspected – contributes to the scene's peculiarly sensual, almost sexual, quality. This is particularly apparent in the climactic exchange of eggs: Lupe drops one inside the front of Ollie's trousers, then smashes it with her hand from the outside – an action which symbolically reverses the process of heterosexual intercourse. A close-up shows Ollie's face charting the egg's downward progress, contortions of pain and disgust finally yielding to a sigh of relief as the extraneous matter is expelled from his body (another egg, placed down the back of his pants, has made a parallel journey at the rear). The duo's revenge for this is to trick Lupe into sitting on an egg, the comparison with a hen symbolically putting her in her female place. In another way, the moment is reminiscent of that scene in *The Battle of the Century* when Anita Garvin's posterior lands on a pie. In both films the mock-erotic and scatological aspects are only implied, yet they surely contribute to the disturbing quality of the humour.

The team's next short, **Oliver the Eighth,** was the last of their three-reelers, and one of the darkest and most complex of all their movies. Superficially a horror-comedy cashing in on the American success of Korda's *The Private Life of Henry the Eighth* (1933), its real inspiration was probably the popular song, 'I'm Henery [*sic*] The Eighth, I Am', first performed in 1910 by the cockney comedian Harry Champion. In the Laurel and Hardy film, as in the song, the story of the Tudor king and his six wives undergoes a gender twist to become one about a widow's disposal of seven-going-on-eight husbands all called Henry or, in the film, Oliver. The eighth Oliver is of course Hardy, and the widow is played by his most frequent spouse, Mae Busch, whom he calls 'my queen' at one point in the film.

The main and most disturbing part of the narrative – in which Ollie goes to marry the wealthy widow who secretly intends to cut his throat – turns out to have been 'a terrible dream'. It therefore encourages a psychological interpretation and reveals itself as an explicit male fantasy – both masochistic and misogynous – about a woman's revenge on men. Mae's motive is that another Oliver once jilted her on the eve of her wedding, but from Ollie's viewpoint (and after all she is merely a figment of his imagination) her actions seem to be his self-punishment for pursuing a woman for money. He answers Mae's lonelyhearts ad only after Stan explains that the financial benefits of marrying the widow would outweigh any considerations about her possible ugliness.

Ollie's dream, experienced while being shaved by Stan in their co-owned barbershop, is also a guilt-trip for breaking his 'gentlemen's agreement' with Stan: both reply to the widow, but Ollie only sends his own letter. After he returns from the mailbox, concealing the unposted letter, Ollie is hit on the head by a spitoon. This is an accident, caused by Stan, but the blow acts like a physical punishment for his deceit and it's possibly the cause of the mental one (the nightmare) which begins as he sits down to be shaved. The end of the film, when Ollie wakes up as Mae is about to slit his throat, implies that he identifies Stan, holding a razor, with the widow: both, in Ollie's mind, have cause to punish him. Their interchangeability is also suggested earlier in the film when the widow uses Stan's scissors to cut off Ollie's tie, a mock castration.

Mae and Stan are perhaps linked in other ways. Although the boys are sexual rivals for her, the film is also about Ollie's desertion of his existing (business) partner for a new one. He rebuffs Stan's request to accompany him, but instead of a 'three's a crowd' justification he explains, 'My social position won't permit it.' As in *Early to Bed* and *Me and My Pal*, Ollie prioritizes financial and social gain above friendship. However, Stan follows him to the widow's house, making this another variation on the 'bachelor intruder' theme as Stan threatens to destroy Ollie's existing or (as here) impending marriage. Stan's unexpected appearance represents the return of the repressed (and, when he confronts the groom with the unposted letter, the suppressed), which could be seen as the eruption of Ollie's homosexuality at the moment he's about to marry. Indeed, the groom ends up spending his wedding night in bed with Stan instead of the bride. In this climactic sequence Ollie and Mae undergo a symbolic gender reversal, the groom resembling a virginal bride who nervously awaits her spouse's entrance, as Mae prepares to bloody the bed sheets by slitting Ollie's throat. While she unleashes the horrors of heterosexuality on Ollie, Stan gets locked in the closet, repressed once again and unable to assist his partner. Fear of sexuality generally is also suggested just before the boys go to bed, when Stan accidentally fires a shotgun into the seat of Ollie's pyjamas, draped over a chair: 'It's a good thing you weren't inside them,' he comments as they inspect a massive hole around the crotch.

But Ollie's guilt about deceiving and rejecting Stan is tied up with further guilt about his fortune-hunting. Stan's motive for following him to the widow's house is to obtain half of everything Ollie will get – 'I want my cut,' he insists, unaware that what Ollie will get is a cut throat. Stan has swapped the barbershop for some nuts and a brick described as 'solid gold' by the other party, who told him to keep it 'until we got back on the gold standard'. (The United States had abandoned the gold standard in April 1933 – about nine months before this film was made – as part of Roosevelt's first phase of reform, which also prohibited the hoarding of gold.) At the film's climax the brick – a symbol of illusory wealth –

becomes an agent of punishment for Ollie's greed when it falls on his head, rendering him unconscious and in a submissive posture for the widow's revenge.

Appropriately for a film with psychological overtones, much of the comedy derives from the insanity of the widow and her butler, Jitters (Jack Barty), each of whom privately accuses the other of being 'crazy'. In practice, both are: Jitters plays with imaginary cards and serves imaginary soup, which the widow 'eats'. Like the 'breakaway' bottle routine in the later *Pick a Star*, the scene may be intended as a humorous comment on the illusory nature of acting – or, specifically, miming with invisible props – which here is equated with madness. The boys humour their hosts, Stan even returning a 'dropped' card to Jitters and loosening his waistcoat during the meal. However, he eventually exposes the sham (like the boy in *The Emperor's New Clothes*) when he flatly tells them, 'You're nuts!' His choice of metaphor recalls the nuts he received with the 'gold' brick and the imaginary 'crackers' offered with the soup.

Dreams are also central to this film (unlike the earlier *The Laurel-Hardy Murder Case* where the dream ending seemed a cop-out). As the boys lie in bed, awaiting the knife-wielding widow's arrival, the preservation of Ollie's life depends – in a precursor of the 1984 horror movie *A Nightmare on Elm Street* – on his ability to stay awake. They decide to take turns at keeping guard, but Stan falls asleep. Ollie, terrified, wakens him but Stan explains, 'I was dreamin' I was awake and then I woke up and found meself asleep!' The fact that this occurs within Ollie's larger dream testifies to the film's comic complexity about dreaming and waking states.

Oliver the Eighth, like the two films preceding it, was fundamentally a battle of the sexes. But in their next six movies Stan and Ollie's chief adversaries were male, allowing Mae Busch to play relatively sympathetic roles in these films (excepting the feature *Babes in Toyland* in which she did not appear). In the two-reeler **Going Bye-Bye!** she is the vampish girlfriend of a gangster (Walter Long) who has broken out of jail in order to exact revenge on the boys for providing the evidence that put him behind bars. The bones of the plot are borrowed from the silent, *Do Detectives Think?*, but the more interesting comparison is with *Scram!* All three films begin in a courtroom but, whereas the earlier talkie presented the boys as vagrant defendants, here they are upstanding members of the community whom the Judge thanks on behalf of the state for their cooperation in convicting Butch Long. Like *The Midnight Patrol*, *Going Bye-Bye!* – inspired by the John Dillinger manhunt – follows the example of the cop movie cycle in repositioning its heroes on the right side of the law. However, the boys are unaccustomed to this new role: when the Judge asks the defendant to stand up, they automatically rise.

As in *Scram!*, Stan and Ollie need to leave town in order to escape the wrath of their enemy – in this case, the defendant rather than the Judge. But again a fatalistic coincidence takes them to the very place – Mae's apartment – where their adversary lurks. Even after their arrival they remain unaware of this, since Butch, in an effort to hide (he had mistakenly assumed the visitors to be the police), has accidentally been locked in a trunk. His confusion is ironically apt in view of the fact they sent him to jail. Indeed, they are indirectly responsible for imprisoning him for a second time – inside the trunk. Their manly endeavours to extricate Butch are hindered by their feminine association with a bunch of flowers, brought for Mae, which they repeatedly hand to each other during their task. All they manage to do is to provide him with air (by drilling holes), fire (from a blowtorch) and water (from a hose), elements which only fuel Butch's desire for revenge when he realizes the identities of his assistants. Eventually, he escapes from the trunk and rewards the boys for their good turn by breaking off their legs and tying them around their necks, one of the body-distortion gags that end several of the team's films.

Assaults on the body play a major part in their next two-reeler, **Them Thar Hills,** the climax of which reactivates the extended tit-for-tat sessions of silents such as *Two Tars* and *Big Business*. But now people are targeted rather than property, and the motive for the violence is also more personal: the boys come into conflict with Charlie Hall over their (innocent) involvement with his wife Mae Busch – again in a sympathetic role, for she simply lets the 'men o' war' get on with their fighting.

Taking a vacation in the mountains, the boys have got drunk on moonshine (dumped in a well by bootleggers), which they believe to be mountain water – a reversal of the cold tea/liquor confusion in

Blotto. Like the youth-restoring drug in Hawks's *Monkey Business* (see Chapter 1), which everybody thinks is water, the moonshine releases suppressed violence. Hall, however, is not drunk, and resents the fact that his wife has become so in the boys' company. The humour arises largely from the juxtaposition of his grim, silent sobriety with their happy, noisy inebriation, and from the contrast between his straight-laced masculinity ('What do you mean getting my wife drunk?') and the gay abandon of their gender-bending (both the boys wear aprons, and Ollie and Mae have swapped hats).

The weapons consist primarily of food and household items, applied to the body with such creativity that the indignities are usually even greater than the physical discomfort. Stan cuts hair from Hall's forehead, suggesting Samson-like emasculation, and glues it to his chin. The bestial nature of the savagery is also implied: a large plunger is attached to Hall's forehead, so he resembles the legendary unicorn (or is it the horn of the cuckold?); feathers are then applied with molasses to the whole of his body, giving him a bird-like appearance (reminiscent of the evil Olga's state at the end of MGM's 1932 *Freaks*). Hall's actions are less imaginative but more direct and drastic: he upends Stan and Ollie's trailer so they and all their belongings roll out; then he douses Ollie's behind in kerosene and ignites it. Stan obligingly provides the match, an action that may be partly explained by his inebriation and natural dumbness, but is also motivated by the masochism involved in the tit-for-tat ritual.

The sequel, **Tit for Tat**, made six months (and two films) later is rather mechanical and self-conscious, as suggested by its title, which is even incorporated into the dialogue. Stan and Ollie are about to open an electrical store. Their sign, proclaiming 'Open for Big Business', recalls their silent classic even before the link with *Them Thar Hills* is introduced. This occurs when they visit the adjacent shop, a grocery run by the Halls. Recalling their earlier conflict, Hall rebuffs Ollie's olive branch and each party decides to ignore the other. But soon Ollie is accidentally stranded on the window-ledge of the Halls's bedroom and comes downstairs laughing about his predicament with Mae: in a startling double entendre, he tells her, 'I've never been in a position like that before!' Hall misunderstands, warning Ollie in Stan's presence, 'If I ever catch you even looking at my wife again, I'll hit you so hard that *he'll* feel it!' – an unusually explicit acknowledgement of the intense bonding of Stan and Ollie, so close that they feel each other's pain.

And plenty of pain is inflicted by both parties during the rest of the film, as a long tit-for-tat exchange ensues between the 'men o' war' – Mae is excluded again, her husband instructing her to 'keep outta this!' Hall's first physical act is to thrust Stan into a crate of light bulbs, while the boys' last one is to push the grocer into a crate of eggs – the similarity of the acts and the shapes of the objects underlining the cyclical nature of the violence. The goods of both shops are used as weapons against the body: Hall grips Ollie's nose in a curling iron; Ollie flicks cottage cheese into the centre of Hall's face, emphasizing the 'nose for a nose' aptness of the retribution. But some of the exchanges focus on property, the fact that both parties are shopkeepers suggesting a 'trade war' more overtly than *Big Business*. Goods are converted into weapons to destroy other goods, as when Hall mixes several watches in a milk shaker. The boys retaliate by pouring honey onto the money (a combination perhaps inspired by 'The Owl and the Pussycat') in Hall's cash register – an even more direct attack on his business.

Eventually, Hall goes on a rampage of destruction, smashing as many of their goods and fittings as possible. 'Now will you stop?' he suggests, apparently unaware that conflicts are escalated rather than ended by great demonstrations of force. And, despite Hall's vandalism, the boys lose even more of their property in a rather different way: each time they leave their store unattended to go to the grocery, a polite little man calmly steals some of their electrical stock. They witness this, but Ollie decides, 'There are more important things to think of – my character.' Finally their store is totally cleaned out: the price of avenging 'a gross insult' to Ollie's character – and achieving an uneasy truce with the grocer following the intervention of a cop – is enormous material loss. Like *Big Business*, the film portrays as clearly as any anti-war tract how the cost of physical conflict is out of all proportion to the trivial transgressions which cause it. It also suggests the perverse self-destruction of warfare, most tellingly when Hall sprinkles alum over his own marshmallows rather than allow Stan and Ollie (who have been brazenly eating one after another) to continue enjoying them.

Between the production of *Them Thar Hills* and its sequel, the team completed two more films, including their fifth feature, **Babes in Toyland**, an adaptation of Victor Herbert's operetta. A curious movie, it exaggerates some of the contradictions implicit in other Laurel and Hardy films. More than any other, it is set in an escapist fantasy world, created totally (and very stagily) within the studio, yet it reflects the real hardships – even under Roosevelt – of life for many people in 1930s America. Mother Peep is thrown into the street after the mortgage on her home (a shoe) is foreclosed, while Stan and Ollie become unemployed after upsetting their boss. Another strange contrast is made between the childlike innocence of Toyland and the violence of the climactic invasion by the Bogeymen, more gruesome in its detail than anything in the team's horror-comedies. This nice 'n' nasty mixture makes the film the most Disneyesque of Laurel and Hardy comedies, a link emphasized by its incorporation of both plot and musical elements from the famous 1933 Silly Symphony *Three Little Pigs* (in which the Big Bad Wolf was perceived even at the time as a symbol of the Depression). Disney, in turn, borrowed from the 1934 *Babes in Toyland* when he came to remake it in 1961, with comic characters evidently based on Stan and Ollie.

In *Babes in Toyland* they are named Stannie Dum and Ollie Dee, which suggests a comparison between Toyland and Lewis Carroll's Wonderland, which featured Tweedledum and Tweedledee. Indeed, the movie was probably inspired by Paramount's 1933 film *Alice in Wonderland* (Charlotte Henry played the female lead in both). As in their previous musical, *The Devil's Brother*, the boys do not wear their suits and bowlers, but in other respects they retain their usual personas. Their introduction as bed-sharing lodgers (in Mother Peep's shoe) underlines the general continuity, and a more particular connection is made with *The Devil's Brother* through Stan's recollection of the two games he played in that film.

Also present is Stan's gender ambiguity, in yet another variation on the theme of the sabotaged wedding, this time with Ollie as best man. Stan, heavily veiled, replaces the reluctant

Bo-Peep for her enforced marriage to the villainous Barnaby (Henry Brandon). After the ceremony Ollie tells Stan, now unveiled, that he must stay with Barnaby since he's married to him. Stan, a tearful bride, protests, 'I don't want to stay here with him.' His objection, however, is not that Barnaby is a man; instead he blubbers, 'I don't love him.' That he does love Ollie is conveyed in a scene towards the end of the film when, having (apparently) defeated Barnaby again, Stan jubilantly kisses everyone around him, including his pal. This moment is possibly a remnant of Hal Roach's original story for the film, which climaxed with Stan and Ollie 'fall[ing] in love with each other' (quoted in Skretvedt, 1987, p. 279). Incidentally, a hint of taboo heterosexuality in Toyland occurs when Bo-Peep's real lover, Tom-Tom, playfully places her legs in punishment stocks, refusing to free her until she consents to his proposal of marriage. When she does, they kiss and a close-up shows Bo-Peep's legs writhing in the pleasure of her physical and marital bondage.

But on the whole, Toyland is a place of sickly sweetness from which transgressors are instantly banished to Bogeyland. This is the home of the Bogeymen, half man and half animal, a description reminiscent of Ethel 'the Human Chimpanzee' in *The Chimp*. Like her, the Bogeymen seem to be relatives of King Kong: their invasion of Toyland, led by Barnaby, is a return of the repressed, comparable to Kong's rampage in New York. Even specific images from the 1933 monster movie are imitated here, notably when the Bogeymen burst through the gates of Toyland (like Kong on Skull Island), and when one of them enters a house through a window. Eventually, the Bogeymen (like the giant ape) are defeated by the military (an army of wooden soldiers) and by Stan and Ollie firing darts at them. And so Big Bad Barnaby is finally expelled from Toyland – an optimistic New Deal ending which, like the film's frequent pauses for dull songs and other distractions, prevents it from being the quintessential Laurel and Hardy work that their previous feature, *Sons of the Desert*, had been.

Artistic decline is also evident in their next two-reeler, **The Live Ghost**, yet another horror-comedy and probably the weakest of all. Horror plays no part in the first half, a reworking of Chaplin's 1915 two-reeler *Shanghaied*, in which the boys help a tough captain (Walter Long) to recruit men for his supposedly haunted ship. As usual, money is both their motive – they shanghai the men for 'a dollar a head' – and their downfall: they are shanghaied themselves by the Captain. The second half resorts to various plot contrivances to produce the 'live ghost' (a drunken sailor – Arthur Housman – who has fallen into whitewash), which in turn gives rise to the frantic mugging and running around seen in the team's earlier efforts in this genre. The infantile aspect of their personas becomes self-conscious when Ollie, before he sees the 'ghost', tells Stan, shaking and screaming, 'You're getting to be absolutely childish.' On this occasion, the same is also true of the film.

The Fixer-Uppers, made in February 1935 after *Tit for Tat*, is more interesting. Their penultimate two-reeler, it reworks the plot of *Slipping Wives*, one of their earliest silents. The boys are Christmas-card salesmen who meet a bored wife (Mae Busch) anxious to make her artist husband (Charles Middleton) jealous. Ollie, motivated by the wife's offer of fifty dollars, agrees to be her 'lover' (Stan's role in the earlier version). The idea is Stan's, based on a case he heard about in which the husband was so grateful that he gave a lot of money to the other fellow and kissed his wife. Ollie, still wary of the consequences, asks Stan to repeat the story, which this time, in the teller's confused mind, undergoes a gender mix-up so that the husband 'gave his wife a lot of money and he kissed the other fellow'.

A reversal of traditional sex roles also occurs when Mae uses Stan to demonstrate how she wants to be kissed – a clinch held long enough to be interrupted by several cutaways to Ollie, impatiently glancing at the camera and examining his watch. A parody of the extended embraces seen in movie romances, the scene presents Stan as totally passive in Mae's passionate grip, but the experience is so overwhelming that when she releases him he faints. When he revives, he reciprocates the kiss on Mae, producing the same effect. 'Well, she started it,' he points out, to justify his oscular tit-for-tat.

A more serious conflict erupts when the plan is put into action and the husband, instead of forgiving Ollie, challenges him to a duel. In the final sequence Mae's substitution of blanks for the bullets in the pistols allows Ollie to complement his role as lover by playing the gallant hero who faces his opponent fearlessly. A histrionic death scene follows, but Ollie quickly returns to life, and reality, when the victor announces his intention to cut up the body.

The excellence of **Thicker than Water**, the last two-reeler in which Laurel and Hardy starred, makes their total abandonment of this format in favour of features all the more regrettable. A summation of their domestic comedies, it returns to the 'bachelor intruder' theme, Stan's presence as the Hardys' lodger highlighting the power struggle between Ollie and his wife. When Mrs Hardy (Daphne Pollard) asks for the payment for his board and lodging, Stan replies that he gave it to Ollie because 'he said he was boss'. Despite her small stature, the wife quickly clarifies her supremacy, not least by the bird-like action of biting the finger on which her husband attempts to transfer a kiss from his mouth to hers. Furthermore, when Ollie announces that he and Stan are going out to a ball game – 'We businessmen have to relax sometime' – Mrs Hardy compels him to forfeit that masculine pursuit for the feminine one of washing the dishes. Ollie, in turn, dominates Stan by insisting that he dries them. In the kitchen Ollie puts on a floral apron, which emphasizes his submission and feminization. Like *Oliver the Eighth*, *Thicker than Water* appears to have been inspired by a famous cockney music-hall song ('It's A Great Big Shame', sung by Gus Elen), in which the first-person narrator mourns the loss of his pal to a woman 'not four foot two' who bullies her husband into putting on an apron and performing various domestic chores, thereby preventing his involvement in masculine leisure activities.

A lengthy confusion develops between Stan's board and lodging money and the latest payment on the Hardys' furniture. To avoid further payments, Stan suggests that Ollie should buy the furniture outright by withdrawing the entire savings in the Hardys' joint bank account. By encouraging Ollie to take control of the family finances, he sows discord between husband and wife in the area where (in the absence of love) it hurts most of all. From this moment, the film charts a typical downward spiral of events, as Ollie uses the withdrawn savings to purchase an antique grandfather clock at an auction on behalf of a bidder who has forgotten her money. He loses the savings, the clock (crushed under a truck) and finally his consciousness when Mrs Hardy exacts retribution by walloping him on the head with a frying pan – a weapon again obtained from the feminine arsenal of kitchenware, and wielded with masculine force.

Ollie is rushed to hospital, where he is given a blood transfusion, having requested that the blood be taken from his 'best friend' Stan. A mix-up in the operation – a culmination of all the hat, jacket and pants mix-ups in earlier films – means that the boys' appearances, voices and mannerisms interchange in the last, oddly poignant scene of this final two-reeler (perhaps the inspiration for this role-play was Ollie's brief mimicry of Stan in the previous year's *Going Bye-Bye!)*. As the two familiar yet strange figures leave the hospital, the nurse bids them goodbye. They turn to look back at her – and the audience – as they reciprocate the farewell, Stan behaving like Ollie and vice versa. Having transformed into animals, children and women, Laurel and Hardy made their short subject valediction with the most appropriate metamorphosis of all. They simply became each other.

Chapter seven

Decline and Pratfall: The Features (1935–51)

FROM mid-1935 commercial pressures dictated that Laurel and Hardy made only feature-length movies. This new policy, enforced on Roach by the decreasing demand for shorts, undoubtedly contributed to the decline in quality of the team's films, though it need not have done. *Sons of the Desert* had proved they were capable of sustaining a feature without the dubious assistance of heterosexual love interest from other characters, as had occurred in *The Devil's Brother* and *Babes in Toyland*. But **Bonnie Scotland**, a feature shot before the final short *Thicker than Water* but released soon after it, returns to the formula of alternating gag sequences with a serious thwarted-young-lovers plot which is even more irrelevant and intrusive than those in the two musicals. We can only be grateful that a few soppy songs were not also tossed into this jumbled film.

Even Stan and Ollie's scenes are pretty eclectic, borrowing from several of their established genres. The will-reading of the opening scenes recalls the horror-comedy, *The Laurel-Hardy Murder Case*, though since it occurs here in an idealized Scottish village, the horror arrives only with the duo's discovery that they have travelled from America merely to collect an inheritance of bagpipes and a snuffbox. As credentials, they offer the Scottish lawyer their prison records, a reference to their first feature *Pardon Us*, since the cards they produce bear the same numbers that they were assigned in the jail of that film. Before long, however, we are in boarding-house territory as the boys become the bed-sharing lodgers of a formidable Scottish landlady (Mary Gordon) to whom they are unable to pay their rent. As a delaying tactic, Ollie feigns illness, recalling his ruses in earlier domestic comedies. But when this fails, and the duo are evicted, the film enters yet another genre as they join the British Army (by mistake) and the action switches to India!

The movie's second half is therefore another of the team's military spoofs, in this case of Paramount's recently released *Lives of a Bengal Lancer* (1935), though the scenes which appear to have parodied it most closely were scrapped during the editing stage. As a Laurel and Hardy film, *Bonnie Scotland* adds little to their earlier military movies, though it does find a new way of feminizing the boys in this genre: since they belong to a Scottish regiment they wear kilts as part of their uniform.

This contributes to the gloriously camp effect of the sequence in which, ordered by their sergeant (James Finlayson) to clear up litter while a regimental band rehearses 'One Hundred Pipers', they convert their menial task into an impromptu dance, as they did in *The Music Box*. Using their sticks and broom like Fred Astaire with his cane, or holding them to their mouths like wind instruments, they dance gaily round the dustcart. Sometimes they link hands or form a partnership in which one twirls round with the other's finger on his head. When Fin returns, Ollie hastily departs but Stan, so carried away that he fails to notice the sergeant, dances on, lifting his kilt like a provocative can-can girl. But all this frivolity makes a serious point: the improvisation and self-expression of their dance, performed during the military band's rehearsal of a set piece, is a rebellion against the dull conformity and rigid march rhythms of the army. As the sequence closes, the duo dance automatically into a cell, locking themselves in and tossing away the key. They know they must be punished for their transgression of military masculinity (they've also caused Fin to fall in a horse trough), but apparently they feel it's a price worth paying for their gender liberation. Indeed, they defiantly continue their dance inside the cell, insolently throwing the backs of their kilts towards Fin.

An earlier sequence, which might be likened to a dance, also demonstrates the boys' ability to undermine military conformity. As their company march along a road, Stan – whose inability to keep in step has been a running gag – decides that his rhythm is right and everyone else's wrong. He persuades Ollie and other nearby comrades to synchronize with him through a rather effeminate skipping movement, and gradually the rest of the company alter their step accordingly. On a symbolic level at least, it suggests that the duo's anarchy has the power to effect change. The film's final gag is a variation on these two sequences. The boys upset some beehives, the inhabitants of which pursue them through a column of soldiers coming from the opposite direction. The orderly unit is disrupted and the kilted troop transformed into a troupe of dancers who perform exuberant Highland flings (with musical accompaniment) as the bees attack their exposed flesh.

The next feature, **The Bohemian Girl**, was an adaptation of Balfe's 1843 opera about gypsies who kidnap a brutal nobleman's child. Obviously inspired by the previous operatic adaptation, *The Devil's Brother*, it casts the boys again as robbers. This time they are successful ones, particularly when they pick the pockets of an effeminate dandy, whom Ollie (pinching Stan's usual gag) addresses as 'madam'. Ollie convinces an officer that the dandy has robbed *him*: his appropriation of the victim's belongings, including a lorgnette and cane, revives his gentrified tramp image from earlier movies.

Despite the nineteenth-century setting, the film also returns to the formula in which Ollie plays the henpecked husband of Mae Busch, who responds to his affectionate greeting with, 'Don't "honey" me, you big bag of suet – I told you five minutes ago not to talk to me.' Reversing traditional marital roles, she treats Ollie like a slave, making him – and Stan – peel vegetables in front of the caravan while she retires behind it with her lover Devilshoof, suggesting a mirror-like equation between the two couples. Indifferent to her assignation, Ollie does resent her verbal humiliation of him in front of Stan: if Mae prioritizes her lover over her husband, Ollie prioritizes his friend over her. Stan reciprocates later in the film: when Mae tries to seduce him into stealing Ollie's money for her, he replies to her offer to be 'very, very nice' to him by asking, 'Are you gonna be nice to Oliver too?' Stan and Ollie are more important to each other than anyone else in their lives.

Mae deceives her husband in another way too. After she snatches the nobleman's infant daughter Arline, she tells Ollie that he's the girl's father. Gullibly, he believes this despite the fact she's already several years old. When he introduces the child to 'Uncle Stanley', the latter copies the girl's curtsey and tells *Ollie*, 'I hope you grow up to be as good a mother as your father' – a line which crystallizes as well as any Stan's gender and generational confusion. As in *Pack Up Your Troubles*, Ollie does indeed have to play the role of mother, making clothes for Arline and putting her to bed. Mae, who might have taken that role, deserts them both for her lover, informing Ollie in her farewell note that he isn't the father – though grown-up Arline, twelve years later, calls him 'daddy'. By now, however, *she* has assumed a maternal role, cooking breakfast for the boys. Or has Arline, in a sense, become Ollie's new wife? When she gives a rendition of 'I Dreamt I Dwelt in Marble Halls', a song which the Arline of Balfe's opera addresses to her lover, she embraces Ollie after the words, 'you'll love me still the same'. Of course, it doesn't really matter; despite, or because of, the ambiguity, Ollie loves her the same, whether as father, son or husband.

Stan's role in all this is equally ambiguous. When the duo set about rearing the infant, the vacancy caused by Mrs Hardy's departure is implicitly filled by him: as in *Pack Up Your Troubles* and *Their First Mistake*, he becomes Ollie's co-parent. But Stan refuses to be defined as father or as mother: when he sings, his voice alternates between bass and soprano, according to whim. In other respects, he's not a parent at all but still a child in relation to Ollie's father-figure, a situation that is suggested by the latter's paternal speech about how he raised him out of the gutter. Stan's infantile qualities are reinforced by a wine-bottling scene in which he places the siphon, still spouting wine, into his mouth, an image suggestive of a baby sucking on a teat.

The childlike and feminine aspects of Stan's persona invite a comparison between him and the girl, particularly in the scene where the mature Arline kisses Ollie goodbye in response to his question, 'Haven't you forgotten something?' Moments later, Ollie hints that Stan too has 'forgotten something'; he means a dishpan, but instead he receives another smacker. The interchangeability of Stan and Arline becomes explicit in the film's climax when he rescues her from prison by wearing her cloak, though the opportunity for an extended female impersonation is not exploited. The climax proposed in the original script did present him in drag: the boys were to attend a ball at the nobleman's castle by masquerading as a duke and duchess. However, this idea was abandoned, as was the second script's cheaper variation in which Stan, in skirt and shawl, was to become 'Mrs Hardy' for an interrogation at the castle (see Mitchell, 1991).

For **Our Relations**, shot in the Spring of 1936, the team returned to the double-identity theme previously used in *Brats* and *Twice Two*. Having played their own children and each other's wives, they now appeared as themselves and their twin brothers Alf (Laurel) and Bert (Hardy). The film's problem is that its plot, based on a W. W. Jacobs story, requires the two pairs to be sufficiently alike to elicit confusion from other parties. As a result, it soon becomes a disappointingly conventional mistaken-identity farce into which more typical Laurel and Hardy material, such as tit-for-tat, is uncomfortably shoehorned. It demonstrates that a complex plot centred on the duo could be at least as inhibiting as one focused on other characters.

The two sets of twins are at least distinguished by their lifestyles. Stan and Ollie are respectable married men whose bourgeois bliss is established in the domestic opening scene. As they enjoy high tea with their wives, the carousel of teacups which the four endlessly pass to each other suggests the circular, repetitive nature of their lives (recalling the reciprocal goodbyes in *Perfect Day*). By contrast, Alf and Bert are outdoor types, sailors who are described as 'bad lads' by Ollie's mother in a letter he receives from her. She encloses a photograph of the foursome as children but this, and all other evidence of the 'bad' brothers, has to be concealed from the wives. Ollie fears that their wives would sue for divorce if they were to find out about the twins, and he cannot countenance such social disgrace. As he sets the photograph alight, Ollie declares, 'We'll burn our past behind us.' This statement, and Stan's reference to 'a black sheep in their closet', suggests that Alf and Bert are the obverse, rather than the opposite, of Stan and Ollie. The sailors, whose uniforms are black, are the 'dark' side of the bourgeois brothers, soon to be uprooted from their safe world of marital domesticity. Through mistaken identity, Stan and Ollie are plunged into a world of chaos where they become entangled with good-time girls and gangsters.

The use of double identity dramatizes the conflicts that usually exist within the boys by dividing their personas into two, thereby separating their desire for respectability from their devious hedonism. As such, it is an extension of the dichotomy suggested in the mirror scene of *Helpmates*, where Ollie gazes in disbelief at the organizer of the previous night's wild party. *Our Relations* displays several narrative similarities with *Their Purple Moment*, but the girls, entertained in the earlier film by deceitful husbands, are now picked up by bachelor 'bad lads' Alf and Bert, leaving Stan and Ollie's bourgeois morality intact – though that doesn't prevent them being blamed by their wives. The fact that the married men of *Our Relations* are not responsible for their apparent waywardness makes them less fallible and therefore less human. The artificiality of their world is represented by the Pirate Club (where the staff dress as buccaneers), which Stan and Ollie, accompanied by their wives, decide to visit. This contrasts with the unpretentious beer garden frequented by Alf and Bert, real sailors for all their faults.

The wives assault both sets of twins for their apparent misdemeanours: Mrs Hardy (Daphne Pollard) hits Bert on the head with a champagne bottle and Mrs Laurel (Betty Healy) cows her husband into submission by wagging a finger at his face so vigorously that he literally has to bend over backwards. The good-time girls, jealous of their new boyfriends' involvement with these older women, are scarcely less aggressive. Before the final reel, the narrative casually dumps the women to concentrate on the reunion of the two sets of twin brothers, leaving Stan and Ollie's marriages in a very fragile state. But in their male-centred world, underscored in this movie by hints of Freemasonry, women are merely a means to attain respectability. In the film's closing scene each set of twins walks side by side, suggesting that Stan and Ollie are more easily reconciled with their 'dark' side than with their wives. Here, the bonds of brotherhood and masculinity are stronger than those of class and matrimony.

After making a brief, silent cameo appearance as hitchhikers in the Charley Chase two-reeler, **On the Wrong Trek**, Laurel and Hardy began production on the comedy-Western, **Way Out West**. On their way to deliver the deed to a gold-mine, they are again cast as hitchhikers, in a scene which parodies the famous episode of Frank Capra's *It Happened One Night* (1934) where Claudette Colbert halts a passing motorist by raising her skirt. Unsuccessful in his efforts to thumb a lift on passing stagecoaches, Stan rolls up one of his trouser legs and the result, as in the Capra film, is a sudden screeching of brakes.

This moment of explicit feminization is developed later in the movie when, having mistakenly delivered the deed to the devious Lola (Sharon Lynne) and her husband (James Finlayson), the boys attempt to retrieve it. Lola pursues Stan and the deed into her boudoir, where the ensuing struggle parodies film portrayals of heterosexual rape by reversing the genders. As the vampish Lola, shedding the fur from her neck, approaches Stan, he conceals the deed under his shirt, like a silent-movie heroine hiding a valuable in her bosom. Terrified, he attempts to escape by running over the bed, but Lola soon catches him and forces her arm down his shirt. In the ensuing tussle, the pair go under the bed which bounces up and down on top of their writhing bodies – a mock-erotic moment which inverts the traditional positions of bed and bodies during sexual activity. Even more startling is the scene's climax, which cheerfully defies the Hays Production Code's puritanical decrees on bed scenes: after a brief chase around the room, Stan jumps onto the bed and lies down, quickly followed by Lola who, on top of him, thrusts her arm inside his shirt and tickles him into submission, finally divesting him of the deed. However, Stan, still affected by the tickling, continues to laugh hysterically – a sharp contrast to his weeping after the mock-rape in *Putting Pants on Philip*.

Stan's submissive femininity in this film is complemented by Ollie's adoption of a more dominant and masculine role than usual. In the duo's introductory scene Ollie relaxes as he is pulled along on a makeshift land raft by their mule, guided by Stan who carries a backpack similar to that of the servile beast. Much later in the movie, Ollie becomes a schoolmaster to Stan's misbehaving pupil in a variation on traditional corporal punishment. Instructing the miscreant to hold out his hand, Ollie waves the end of a rope threateningly as Stan, cringing and looking away, nervously alternates between proffering and withdrawing his right hand. Finally, Ollie hits him on the head with the rope, but Stan, following the schoolboy ritual to the end, shakes and blows on his hand to reduce the pain, psychologically felt. Unlike the 'schoolroom' scene in *Pardon Us*, this one is effective because the teacher–pupil associations are only implicit.

Yet in the musical numbers Ollie as well as Stan brings a feminine lightness and grace to the traditionally masculine genre of the Western. During an impromptu dance (reminiscent of *Bonnie Scotland*) in accompaniment to 'At the Ball, That's All' sung by a cowboy quartet, they lift their coats as if they were skirts, hold hands and press their bodies against each other. Their second number takes place in a saloon when a cowboy begins to sing 'The Trail of the Lonesome Pine' and Ollie takes over. Stan joins in with his normal voice, then the visual androgyny of the earlier dance receives its vocal equivalent when, by clever dubbing, he continues in the gruff tones of a bass followed by the silvery ones of a lyric soprano (a repetition, in reverse order, of his extreme vocal identities in *The Bohemian Girl*). Song and dance, as in the team's military movies, undermines the genre's masculine values.

Stan's androgynous singing is one of numerous gags in this film which defy reality. The naturalistic games that he played with his hands in *The Devil's Brother* and *The Bohemian Girl* are now replaced by one in which he magically converts his naked thumb into a lighter (an ironic contrast with his inability to perform the simple act of thumbing a lift). He is also able to eat Ollie's hat – in punishment for a rash promise – without ill effects; indeed he makes a meal of the derby, complete with napkin and the addition of salt and pepper. These are moments of spectacle in a film which, in contrast to *Our Relations*, is paced very leisurely and contains a minimum of plot. Even the narrative is converted into spectacle when Stan, towards the end of the film, performs a mimed recapitulation of the story so far, each highlight indicated by a brief gesture or two.

During the production of *Way Out West*, Laurel and Hardy took one day off from their main project to make a guest appearance in Roach's Hollywood-set musical, **Pick a Star**. Their few scenes are rather strange in that they present an image of the team in (the film's version of) real life which is almost identical to their movie personas. As Stan, about to shoot a scene, asks their director (James Finlayson!), 'When am I supposed to look dumb?', his typically vacant look and vocal tone indicate that he will not need to act. In the team's ensuing performance for Finlayson's cameras, they go into a bottle-breaking routine with their old nemesis Walter Long. After the filming is finished, Stan and Ollie (overlapping and perhaps improvising their dialogue) demonstrate to a visitor (Patsy Kelly) that they use harmless breakaway bottles, but a 'real' one is accidentally substituted and the boys are both knocked out. In its play on the confusion between illusion and reality, the bottle gag parallels the film's deceptive representation of Laurel and Hardy. Their final scene, a harmonica-playing contest between the duo, is more overtly fantastic and culminates with Ollie swallowing a tiny harmonica which plays a tune when Stan prods his belly.

The increasing importance of musicals at the Roach studio was reflected in the team's next starring feature, **Swiss Miss**. Laurel and Hardy's scenes are interspersed with several vacuous songs, performed mainly by an operetta composer and his soprano wife whose tedious bickering also holds up the comedy. The result is the weakest feature Laurel and Hardy had made to date. Even their own material is seldom inspired and suffers from its extremely artificial setting, a stagily prettified portrayal of the Swiss Alps. Although the duo are back in their old occupation of door-to-door salesmen, it is hard to care about their efforts to sell their unlikely merchandise (mousetraps) in a context that bears no relation whatever to reality. Having finally sold all their stock to one customer, who pays them with fake banknotes, they order a huge meal at the Alpen Hotel. Informed that there is no apple pie, Ollie asserts his bourgeois pomposity and reprimands the chef. But the discovery that their money is worthless turns the tables: the boys are forced to become hotel skivvies under the supervision of the vengeful chef. The duties they perform for the rest of the film include washing dishes, scrubbing stairs and sweeping floors – 'woman's work', which intensifies their humiliation by feminizing them. Alongside this are suggestions of boyishness, particularly in the short trousers of their Tyrolean costumes and Ollie's bashful courtship of the composer's wife.

The film's two most memorable sequences both involve animals. In a superb piece of solo pantomime, Stan persuades a St Bernard to give him a drink of brandy by playing the role of a stranded climber freezing to death in snow (actually chicken feathers). Still tipsy from the brandy, Stan has to help Ollie move a piano from the hotel to a tree house that lies at the other end of a suspension bridge across a mountain gorge. Halfway, they meet a gorilla, played by Charles Gemora who had played the title role in *The Chimp*. But, unlike Ethel of that three-reeler, the gorilla here is an unsubtle and anonymous creation, its introduction forced and its aggressive behaviour motiveless.

If *Swiss Miss* is one of the poorest of the team's features, their second movie of 1938, **Block-Heads,** is among the best. Eschewing musical numbers and conventional love interest, the film recreates the atmosphere of the shorts by focusing on Stan and Ollie. Indeed, the opening scene, set in a World War I trench in 1917, adapts the separated-young-lovers sub-plot of *Bonnie Scotland* and other features for the boys themselves: Ollie, going over the top with his company, says farewell to Stan, who has been ordered to stay behind and guard the post. Twenty-one years later, Stan is still there, his daily routine including a breakfast of beans eaten at a makeshift table.

When we catch up with Ollie, he is also at the breakfast table, but with his wife (Minna Gombell) in their luxury apartment. Despite the stark contrast with Stan's circumstances, a parallel between the two breakfast scenes gradually emerges: after only one year of marriage, Ollie's lifestyle has become almost as grinding a ritual as Stan's twenty-one-year stint. Wearing an apron for his morning duty of cooking the breakfast, Ollie is not only feminized but treated like a child by his wife, who gives him a daily allowance of seventy-five cents; no wonder he calls himself her 'baby Oliver'. Although the marriage is depicted as reasonably harmonious at this stage, the husband has to be heavily prompted by the wife to remember that today is their first wedding anniversary. Moreover, the uneventfulness of married life is tellingly conveyed by Ollie's banal remark that he 'almost' burned his finger on the bacon this morning.

When he reads a newspaper story about the discovery of Stan, he goes to the soldiers' home to see his old pal. Sitting in a wheelchair with a shortened leg support, Stan has doubled his right leg underneath him. In the long reunion scene which follows, Ollie assumes that his friend has lost a limb in combat. He insists on pushing Stan in the wheelchair and, when told that the chair belongs to another soldier, he even carries him like a babe in arms – a startling visual affirmation of their child–parent relationship. Far from being in bad taste, the 'lost' leg gag (an earlier version of which can be seen in Laurel's 1923 solo comedy *White Wings*) mocks patronizing attitudes to the disabled. Ollie stoically endures Stan's stupidity, his pity outweighing any sense of irritation as long as he believes his pal is wounded. Only when he finally realizes that Stan is able-bodied does he allow his normal feelings to surface. Moreover, Ollie is largely responsible for the misunderstanding due to his embarrassed silence on the subject of the supposedly missing limb. When he asks, 'Why didn't you tell me you had two legs?' Stan's reply, 'Well, you didn't ask me,' is perfectly valid.

Despite this set-back to their renewed friendship, Ollie carries out his original intention of taking Stan home for a slap-up meal. 'My home is your home,' he insists, confirming the ominous suggestion of *ménage à trois* by adding, 'I'm never going to let you out of my sight again.' But in order to reach the Hardys' thirteenth-floor home, the boys must climb numerous flights of stairs, the lift (apparently) being out of order. The exhausting ascent, comparable to that in *The Music Box*, is complicated by several people they meet on the way. A smartly dressed gent (James Finlayson) picks a fight with Ollie, who, observing social convention, tells him they will settle the matter outside. To do this, they have to march down the stairs they have just ascended (the cross-sectional staircase set recalls that in Keaton's *The Cameraman* (1928)), gathering a crowd of spectators en route. 'There's gonna be a fight,' Stan tells everyone in the building: it's one of several events in the film which suggests that the war he didn't know had ended has indeed continued in everyday domestic life. Outside, the fight is soon over, but this display of childish masculine aggression has delayed the husband's re-entry to the potential maturity of his marital home.

At the start of their second ascent, the boys meet Lulu, an old flame of Ollie's from the war. Unaware that he's now married, she has put a note under his door detailing indiscreet reminiscences. Lulu is Stan's female counterpart, a 'friend' from the past who threatens Ollie's present marital harmony. After hurriedly climbing the stairs again, the boys' recovery of the note (before Mrs Hardy sees it) is delayed by a violent encounter on the landing with a young boy who accidentally kicks his football into Ollie's face. In retaliation, Hardy kicks the ball to the ground floor, the boy proceeds to tell his father, who forces Ollie to go downstairs to retrieve the ball. The tale-telling brat, eliciting and mirroring Ollie's infantile pettiness and aggression, is an obstacle, a projection of himself, which must be overcome if Ollie's adult union with his wife is to have any chance of preservation.

But this still leaves the childlike Stan, whose entry into the Hardys' home, after their twelve months of marriage, is like the arrival of a baby (a comparison intimated when Ollie carried him at the soldiers' home). However, this 'baby' will fracture rather than solidify the marriage, for Stan simultaneously assumes the roles of a child and a lover in relation to Ollie (just as 'baby Oliver' did in relation to his wife in the breakfast scene). As the pair enter the apartment, Ollie's key, which is attached to a chain, jams in the lock and he is forced to remove his trousers: 'Gee, that's pretty underwear,' observes Stan, unconstrained by the codes of heterosexual masculinity. At this embarrassing moment, Mrs Gilbert (Patricia Ellis), a neighbour, appears with Lulu's indiscreet note, delivered to her door by mistake. As the movie goes into a remake of the team's first talkie, *Unaccustomed as We Are*, Mrs Hardy, now the nagging wife typical of Laurel and Hardy films, returns from shopping and berates Ollie for bringing home another of his 'tramp friends'. The double meaning implicit in the word 'tramp' suggests that her contempt for Stan is motivated partly by sexual jealousy (she behaves as if the tramp is a lady). After a massive marital row – during which Stan is accidentally locked in the closet – Mrs Hardy packs her bags and storms out to her mother's. 'Let that be a lesson to you,' Ollie advises Stan after her departure, 'never get married.'

Now single, Ollie is determined to cook the promised meal himself, but between them the boys manage to blow up the kitchen and Mrs Gilbert becomes involved in a similar way to her counterpart in the 1929 prototype. Wearing Ollie's pyjamas, she hides as Mrs Hardy returns, more irate than ever on discovering the state of her kitchen. When Ollie announces that he is leaving for Honolulu (an echo of *Sons of the Desert*), she tells Stan, 'Not content with wrecking my home, you want to take my husband away from me.' Mr Gilbert (Billy Gilbert), a big-game hunter, hears the commotion and repeats Mrs Hardy's accusation that Stan is 'a homebreaker' – which, literally, he is, having unwittingly wrecked the kitchen and, earlier, smashed the Hardys' car and garage. Unfortunately, the film peters out with Mr Gilbert's discovery of his wife in Ollie's trunk. The final gag reworks the end of *We Faw Down* – half-dressed men jump out of apartment windows as the hunter fires at the boys, returning the film to the state of war with which it began.

Conflict between Laurel and Roach caused a temporary break-up of the team in 1938–39, during which time Hardy appeared with Harry Langdon, the comedian whose work had been so influential a decade earlier, in Roach's *Zenobia*, a sentimental and appallingly racist comedy set in 1870 Mississippi. Langdon, who had contributed to the script of *Block-Heads*, would also be a writer on the next three Laurel and Hardy films, including **The Flying Deuces**, made in 1939 for the independent producer Boris Morros. Largely set in the Foreign Legion, it begins with a romantic disappointment for Ollie in Paris. His lovelorn manner has distinctly feminine overtones: rejected by Georgette, his intended, Ollie utters, 'I want to be alone' with Garbo-like gravity. However, Stan accompanies him to their hotel room where, as they sit together on a bed, he puts a comforting arm round Ollie. Stan's physical proximity and his gradual consumption of the chocolates bought for Georgette express his restoration (and displacement of her) as Ollie's partner. But the cuddle brings little solace; Ollie lies down and requests smelling salts, like a lady suffering from the vapours.

When Stan jokingly suggests suicide, Ollie takes him seriously, even insisting that his pal accompany him to the bottom of the Seine. Stan baulks at the idea but Ollie counters: 'Do you realize that after I'm gone that you'd just go on living by yourself . . . there'd be no one to protect you?' Indeed, the scene where they try to drown themselves plays like a parody of a lovers' suicide pact, confirming the shift of emotional emphasis from the fantasy heterosexual coupling of Ollie and Georgette to the established relationship between the boys. A curious mock-erotic moment occurs when Ollie's behind, hanging over the edge of the river bank, is stroked by the fin of an escaped shark as it swims by. Initially puzzled, Ollie turns to Stan and indignantly reprimands, 'Don't do that!'

Instead of committing suicide, the boys join the Legion to forget Georgette. On the parade ground they lose themselves in a maze of marching men, reducing the disciplined rows of soldiers to a heap of wandering individuals. They confront the Commandant (Charles Middleton, as in *Beau Hunks*) in his office, adamantly refusing to work for the three cents a day he is offering. But, far from withdrawing their labour, they submit to the humiliating punishment of 'woman's work': washing and ironing the Legion's (almost literal) mountain of laundry. However, Ollie's ironing in this film has none of the feminine finesse he brought to the same chore in *Pack Up Your Troubles*. Their opposition to the Legion's authority is not from the bourgeois feminine standpoint they adopted in *Beau Hunks* but is one of masculine plebeian self-confidence: they address an officer on the parade ground in matey language ('Well, look who's here!') and, to underline their demand for higher wages, they bang on the Commandant's desk. This coarsening of Stan and Ollie's personas forebodes the crudity of the movies they would begin to make a couple of years later.

A rare exception to the movie's prevailing tone is the boys' musical number, which occurs in the context of their decision to leave the Legion. Wearing civilian clothes, they hear a band playing 'Shine On, Harvest Moon'. Ollie sings the lyrics (the themes of nature and heterosexual love contrasting with their man-made environment and recalling the outside world for which they are heading), while Stan dances in front of him. Then Ollie joins his partner to perform a soft-shoe shuffle, raising the bottom of his jacket like a skirt towards the end of the number. The duo's grace and freedom of movement, with its feminine overtones, expresses their opposition to the constricting masculine authority of the Legion they intend to desert. Another moment of feminization occurs later in the film when, Georgette having re-entered the story, the boys hide in her wardrobe which topples over; emerging from the closet, they are clad in her frilly clothes, a more appropriate dress than the legionnaire uniforms they are wearing underneath.

After a disappointing back-projected climax in an out-of-control plane, the film closes with a charming metamorphosis gag: Ollie, killed when the plane crashed, reappears to Stan reincarnated as a horse, complete with moustache and derby. Stan, delighted, hugs the horse, echoing his cuddling of Ollie early in the film and affirming that the duo's love for each other – unlike the heterosexual kind that can be 'forgotten' in the Legion – transcends both death and physical form.

Earlier in 1939 the team had completed a four-reeler for Hal Roach, who was now releasing his product through United Artists instead of MGM. **A Chump at Oxford**, later extended to six reels for the European market, is nominally a spoof of MGM's *A Yank at Oxford* (1938) but it is really no more about university life than *The Flying Deuces* is about the Foreign Legion. Indeed, the opening two reels, shot after the completion of the independent production, conflate the plots of *From Soup to Nuts* and *Another Fine Mess* to allow Stan and Ollie to masquerade as a maid and butler at a high-society dinner party.

Like their films of the early 1930s, the opening scenes establish the social circumstances which have forced the duo to adopt this desperate measure. The initial shots of the boys riding in a chauffeur-driven limousine suggest that they are wealthy, but the image is illusory: they have merely hitched a lift with the friendly driver. Out of work, they go to an employment agency where Stan expresses their willingness to take 'anything you got . . . we're down to our last six bucks'. As they wait, they overhear the clerk's phone conversation with a client, Mrs Vandevere (Anita Garvin), who wants a married couple to serve at her dinner party. Immediately, Ollie – presumably feeling that he and Stan at least fulfil the 'married couple' requirement – says to his other half, 'Too bad you wasn't a woman, that'd be a swell job for us.' Having established the link between gender conventionality and economic security, he glances at Stan's face and tells the clerk that he knows of a suitable couple. Ironically, gender transgression results from the duo's need to conform to society's rules.

By the time they arrive at the Vandeveres, Stan has transformed into 'Agnes', the name and curly wig recalling his maid masquerade in *Another Fine Mess*. However, whereas much of the earlier film's humour derived from his ease and enjoyment in drag, here the comedy arises from Stan's unconvincing assumption of a female role. 'What a strange-looking person!' remarks Mrs Vandevere, who is later even more perplexed by Agnes's uncouth manner of serving the hors-d'oeuvres. More of Stan's masculinity erupts when, his wig slipping off, he wanders tipsily into the dining-room smoking a pipe; the fact that he still wears the maid's uniform makes his appearance bizarrely androgynous. Yet another layer of femininity is shed when he carries out his instruction to serve the salad 'undressed' – a double-entendre gag reprised from the silent, *From Soup to Nuts*. Meanwhile, Ollie has upset the Vandeveres by disrupting the seating arrangement and addressing them and their guests in a relentlessly informal manner ('Come and get it! . . . Okay boys, si' down'). Like much of his behaviour in *The Flying Deuces*, this is a strange departure from the resolute, if flawed, refinement he normally displays.

Having been expelled by the Vandeveres, the boys reappear as street cleaners. 'Well, here we are at last – right down in the gutter!' declares Ollie. But they are not there for long: having accidentally foiled a bank robbery, they are rewarded with an education at Oxford! They arrive at the university in Eton uniforms, an image which – unlike the laboured 'schoolroom' scene in *Pardon Us* – betokens their mental age without forcing the point. Even the pun contained in Stan's response to the criticism that they're dressed for Eton – 'Well, that's swell, we haven't eaten since breakfast' – conveys the priorities of a child hungrier for food than education (crucially, Stan is not aware of the pun). Indeed, there are no scenes of education in the film, the Oxford section of which chiefly consists of the other students' practical jokes of directing the freshers into a maze and to quarters which in fact belong to the Dean.

More interesting is the final section in which Stan, having been hit on the head, transforms into his alter ego Lord Paddington, whose supreme intellect is matched by his athletic prowess. In short, Stan becomes everything that normally he is not. Laurel's characterization is, however, a complex one, reminiscent of his *Putting Pants on Philip* persona in its synthesis of apparently contradictory identities. Lord Paddington bears many hallmarks of Wildean effeteness that border on effeminacy: the nasal tones of his upper-crust English accent; his reference to Ollie as 'old dear'; fussy mannerisms with a long cigarette-holder and a handkerchief; his fastidious taste in tea; the lazy demand to be handed the diary that lies on the table before him. Yet his many sports prizes testify to his physical masculinity, as does his single-handed ejection of a stream of students, including Ollie, through the window of his room.

Moreover, in an inversion of the power dynamic implicit in the boys' normal relationship, the haughty Lord dominates Ollie by making a manservant of him and humiliating 'this coarse person with the foreign accent' through personal criticisms. As in the silent, *Early to Bed*, the duo's friendship is severed by class distinction, but in this case it's Stan who has the upper hand. 'Don't you know me?' pleads Ollie. However, the abrupt resolution, brought about by an external force, has none of the subtlety of the earlier movie's gradual reconciliation: Stan, hit on the head again, suddenly reverts to his normal dumb persona. Ollie, delighted, exclaims, 'Stan, you know me!' and the film ends with him hugging his old pal, just as *The Flying Deuces* concluded with Stan hugging the equine Ollie. Both scenes celebrate the duo's reunion (after a real-life period in which the continued teaming of Laurel and Hardy had been in doubt); if *Deuces* suggested that their friendship could survive Ollie's physical death and transformation, *Chump* shows that Stan's spiritual demise and metamorphosis into an alter ego is a barrier which must be eradicated before reconciliation can be achieved.

The team's last film for Roach, **Saps at Sea**, is a disappointingly crude effort. Made in the last months of 1939, it seems determined to tune into the brassy loudness of the 1940s right from the early scene in a noisy horn-testing workshop. With hindsight, the team's resistance to this brash new world appears to be symbolized by Ollie's 'hornophobia', although this film – unlike its big studio successors – was made under their own creative control. Besides the many gags built around horns, it has a distractingly emphatic musical score and exhibits a tiresome reliance on sound effects. But the most misjudged scene is that outside the horn factory when (as soon as the car horn abates) a crowd of spectators are introduced to laugh loudly at the boys' antics in their car – presumably, an inducement for the movie's audience to do likewise. Earlier films had also included amused bystanders, but either for naturalistic effect (as in the boxing match of *Any Old Port*) or to enhance a character trait (such as Ollie's embarrassment during his problematic phone call in *Blotto*). Here, their presence seems almost as forced as canned laughter on a TV sitcom.

For too much of the film, Stan and Ollie's characters are pushed into the background by gimmicky, mechanical gags that could be executed by any comedian. The best sequence occurs in the cabin of a small boat, tied to a quay, to which the duo have come for the fresh sea air that will improve Ollie's health. Stan, reading 'Old Mother Hubbard' at the patient's bedside, seems to adopt a parental role. Ollie, too old for nursery rhymes, turns over in disgust, but Stan reveals the predominantly childlike part of his own nature by his increasing absorption in the story of Mother Hubbard's 'poor dog'. He's confused, but fascinated, by the anthropomorphic animal whose fluidity – one minute dead, the next 'smoking a pipe' – mirrors his own. This scene also features a real animal, a goat the duo have brought for its milk. Named Narcissus, the goat sleeps in Stan's bed, at one point sharing it with him. Like so many animals in the team's movies, Narcissus seems to be a reflection of Stan, something he loves in order to love himself.

In the film's final section, as in *A Chump at Oxford*, Stan and Ollie are dominated by an outsider. But Lord Paddington's rule was benign compared to that of Nick Grainger (Rychard Cramer), a vicious fugitive whose sadistic brand of masculinity forces the boys into submissive feminine roles. He calls Ollie 'cream-puff', a 'sissy' jibe accompanied by a nose-twisting action that produces an appropriate nasal whine from the victim. Divested of their dignity, the boys become Nick's kitchen slaves, forced to cook a meal for him despite the absence of food on the boat (now out at sea). 'You'll have to take pot luck,' warns Ollie, wagging his finger, like a flustered wife confronted by an unexpected dinner guest.

Having concocted a 'synthetic meal' from string, paint, sponge and other inedibles which they hope will poison their persecutor, the duo are forced at gunpoint to eat it themselves – a particularly masochistic form of tit-for-tat. The realism of this protracted meal scene contrasts oddly with the fantasy of the film's first half and indeed with that of the hat-eating in *Way Out West*, where the joke was that Stan, endowed with magical abilities, enjoyed his bizarre food. But after filming the 'synthetic meal' scene in *Saps*, Laurel recalled, 'It was the first time I gagged, literally, on a gag' (Skretvedt, 1987, p. 368) – and during this nauseating spectacle the viewer has to make an effort not to follow his example.

The boys finally defeat Nick when Stan's playing of a trombone activates Ollie's 'hornophobia', enabling him to punch the thug's face repeatedly – a violent climax somewhat deficient in inventive humour. Released in May 1940, *Saps at Sea* is an unworthy conclusion to the Laurel–Hardy–Roach partnership. Despite its production context, it forebodes the comedians' subsequent 20th Century Fox and MGM movies with Nick's reference to the boys as 'jitterbugs' (the title of one of the Fox films) and his insistence on replacing their real names with 'Dizzy' and 'Dopey' (the big studio movies would sometimes dub them as 'dopes'). This contemporary slang exemplifies the film's attempt to accommodate the superficial values of the new decade; the fact that it does not entirely succeed is its saving grace.

By the summer of 1941, when the team made **Great Guns**, their first movie for 20th Century Fox, the new values have almost totally subjugated the Stan and Ollie we know. The film seems, with hindsight, to be part of Hollywood's preparation for the involvement of the United States in World War II from December 1941. The anti-militarism of the earlier army comedies is no longer permitted and, like the typical early 1940s movie war hero who was 'certain of his identity' (Mellen, 1977, p. 139), Stan and Ollie are required to present fixed rather than fluid personas. Even the comic tensions between the adult and the childlike aspects of their behaviour have been ironed out. Both are unsuitably cast in parental roles (though they are actually servants) to Daniel, a young millionaire. When he joins the army, they also enlist to continue the pampering he has always received from his family, who mistakenly believe he is ill. The supposed humour in this situation, the mainstay of the movie, is that they treat him like an invalid child ('We've been worrying about you – d'you know it's after eight o'clock?') when in fact he's a red-blooded young man, eager to handle guns and gals. The enthusiastic Daniel is a precursor of the ideal male who 'subordinated everything to winning the war' (Mellen, 1977, p. 139). Stan and Ollie are required to emulate his patriotic optimism, even to participate in a triumphant parade after they help to win a mock-battle.

The focus has been shifted from the Stan–Ollie relationship to that between Daniel and the duo, who tend to behave in unison: both of them masquerade as tycoons in order to buy off the girlfriend they see as unsuitable for him. When, in another over-protective effort to prevent Daniel dating her, they get him into trouble with their sergeant, they cry in each other's arms over their cruel-to-be-kind action. But the irony of such childlike behaviour coming from parental figures is lost in this film, where the characterizations enforced by Fox do not possess the subtle ambiguities of the Roach films. The duo are now just silly adults who are not even allowed to show affection for each other. Perhaps Fox were anxious that no homosexual interpretation should be made of their friendship for, in contrast to the Roach military films, Stan and Ollie sleep not only in separate beds but on opposite sides of the room! Meanwhile, a tedious sub-plot of romantic rivalry between Daniel and the sergeant is allowed to develop.

The most characteristic aspect of the film is Stan's close relationship with his pet crow called Penelope. It is an unlikely pet with an unlikely name, but 'Stan and Penelope are inseparable,' avers Ollie. From this bonding arises a gag, when the crow has to be concealed in Ollie's pants during an inspection parade. As Penelope tries to peck her way out of the constraining uniform, she – rather than the boys – disrupts military discipline. Ollie is forced to wriggle, yell and finally jump out of the parade line into the arms of the tough sergeant. 'We like him, sir, he's very nice to us,' explains Ollie to an officer, but the joke is in the tradition of privates' sarcasm about sergeants, not that of subversive sexuality. Indeed, the whole film – apparently conceived as a cash-in on Abbott and Costello's first starring vehicle, *Buck Privates* (1940) – is nearer to a conventional army comedy than a typical Laurel and Hardy movie.

The second Fox film, **A-Haunting We Will Go**, made in 1942, involves the boys with gangsters, con men, insipid young lovers and a stage magician (it has nothing, however, to do with haunting). In between all this the team manage to insert some characteristic bits of business, such as Stan's difficulties with an umbrella and their belated discovery that they cannot pay a restaurant bill. Indeed, the opening scenes are promisingly reminiscent of the Roach years: the duo, having been jailed overnight for vagrancy, are told by the cops to leave town, but their hitchhiking efforts are spectacularly unsuccessful. Dante the magician, to whom they become assistants, restores the otherworldly aspect of their humour, but the gags, involving too many stage props and cinematic special effects, seem forced and very remote from Stan's casual conversion of his thumb into a lighter in *Way Out West*. The final reels are largely devoted to a dreary resolution of the plethora of plots.

Having made two bad movies for Fox, the team turned in late 1942 to MGM, a studio for whom they had worked several times before. However, that had been a decade earlier, and with the creative freedom negotiated by their old boss Hal Roach. **Air Raid Wardens**, the first product of the new deal with MGM, attempts to recruit the duo for the war effort without resorting to the military context of *Great Guns*. That film, made before the United States entered World War II, at least avoided the banality of overt propaganda, but in *Air Raid Wardens* Stan and Ollie are forced to foil Nazi spies – and in a way that allows precious little time for their bumbling brand of comedy. The loss of irony in Laurel and Hardy's humour is therefore even more marked than in the Fox films whose stridency is replaced by dollops of MGM sentimentality, especially when the duo, wrongly accused of being drunk on the job, are dismissed from their posts as wardens. In an excruciating sequence that tries for undiluted Chaplinesque pathos, Stan, on the verge of tears, makes an apologetic speech: 'I guess we're not smart like other people. But if we can do something for our country by not doing this work, we'll do that too. We'll do anything that Uncle Sam tells us to do.' The genuine tragedy here is that the words mirror Laurel's unhappiness about working on this movie: 'We do what they tell us and we go home. They don't care whether we're funny or whether we're not.' (Recollected by the Roach studio editor Bert Jordan and quoted in Skretvedt, 1987, p. 392.) When the boys return their warden equipment, we could equally be watching two great film-makers being forced to relinquish the tools of their trade – and the souls of their characters – in order to produce garbage like *Air Raid Wardens* for Uncle Sam.

Perhaps due to the presence of two members of the old Roach stable on the writing team, the film is, superficially, closer to those of the classic years than its Fox predecessors. Its narrator introduces Stan and Ollie as a 'couple' and, later, the boys have a bed-sharing scene. Edgar Kennedy is brought in for two tit-for-tat routines, both poorly conceived and directed (the absence of background music does not help either). Oddly, the film's best scene is a reworking of the crow-in-the-pants gag in *Great Guns*. Stan befriends a stray dog in the street as he and Ollie are about to enter a public meeting. 'I'll see you when we come out,' he informs the mutt – the point being not so much that Stan treats it as a human but that he regards it as his equal. However, the dog follows them into the meeting and its barking contributes to their (accidental) disruption of the proceedings. The boys try to muzzle the mutt by stuffing it under Stan's jacket but, like the crow, it tries to break out of its confinement, poking its tail through a gap. The animal within Stan finally erupts: the dog jumps to the floor, Stan echoing its movements by following on his hands and knees. They move towards the town's banker, who is in the middle of delivering a pompous speech, and between them the dog and Stan literally topple him. Perhaps the banker was originally supposed to be one of the Nazi spies: his reference (in the finished film) to Stan and Ollie as 'misfits ... accidents ... with these men we can never achieve perfection' smacks of fascistic racism. Anyway, it seems to have been clear to Laurel and Hardy that they could not achieve perfection – or even mediocrity – at MGM. They returned to Fox.

Jitterbugs, made there in 1943, has often been rated as the best of their post-Roach films. Yet – as the title suggests – it is the one which, more than any other, tries to create humour from their clash with the stridency of the 1940s. During the opening credits swing music blares from the soundtrack, heralding the several production numbers that appear later in the movie, designed to showcase the singer Vivian Blaine. We are also asked to believe in the boys as a two-man 'zoot-suit' band with a swinging sound comparable to that of Harry James. As Ollie blows a hot trumpet and Stan bashes percussion, the distance from the desperate street musicians of earlier films seems immeasurable. Fortunately, the band gimmick is soon ditched, albeit in favour of an over-complex plot about con men trying to outwit each other.

This does at least allow the duo to perform a series of impersonations. In the first Ollie is Colonel Bixby, an old-style Southerner, and Stan is his 'butler, valet and general factotum Potts' – a revival of the master–servant masquerade in *Another Fine Mess*, but without the gender complexity of Stan's interchangeable butler and maid. As Potts, Stan is mistaken for 'Bixby' by a scheming vamp, but the material here is feeble. The scene develops by bringing in Ollie, as the 'Colonel', while Stan, gradually getting drunk, hides under the sofa on which 'Bixby' and the woman (both trying to seduce each other) are sitting. From under the sofa emerges Stan's hand, which Ollie fondles and kisses, believing it to be the woman's. But the gag is virtually ruined by the direction and editing, which fail to clarify the reason for Stan's proffering of his hand. Is he reaching for another drink (in which case the trajectory of his arm is unconvincing) or has his inebriation made him playful? Compared to Ollie's massaging of Stan's foot, mistaken for his own, in *Beau Hunks*, this gag seems muddled, contrived and lacking in emotional and sexual resonance.

More amusing is the film's second half in which Stan eschews the role of Potts for that of Blaine's Aunt Emily from Boston, supposedly 'Bixby's' future wife. Stan is initially resistant: 'I'm not gonna be a dame,' he avers, and his first efforts (in private) show him doggedly preserving his masculine gait. However, Ollie is able to give him lessons in ladylike deportment. Walking, hand on hip, with an elegant wiggle, Ollie draws on the fund of femininity underlying his own persona, the facile incorporation of 'Bixby's' cane in his demonstration suggesting that, on this occasion, he can transfer genders more easily than Stan. But later in the film, Stan becomes absorbed and carried away, as usual, in his female impersonation: giggling with the gangsters they are trying to outsmart, he exclaims, 'I feel so gay!' Generally, though, his performance as Aunt Emily emphasizes upper-class rather than feminine details: the English accent he assumes for the role is similar to that of Lord Paddington in *A Chump at Oxford*.

In the final sequence, set on a showboat, Stan's impersonation becomes the basis for jokes which reflect 1940s popular culture. As Ollie walks with an apparently tipsy 'Aunt Emily', a passer-by observes, 'Nice goin', sister.' Ollie retorts, 'It's not my sister – my mother': one of several instances in the film when the slang of the period is interpreted literally by the boys (though usually by Stan). A little later, the duo are forced onto the boat's dance floor where they perform an updated version of the scene in *That's My Wife* which satirized 1920s dance crazes. Here, the swing era's jive styles are even more wildly athletic, but the overall effect is marred by obvious use of doubles in long shots.

Around this period, the team made a five-minute silent appearance in **The Tree in a Test Tube,** a documentary colour short for the US Department of Agriculture. Like naughty schoolboys, they empty their pockets (and a suitcase), to enable the pedagogic narrator Pete Smith to explain the use of wood products in a wide variety of everyday objects. The contrast between Laurel and Hardy's leisurely mime and Smith's rapid-fire, wisecracking commentary exemplifies the collision between the duo's visual style of humour and the verbal approach demanded by the brash 1940s. As they hold the items before the camera, the viewer senses that the comedians could build a sight gag around each one, but the garrulous narrator hurries them on to the next object.

In their next effort for Fox they play the eponymous roles in **The Dancing Masters.** We are told that they teach all types of dance, but the hectic modern style seen in *Jitterbugs* is now replaced by demonstrations of ballet – much more suited to the team's old-world refinement. 'Gracefulness is everything,' is the advice given to the all-female students by Ollie, clad in a baggy satin costume with frills at the front. Meanwhile, Stan, in tights and a tutu, performs 'The Dance of the Pelican', curtseying to his girls at the end of his demonstration. The name of Stan's number suggests his affinity with the animal world (more specifically, it continues his bird association from *Great Guns*), but the high camp of the film's dancing-school segment emphasizes the boys' feminization. When Stan gets his foot stuck to the wall during a bar exercise (a gag sloppily set up with a close-up of glue being spilt by an otherwise invisible man), aid is provided by Ollie, now wearing a grass skirt for his hula dancing class. And, later, Stan tucks banknotes – received from one of the few pupils who pay – under his bodice.

Financial difficulties dominate from this point on. The original story outline was called 'A Matter of Money', but in the finished film, at least, there is little sense that money really matters. The boys' need for it (to pay their landlord and to assist an inventor friend) simply provides a pretext for squeezing a number of routines from the Roach years into the narrative, notably the auction sequence from *Thicker than Water* which now has some extra details. When the auctioneer brings down his hammer on a sale, Stan rises and says, 'Yes, your honour' – a relatively subtle joke which is unfortunately wasted in this movie where the duo are not vagrants.

Indeed, they are highly domesticated, judging from a sequence which reinforces their feminization through housework. Ollie uses a feather duster while Stan, wearing his ballet costume like an apron, attempts to operate a vacuum cleaner. Another scene provides a more subtle hint of the duo's marital status as they hide under separate beds in which a husband and wife are trying to sleep. The imagery suggests a comparison between two middle-aged couples, the heterosexual one on top dominating and concealing the pair of men. Unfortunately, such moments are rare in a poorly constructed film that climaxes with another back-projected sequence, the runaway showboat of *Jitterbugs* here replaced by a runaway bus that somehow finds its way onto a rollercoaster.

The penultimate Fox movie, **The Big Noise**, made in 1944, marks the nadir of the series. The writer's dearth of imagination is foreboded by the duo's introductory scene, virtually repeating one from *The Dancing Masters*, in which Stan (with vacuum cleaner) and Ollie (with feather duster) confuse a doorbell with a ringing telephone. The boys soon abandon their job as cleaners to become private detectives, engaged by a crazy inventor who has developed a super-bomb (shades of the atomic race). Several routines are clumsily reworked from Roach pictures, including the cramped sleeping-car scene in *Berth Marks*. Here, it is even more tedious than in the original, despite extra touches such as Stan's admonition, 'You're on my side' (the boys have slept together so often that they now have regular 'sides') and the introduction of a drunkard which leads to a three-men-in-a-bed routine. The movie concludes with yet another back-projected climax, this time in a runaway plane, out of which the boys parachute just in time to drop the bomb on an enemy submarine. Little to interest Laurel and Hardy connoisseurs here.

There is not much more to recommend in **Nothing But Trouble,** the product of a disastrous return to MGM. Like *Air Raid Wardens*, the film differs from the Fox films only in its obnoxious attempt to introduce pathos, on this occasion in the shape of Chris, a boy whom Stan and Ollie befriend without realizing he is a king. They are assigned sentimental dialogue which crudely tries to enforce and explain their relationship to children. Having refereed a football match for a group of boys, Ollie remarks, 'We just like to see kids have fun,' followed by Stan's even blander statement, 'Yeah, we think kids are nice.' Most of the film follows this pattern, but the script seems unclear whether it wants them to be the orphaned Chris's pals or his surrogate parents. During the football match, Stan is bewildered and frightened by the speed and aggression of the players – like a small child out of his depth with older lads – but this hardly accords with the more 'serious' scenes in which he adopts a paternal role, protectively putting his arm round Chris when the three spend a night in a mission. Yet even the role of parents is denied the duo in this film: when they discover Chris's true status, Stan observes, 'He's a king and we're just nobody.'

Even if the writers of these later films had recognized Stan's subtler childlike qualities, his age – he was now in his mid-fifties – made it increasingly difficult for him to display them. This would have been less problematic if he had been allowed to return to the whiter make-up used at Roach instead of the more naturalistic one now forced on him. Although King Christopher does not reject his old pals, as Shakespeare's King Henry rejects Falstaff, Henry's famous words are as sadly appropriate for Laurel as for Falstaff: 'How ill white hairs become a fool and jester!'

The duo were more successful when it came to suggesting their animal qualities. In one particular scene they attempt to steal a steak from a caged lion in a zoo. Ollie tries to distract it by pretending to be another lion; he crouches and yowls. Stan suggests he should be 'a lady lion' so Ollie, after an effeminate wiggle of the head, yowls at a higher pitch. But it is Stan who undergoes the more complete metamorphosis when, frightened by the real lion, he suddenly leaps like a terrified cat onto the top of a very high wall, where he is found on all fours.

In the movie the duo play a chef and butler, and in the opening shots we find them queuing with other unemployed men. Unable to find any vacancies, they travel around the world, fruitlessly searching for work. On their return, they find the queues at the employment agency are longer than ever. 'It's even worse than in 1932,' comments Ollie, unaware that now the queues are composed of wealthy householders competing with each other during the wartime shortage of servants. The social context of the Depression shorts is therefore explicitly reversed, though the food shortage (from which the steak-stealing scene arises) is common to both eras. But once the boys find employment, credibility goes out the window – as do Stan and Ollie themselves in a poorly staged vertiginous climax that recalls Harold Lloyd and their own silent, *Liberty*.

In the autumn of 1944, the team returned to Fox to make **The Bullfighters**, their final American film and arguably the best of their post-Roach efforts, partly because the secondary characters on this occasion do seem to be there to support Laurel and Hardy, not vice versa. Although the boys are private detectives in Mexico City on the trail of a certain Larceny Nell, the film is really a reworking of *Going Bye-Bye!* as they try to escape the revenge of an innocent man who was once sent to prison on the strength of their testimony. It's also another of their dual-identity films, but this time only Stan, the exact double of Spanish matador Don Sebastian, has two roles. Like Lord Paddington in *A Chump at Oxford*, the haughty Sebastian is the antithesis of Stan's normal persona. The macho matador is the idol of Mexico City's ladies, so Stan, arriving there before him, becomes the object of their sexual interest. But when a female admirer kisses him, Stan's only response is to faint. Revived by Ollie, he puts his arms round his pal and kisses him instead of the woman. Much later, we see the real Sebastian answer a female advance with a devastating heterosexual embrace. The matador's heroic manner is also alien to Stan who is nevertheless – by virtue of a string of plot contrivances – forced to impersonate him. Bowing to his public in a nightclub, Stan punctures the image he is trying to project by banging his lowered head on a table. Unfortunately, the film's climax is feeble and confused, with both Sebastian and a drunken Stan sent into the bullring.

Earlier, there are a couple of tit-for-tat sequences worthy of mention, the best of which is a nicely paced water-throwing altercation at a fountain in a hotel lobby. The other, a reprise of the *Hollywood Party* egg-breaking scene, suffers from crude sound effects and intrusive musical comments. The routine is also bowdlerized – no eggs are put down Ollie's pants this time – and the overall effect is to remove the sensuality that makes the original so memorable.

A final reminder of earlier days comes with the film's bizarre ending (a variation on that of *Going Bye-Bye!*), which defines it as a 'narrative of failure' like most of the Roach movies. The boys are caught by their knife-wielding nemesis who fulfils his threat to skin them alive: in the last shot, Stan and Ollie appear as mere heads perched on top of walking skeletons. Laurel and Hardy's Hollywood career thus concluded with a comic, yet sadly apposite, image of death in life; as in all their films of the last four years, only the bare bones of their established screen personas are visible.

After *The Bullfighters*, the team shot no more movies together (Hardy made two solo appearances) until 1950 when work began on **Atoll K,** a troubled international co-production which provided a melancholy coda to their cinematic career. Like several of their Roach films, it begins with an inheritance, in this case chiefly consisting of a yacht and a Pacific island, the estate's money largely disappearing in taxes. Much of the movie takes place on the boat, which eventually founders in a storm, leaving the boys and two male companions on a newly formed atoll. Their Utopian beachcombing existence is complicated first by the arrival of a temperamental female singer, then by the discovery of uranium on the island. The latter part of the movie seems to take its inspiration from the 1949 Ealing comedy, *Passport to Pimlico*, the quintet forming their own republic in which there are no laws or money. Unfortunately, opportunistic adventurers destroy their anarchic ideals and the atoll sinks.

Despite the unusual element of political satire, Stan and Ollie's characterizations and most of the gags are much more in line with their earlier work than their 1940s films. Something of the warmth of the Roach years is rekindled when Ollie, hurt by a remark from Stan, rebukes his surrogate child by shaming him: 'Haven't I always taken care of you? You're the first one I think of.' Stan, suitably chastened, attempts a reconciliation by tentatively tapping the back of his protector, then dabbing Ollie's eyes with a handkerchief and blowing his nose for him – gestures which suggest their father–child relationship is interchangeable. Indeed, later in the film, Stan assumes a proudly parental role in relation to a pet lobster, which he bounces like a baby and burps on his shoulder. But, like a child whose doll is a mirror image, he also empathizes with the crustacean: they sleep together, sharing a pillow.

Enjoyment of *Atoll K* is severely mitigated by abysmal production values, crude dubbing of the supporting players and above all by Laurel's emaciated appearance and slurred speech – very ill, he was hospitalized at one point in the eight months of production. It's a relief when the end of the movie is heralded by the duo's arrival on their inherited Pacific island. This final image of the team's cinematic oeuvre is not a Utopian one (they are faced with more taxes, prompting Ollie's last delivery of the 'another nice mess' line), any more than this film proved to be the paradise of freedom for which they had hoped after their experiences with big studios. Instead, it presents an image of exile for Laurel and Hardy, the comedians whom no film studio understood after 1940, and the ultimate portrayal of their creations Stan and Ollie as society's outcasts, living on their private island yet still harrassed by the law. But it is also an image of togetherness which recalls the emblem chosen for the flag of their anarchic republic: a heart pierced by an arrow.

The magic of Laurel and Hardy is their love for each other. — John Landis (1978, p. 16)

It is safe to say that no one in films has been loved so universally and for so long as Laurel and Hardy. — Charles Barr (1967, p. 6)

Maybe people loved our pictures the way they do because we put so much love *in* them. — Stan Laurel (quoted in McCabe, 1989, p. 205)

Appendix

A Laurel and Hardy Filmography and Concordance

DETAILED filmographies can be found in most existing books about Laurel and Hardy. Instead of duplicating these, I offer something different: a numbered list of the 106 titles in which both comedians appeared, given in the order they were made, followed by a 'concordance' of selected images, gags, props, situations, professions, characters and catch-phrases from these films. Each entry is accompanied by numbers which refer to those preceding the titles in the filmography.

While it is possible that there may be a few unintentional omissions in a listing of this scope and complexity, fault-finders should note that the selection of subjects to be covered, and the depth with which each one is treated, have necessarily been a matter of personal choice. I have not, for example, tried to list every film in which a car appears, only those in which Stan and/or Ollie drive one, or in which the vehicle is integral to a gag. Since the interest of this concordance resides mainly in establishing connections – Laurel and Hardy reworked some of their gags several times – I have concentrated on logging features that recur, rather than those confined to one or two films. However, the briefer entries may enable the reader to identify a film from one remembered image or scene. Naturally, for films where Laurel and Hardy do not appear throughout, the emphasis is very much on their contributions. However, their pre-teaming films are considered in their entirety, since even scenes which do not involve them may have influenced their later work. 'LH' denotes that the entry is definitely restricted to Laurel and/or Hardy's participation.

In the few instances where the complete films are no longer available, I have relied on existing synopses and stills for details of their content. Where films are now available in longer (English-language) versions than the original release prints, I have taken the extra material into consideration. Slight variants are included for the catch-phrases.

Films are two-reel Hal Roach productions except where stated otherwise. The original release date, where known, is given after each title.

Filmography

1. *The Lucky Dog* (1922) Produced by G. M. Anderson.
2. *45 Minutes from Hollywood* (26/12/26)
3. *Duck Soup* (13/3/27)
4. *Slipping Wives* (3/4/27)
5. *Love 'Em and Weep* (12/6/27)
6. *Why Girls Love Sailors* (17/7/27)
7. *With Love and Hisses* (28/8/27)
8. *Sailors, Beware!* (25/9/27)
9. *Do Detectives Think?* (20/11/27)
10. *Flying Elephants* (12/2/28)
11. *Now I'll Tell One* (5/10/27)
12. *Sugar Daddies* (10/9/27)
13. *The Second Hundred Years* (8/10/27)
14. *Call of the Cuckoos* (15/10/27)
15. *Hats Off* (5/11/27)
16. *Putting Pants on Philip* (3/12/27)
17. *The Battle of the Century* (31/12/27)
18. *Leave 'Em Laughing* (28/1/28)
19. *The Finishing Touch* (25/2/28)
20. *From Soup to Nuts* (24/3/28)
21. *You're Darn Tootin'* (21/4/28)

22. *Their Purple Moment* (19/5/28)
23. *Should Married Men Go Home?* (8/9/28)
24. *Early to Bed* (6/10/28)
25. *Two Tars* (3/11/8)
26. *Habeas Corpus* (1/12/28)
27. *We Faw Down* (29/12/28)
28. *Liberty* (26/1/29)
29. *Wrong Again* (23/2/29)
30. *That's My Wife* (23/3/29)
31. *Big Business* (20/4/29)
32. *Double Whoopee* (18/5/29)
33. *Bacon Grabbers* (19/10/29)
34. *Angora Love* (14/12/29)
35. *Unaccustomed As We Are* (4/5/29)
36. *Berth Marks* (1/6/29)
37. *Men O' War* (29/6/29)
38. *The Hollywood Revue of 1929* (23/11/29) MGM. 120 minutes.
39. *Perfect Day* (10/8/29)
40. *They Go Boom* (21/9/29)
41. *The Hoose-gow* (16/11/29)
42. *The Rogue Song* (17/1/30) MGM. 115 minutes.
43. *Night Owls* (4/1/30)
44. *Blotto* (8/2/30) 3 reels.
45. *Brats* (22/3/30)
46. *Below Zero* (26/4/30)
47. *Hog Wild* (31/5/30)
48. *The Laurel-Hardy Murder Case* (6/9/30) 3 reels.
49. *Pardon Us* (15/8/31) 56 minutes. (65 minutes preview print exists.)
50. *Another Fine Mess* (29/11/30) 3 reels.
51. *Be Big* (7/2/31) 3 reels.
52. *Chickens Come Home* (21/2/31) 3 reels.
53. *Laughing Gravy* (4/4/31) (3-reel versions exist.)
54. *The Stolen Jools* (4/31) Presented by National Variety Artists.
55. *Our Wife* (16/5/31)
56. *Come Clean* (19/9/31)

57. *One Good Turn* (31/10/31)
58. *Beau Hunks* (12/12/31) 4 reels.
59. *On the Loose* (26/12/31)
60. *Helpmates* (23/1/32)
61. *Any Old Port* (5/3/32)
62. *The Music Box* (16/4/32) 3 reels.
63. *The Chimp* (21/5/32) 3 reels.
64. *County Hospital* (25/6/32)
65. *Pack Up Your Troubles* (17/9/32) 68 minutes.
66. *Scram!* (10/9/32)
67. *Their First Mistake* (5/11/32)
68. *Towed in a Hole* (31/12/32)
69. *Twice Two* (25/2/33)
70. *The Devil's Brother* (5/5/33) 90 minutes.
71. *Me and My Pal* (22/4/33)
72. *The Midnight Patrol* (3/8/33)
73. *Busy Bodies* (7/10/33)
74. *Wild Poses* (28/10/33)
75. *Dirty Work* (25/11/33)
76. *Sons of the Desert* (29/12/33) 68 minutes.
77. *Hollywood Party* (1/6/34) MGM. 68 minutes.
78. *Oliver the Eighth* (2/34) 3 reels.
79. *Going Bye-Bye!* (23/6/34)
80. *Them Thar Hills* (21/7/34)
81. *Babes in Toyland* (30/11/34) 79 minutes.
82. *The Live Ghost* (8/12/34)
83. *Tit for Tat* (5/1/35)
84. *The Fixer-Uppers* (9/2/35)
85. *Bonnie Scotland* (23/8/35) 80 minutes.
86. *Thicker than Water* (8/35)
87. *The Bohemian Girl* (14/2/36) 70 minutes.
88. *Our Relations* (30/10/36) 74 minutes.
89. *On the Wrong Trek* (6/36)
90. *Way Out West* (16/4/37) 65 minutes.
91. *Pick a Star* (21/5/37) 70 minutes.
92. *Swiss Miss* (20/5/38) 72 minutes.
93. *Block-Heads* (19/8/38) 58 minutes.
94. *A Chump at Oxford* (16/2/40) 63 minutes.

95. *The Flying Deuces* (20/10/39) 69 minutes. Produced by
     Boris Morros.
96. *Saps at Sea* (3/5/40) 57 minutes.
97. *Great Guns* (10/10/41) 20th Century Fox. 74 minutes.
98. *A-Haunting We Will Go* (7/8/42) 20th Century Fox.
     67 minutes.
99. *Air Raid Wardens* (4/43) MGM. 67 minutes.
100. *Jitterbugs* (11/6/43) 20th Century Fox. 74 minutes.
101. *The Tree in a Test Tube* (1943) US Dept. of Agriculture.
     One reel.
102. *The Dancing Masters* (19/11/43) 20th Century Fox.
     63 minutes.
103. *The Big Noise* (9/44) 20th Century Fox. 74 minutes.
104. *Nothing But Trouble* (3/45) MGM. 70 minutes.
105. *The Bullfighters* (18/5/45) 20th Century Fox. 69 minutes.
106. *Atoll K* (21/11/51 – France) Franco London Films
     SA/Films EGE/Films Sirius/Fortezza Film. 98 minutes.
     (1952 UK version 82 minutes.)

Concordance

Aircraft	93, 95, 97, 103, 105
Alcohol	1, 2, 4, 24, 44, 49, 66, 70, 76, 80, 84, 87, 88, 92, 94, 95, 99, 100, 102, 105
Amusement park	12
'Another nice mess'	48, 49, 50, 52, 67, 76, 78, 79, 81, 82, 85, 86, 88, 95, 96, 98, 100, 104, 105, 106
Apes	63, 75, 92
Apple	9, 14, 41, 76, 99
Aprons (LH)	39, 55, 60, 65, 80, 86, 93, 102, 106
Army	7, 65, 85, 93, 97
Attachment officers	33
Auction	57, 86, 102
Axe	41, 52, 57, 62, 80
'Bachelor intruder'	23, 30, 35, 44, 55, 60, 67, 71, 78, 86, 93
Banana skin	17, 20, 38, 87, 94, 96, 102
Bandits	42, 70, 91
Barbers	78
Bat	26, 48, 106
Baths/footbaths	2, 3, 4, 5, 8, 9, 14, 34, 40, 45, 49, 51, 52, 53, 56, 75, 76, 80, 96

Bibliography

In the following list, publication details are for the edition to which page references have been given.

Agee, James (1949), 'Comedy's greatest era', in *Agee on Film*. Perigee Books, New York, 1983.

Barr, Charles (1967), *Laurel and Hardy*. Studio Vista, London.

Bergman, Andrew (1971), *We're in the Money: Depression America and Its Films*. Harper & Row, New York.

Everson, William K. (1967), *The Films of Laurel and Hardy*. Citadel Press, New York.

Everson, William K. (1978), *American Silent Film*. Oxford University Press, New York.

Grierson, John (1946), 'The logic of comedy', in *Grierson on Documentary*. Faber & Faber, London, 1966.

Howes, Keith (1993), *Broadcasting It*. Cassell, London.

Keaton & Samuels (1960), *My Wonderful World of Slapstick*. Allen & Unwin, London.

Kerr, Walter (1975), *The Silent Clowns*. Alfred A. Knopf, Inc., New York.

Landis, John (1978), 'Laurel & Hardy: Brotherly antics', in *Close-Ups* (ed. Danny Peary). Workman Publishing, New York.

McCabe, John (1966), *Mr Laurel and Mr Hardy*. Signet, New York.

McCabe, John (1975), *The Comedy World of Stan Laurel*. Robson Books, London.

McCabe, John (1989), *Babe: The Life of Oliver Hardy*. Robson Books, London.

McCabe, John, Kilgore and Bann (1975), *Laurel and Hardy*. W.H. Allen, London.

Mast, Gerald (1979), *The Comic Mind: Comedy and the Movies*. University of Chicago Press, Chicago and London.

Mellen, Joan (1977), *Big Bad Wolves: Masculinity in the American Film*. Elm Tree Books, London.

Mitchell, Glenn (1991), 'The Bohemian Girl: From script to screen', *The Laurel & Hardy Magazine*, 3(4), Helpmates UK (Sons of the Desert).

Rheuban, Joyce (1983), *Harry Langdon: The Comedian as Metteur-en-Scène*. Associated University Presses, London and Toronto.

Rosow, Eugene (1978), *Born to Lose: The Gangster Film in America*. Oxford University Press, New York.

Russo, Vito (1981), *The Celluloid Closet: Homosexuality in the Movies*. Harper & Row, New York.

Skretvedt, Randy (1987), *Laurel and Hardy: The Magic Behind the Movies*. Apollo Press, London.

Wood, Robin (1968), *Howard Hawks*. Secker & Warburg, London.

Wyatt, David (1990), 'Now I'll tell one . . . the discovery of a new Laurel & Hardy film', *The Laurel & Hardy Magazine*, 2(12).

Other sources

Everson, William K. (1971), *The Films of Hal Roach*. Museum of Modern Art, New York.

Lahue, Kalton C. (1966), *World of Laughter: The Motion Picture Comedy Short 1910–1930*. University of Oklahoma Press, Norman.

Lahue, Kalton C. and Gill, Sam (1970), *Clown Princes and Court Jesters*. A.S. Barnes & Co., New Jersey.

Maltin, Leonard (1972), *The Great Movie Shorts*. Bonanza Books, New York.

Marriot, A.J. (1993), *Laurel & Hardy: The British Tours*. A.J. Marriot, Blackpool.

Paton, Adam (1992), 'The anarchic child: a study of "Double Whoopee" ' *The Laurel & Hardy Magazine*, 3(6).

Walker, Alexander (1978), *The Shattered Silents*. Elm Tree, London.

Index

Italicized page numbers indicate the main discussion of a Laurel and Hardy film. References to supporting actors are normally restricted to comment or specific information.